intensely chocolate

100 SCRUMPTIOUS RECIPES FOR TRUE CHOCOLATE LOVERS

CAROLE BLOOM, CCP

WILEY

JOHN WILEY & SONS, INC.

Published by John Wiley & Sons, Inc., Hoboken, New Jersey

Published simultaneously in Canada

For general information on our other products and services or for technical support, please contact our Customer Care Department within the United States at (800) 762-2974, outside the United States at (317) 572-3993 or fax (317) 572-4002.

Wiley also publishes its books in a variety of electronic formats. Some content that appears in print may not be available in electronic books. For more information about Wiley products, visit our web site at www.wiley.com.

DESIGN BY Vertigo Design NYC

Library of Congress Cataloging-in-Publication Data:
Bloom, Carole.
 Intensely chocolate : 100 scrumptious recipes for true chocolate lovers / Carole Bloom.
   p. cm.
 Includes index.
 ISBN 978-0-470-55101-1 (cloth)
 1. Cookery (Chocolate) 2. Desserts. I. Title.
 TX767.C5B57 2010
 641.3'374--dc22
                              2009049551

Printed in China

10 9 8 7 6 5 4 3 2 1

Dedicated with love to my mother, Florence, and my husband, Jerry Olivas, chocolate lovers extraordinaire. This book is also dedicated to the memory of my friend Robert Steinberg, chocolate pioneer and visionary.

acknowledgments

With grateful thanks to all who have helped bring this book to life:

Susan Ginsburg, outstanding agent, for all her hard work done so graciously.

Pam Chirls, multitalented editor, for the opportunity to work together again.

Rebecca Sherm, Pam's assistant, for keeping the lines of communication flowing smoothly.

Alda Trabucchi, senior production editor, for guiding this book through the publishing process so gracefully.

Suzanne Fass, copy editor, for her attention to detail and excellent queries.

Alison Lew of Vertigo Design for, once again, designing a beautiful, exciting book.

The entire team at Wiley, for their support and work to bring this book into the hands of the public.

Glenn Cormier, incredible photographer, for making it possible for us to work together again and for creating such fabulous photographs.

Ben Carufel, Glenn's assistant, for making our photo sessions so productive and fun and for his enthusiasm for eating what we photograph.

Florence Bloom, my mother, for always being proud of me and for being such a great role model.

My neighbors and friends, for eating my desserts and giving me feedback. And my yoga friends, especially Rachel Leshaw, for so enthusiastically eating my experiments.

All my colleagues who provided me with fabulous ingredients to use to develop and test the recipes in this book:

Art Pollard of Amano Artisan Chocolate

Deborah Kwan of Deborah Kwan Public Relations, representing Valrhona Chocolate

Gary Guittard of Guittard Chocolate

Derek Lanter of Waialua Estate Chocolate

Tom Cavers of Scharffen Berger Chocolate Maker

Land O'Lakes Butter

And Jerry Olivas, my husband, for help with everything, including tasting all the recipes, believing in me, making me laugh, and in general making my life rich and sweet.

contents

introduction

Just when you thought chocolate couldn't get any better, it has. The use of high cacao content chocolate has taken chocolate desserts to a new and more satisfying place. High cacao content chocolate gives desserts a much more pronounced flavor. All the recipes in this book use a substantial amount of chocolate, many use more than one type of chocolate, and most are made with high cacao content chocolate.

Chocolate has been my passion for as long as I can remember. Like many Americans, as a child I first experienced milk chocolate. I liked milk chocolate then, and still do, but after being introduced to dark chocolate while traveling in Europe, my preference changed. And to my delight, many chocolate manufacturers are now producing even darker chocolates, which are referred to as "high cacao content chocolates." It was clear to me when I first started to use these chocolates that I was taking chocolate desserts to greater heights—and everyone who tasted them agreed.

You get a more intense chocolate flavor in desserts made with high cacao content chocolate because these chocolates have more chocolate liquor, cocoa butter, and cacao solids. Most of the recipes in *Intensely Chocolate* use high cacao content chocolate. This includes desserts made with dark chocolate and dark milk chocolate. And to further enhance them, several of these recipes include cocoa powder, cacao nibs, or chocolate extract. Many of the recipes combine different types of chocolate—for example, white chocolate and dark chocolate. The other ingredients in these recipes are what I feel go best with high cacao content chocolate. You will find some new and creative desserts in *Intensely Chocolate*.

The book begins with a chapter on Ingredients, Equipment, and Techniques, including a very informative and up-to-date section titled Understanding Chocolate. The rest of *Intensely Chocolate* is arranged by type of dessert, including cakes and cupcakes; brownies, scones, and muffins; tarts and tartlets; cookies; custards, mousses, and puddings; truffles and candies; ice creams, sorbets, and frozen desserts; and liquid chocolate (beverages and sauces). A short descriptive headnote included with each recipe offers hints for use or serving, along with the yield and any special equipment that is necessary. These are followed by the ingredients section listing the type or types of chocolate, including a range for the cacao content. Step-by-step instructions are next, followed by suggestions for Keeping, and where appropriate, information about Streamlining, Making a Change, and Adding Style.

The recipes in this book do not have to be made in any particular order. You can pick any recipe that you like to start with. Some of them require a little more effort, such as Bittersweet Chocolate and Cacao Nib Meringue Layer Cake (page 24) and Cocoa Pavlova with Cacao Nib Whipped Cream (page 96), while others have fewer ingredients and steps. It's always a good idea to read through a recipe before starting. I like to get all my ingredients and equipment set out before I begin. If you have any questions about ingredients, equipment, or techniques, you can always refer back to the first chapter. And make sure to read through the Glossary where you will find definitions explaining what high cacao content chocolate is, as well as other important subjects like single-origin chocolates and organic chocolates. This way, not only will you learn a lot about chocolate, but you will be able to dazzle your friends and family with your up-to-date chocolate knowledge.

Intensely Chocolate is for all levels of dessert makers. You will find everything written in a clear, easy-to-understand, yet concise way. From my experience I know that some dessert makers shy away from chocolate recipes, thinking that they may be too challenging and will not result in a great chocolate dessert. This is definitely not the case with the recipes in this book. I can assure you that your finished chocolate desserts will be the best that you, your family, and your friends have ever had.

I love to work with chocolate, and I enjoy indulging in and sharing my creations. If you are a chocolate lover and you haven't made chocolate desserts that use a generous amount of chocolate—especially high cacao content chocolate—you must. This book is your easy-to-follow road map to the very best of chocolate.

CHAPTER ONE

ingredients, equipment,
and techniques

ingredients

It's important to use the best-quality ingredients to make the best-tasting chocolate desserts. Since many chocolate desserts are made using only a few ingredients, it's not easy to hide poor quality.

UNDERSTANDING CHOCOLATE

All chocolate comes from cacao beans grown in tropical climates within 20 degrees of the Equator, around the world. There are several types and forms of chocolate: unsweetened, extra-bittersweet, bittersweet, semisweet, milk, dark milk, white, cocoa powder, and cacao nibs. All these types and forms of chocolate are used in the recipes in this book. The basic components of chocolate are chocolate liquor, cocoa butter, and cacao solids, which have been extracted from the cacao bean during manufacturing,

HIGH CACAO CONTENT CHOCOLATE is chocolate that has a high percentage of cacao components: chocolate liquor, cocoa butter, and cacao solids, as compared to most traditional varieties of chocolate. This chocolate is labeled with its percentage of cacao components, such as 62%, 64%, or 70%. The higher the cacao percentage, the smaller the amount of sugar, so chocolate with high cacao content has deeper, more intense chocolate flavor. Because high cacao content chocolate contains more cacao components, which behave in a way similar to dry ingredients, it must be balanced in recipes. Substituting chocolate with high cacao content in a recipe you have been making for many years with regular chocolate will not yield the same results. It's important to always use the type and form of chocolate called for in the recipes in this book.

UNSWEETENED CHOCOLATE, sometimes called bitter chocolate, is pure unadulterated chocolate liquor with no sugar. Unsweetened chocolate is used in baking to add extra deep flavor but is generally not eaten plain because of its strong, bitter taste. Unsweetened chocolate contains 100% cacao components.

EXTRA-BITTERSWEET CHOCOLATE is made from chocolate liquor, cocoa butter, a small amount of sugar, vanilla, and sometimes lecithin (see Glossary, page 207). Extra-bittersweet chocolate has a pronounced, full-bodied chocolate flavor with just a hint of sweetness. One manufacturer's extra-bittersweet may be another manufacturer's bittersweet, but in general, those in the chocolate industry consider extra-bittersweet to have cacao content higher than 73%. It is not unusual to see chocolate labeled as 85 or 87% cacao content. Extra-bittersweet chocolate has the least amount of sugar compared with bittersweet and semisweet chocolates. It is not a good idea to substitute extra-bittersweet chocolate in recipes that call for bittersweet chocolate, because its much higher cacao content reacts differently with the other ingredients in a recipe.

BITTERSWEET CHOCOLATE is made from chocolate liquor, combined with cocoa butter, sugar, vanilla, and occasionally lecithin. Bittersweet chocolate has a strong chocolate flavor with only a mild amount of sweetness. One manufacturer's bittersweet may be another manufacturer's semisweet, but in general, those chocolates the industry considers bittersweet have cacao content between 63 and 72%. Bittersweet chocolate has more sugar than extra-bittersweet chocolate but less sugar than semisweet.

SEMISWEET CHOCOLATE is made from chocolate liquor, cocoa butter, sugar, vanilla, and occasionally lecithin. Semisweet chocolate has a mildly sweet, deep chocolate flavor. In general, those in the chocolate industry consider semisweet to have cacao content between 50 and 62%. Semisweet chocolate has the most sugar compared with bittersweet and extra-bittersweet chocolate.

Labeling for extra-bittersweet, bittersweet, and semisweet chocolate can be confusing because the only standard the U.S. Food and Drug Administration (FDA) has set is that these chocolates must contain a minimum of 35% cacao components. This allows each chocolate manufacturer to label their chocolates as they choose. For my recipes, extra-bittersweet contains cacao components in excess of 72% cacao components; bittersweet chocolate ranges between 63 and 72%; and semisweet chocolate is in the range of 50 to 62%. Different brands of chocolate with the same cacao content may taste different and may have different mouthfeel because of differences in the cacao beans used to make them and the amount of cocoa butter used by the manufacturer. Keep in mind that the higher the cacao content, the smaller the amount of sugar, and the more intense the chocolate flavor will be.

It is not a good idea to substitute semisweet chocolate in recipes that call for bittersweet or extra-bittersweet chocolate, bittersweet chocolate in recipes that call for semisweet chocolate, or extra-bittersweet in recipes that call for bittersweet, because the different cacao contents will react differently with the other ingredients in the recipe.

DARK CHOCOLATE is a catch-all phrase that refers to chocolate other than milk chocolate or white chocolate. Dark chocolate always has less sugar than either milk or white.

MILK CHOCOLATE is the sweetest of all of the types of chocolate. It is made from chocolate liquor, cocoa butter, a great deal of sugar, powdered milk solids, vanilla, and usually lecithin. Milk chocolate contains less chocolate liquor than semisweet, bittersweet, and extra-bittersweet chocolates. FDA standards require a minimum of 10% cacao content, which is very low. Milk chocolate has a creamy texture and is more sensitive to heat than the dark chocolates. It is light brown in color. Milk chocolate is easily distinguishable from semisweet, bittersweet, and extra-bittersweet chocolates because of its strong, sweet, chocolate milk flavor. Some milk chocolates have a slight caramel undertone. It is never a good idea to substitute milk chocolate for any other chocolate called for in recipes because it has much less body than any of the dark chocolates.

Here are several characteristics to look for and be aware of when selecting chocolate.

THE APPEARANCE SHOULD BE SMOOTH AND EVEN WITH CONSISTENT COLOR. CHOCOLATE WITH CRACKS AND SIGNS OF EITHER CHOCOLATE OR SUGAR BLOOM (SEE GLOSSARY, PAGES 206 AND 207) INDICATE POOR HANDLING.

—

THE AROMA SHOULD BE PLEASANT AND MAKE YOU WANT TO TASTE IT. ANY OFF ODORS INDICATE THAT THE CHOCOLATE MAY NOT TASTE GOOD.

—

CHOCOLATE SHOULD BREAK WITH A CLEAN, CRISP SNAP, INDICATING THAT IT HAS BEEN PROPERLY TEMPERED.

—

MOUTHFEEL (HOW CHOCOLATE FEELS IN YOUR MOUTH) IS IMPORTANT. IT SHOULD MELT EVENLY AND HAVE A SMOOTH TEXTURE. CHOCOLATE MELTS AT SLIGHTLY LESS THAN BODY TEMPERATURE SO IT SHOULD MELT RAPIDLY.

—

FLAVOR IS THE MOST IMPORTANT FACTOR. CHOCOLATE SHOULD TASTE GOOD AND HAVE A WELL-BALANCED FLAVOR.

—

AND, FINALLY, AFTERTASTE IS THE LAST CHARACTERISTIC. THE FLAVOR SHOULD LINGER IN THE MOUTH FOR AT LEAST A MINUTE, LEAVING YOU SATISFIED. I recommend tasting several types

and brands of chocolate plain before making a choice of which to use in your recipes. The flavor of chocolate won't change when you bake and make desserts with it, so make sure you like it straight off the bar. In the back of this book is a list of the chocolate types and brands that I used in developing and testing the recipes. Note that chocolate bars are not labeled with the type of cacao beans used to make them (*criollo, forastero, trinitario,* or a blend), but many are labeled with the names of the place of origin of the cacao, such as Jembrana, Ocumare, or Madagascar.

DARK MILK CHOCOLATE has a higher than cacao content and less sugar than regular milk chocolate, which gives it richer, deeper flavor. It is made from chocolate liquor, cocoa butter, sugar, powdered milk solids, vanilla, and usually lecithin. The cacao content for dark milk chocolate usually ranges between 38 and 42%. Some chocolate manufacturers are beginning to increase the cacao content in dark milk chocolate. Dark milk chocolate is my preference when using milk chocolate.

WHITE CHOCOLATE is made with cocoa butter, sugar, and powdered milk solids. Although it has no chocolate liquor, it contains between 31 and 35% cacao components, which come from the cocoa butter. White chocolate has a sweet, subtle chocolate flavor.

Besides bars and blocks, chocolate is also available from some manufacturers in the form of buttons or wafers. Because these are already small, they don't have to be chopped for melting, so they save time. Any form of chocolate can be used to make the recipes in this book. Just make sure that whatever form you use is completely melted, if necessary.

GIANDUIA CHOCOLATE is a blend of chocolate and roasted hazelnuts. It has a velvety smooth texture and is light brown in color. On occasion roasted almonds are used in place of hazelnuts. Gianduia is usually made with milk chocolate, but versions made with dark and white chocolate can also be found. In recipes gianduia is used in the same way as chocolate. The flavor combination of hazelnuts and chocolate is also called gianduia and it is the name of a group of candies and confections made with the same flavor combination.

OTHER CHOCOLATE FORMS

COCOA POWDER is made by pressing most of the cocoa butter out of chocolate liquor, leaving a fine powder. This powder is further dried, sifted, and processed, resulting in unsweetened cocoa powder. There are both low- and high-fat types of cocoa powder, depending on how much cocoa butter remains in the mixture. Cocoa powder is used in baking and candy making both as an ingredient and as a garnish.

There are two types of cocoa powder, **NATURAL** and **DUTCH-PROCESSED.** Both types are used in many recipes. Natural cocoa has a more acidic flavor than Dutch-processed cocoa. The alkali used to make Dutch-processed cocoa powder reduces the acidity, softening its flavor and darkening its color. Because of their differences in acidity, each type of cocoa powder works better with a different leavener. Baking soda neutralizes the acidity of natural cocoa powder, while baking powder is the leavener of choice for Dutch-processed cocoa powder. Also, the alkaline quality of Dutch-processed cocoa powder is balanced by other acid ingredients such as buttermilk, honey, sour cream, and yogurt. It's a good idea to use the cocoa powder called for in each recipe and not make substitutions.

CHOCOLATE CHIPS are manufactured in tiny pieces ranging in diameter from $\frac{1}{8}$ to $\frac{1}{2}$ inch. They are available in many types including bittersweet, semisweet, milk, and white chocolate. They are manufactured to tolerate high heat without burning and to maintain their flavor and texture after baking. Generally they don't melt down completely to a smooth consistency like bulk or bar chocolate and should not be substituted for other forms of chocolate in recipes.

CACAO NIBS are the cracked, roasted, and hulled unsweetened center of cacao beans. They are pure unsweetened chocolate before it is pressed into a liquid and further processed. Cacao nibs add crunchy texture and toasty chocolate flavor when added to recipes. Since they are unsweetened, they have a slightly bitter flavor. Nibs can be used in place of nuts in many recipes.

CHOCOLATE EXTRACT is similar to vanilla extract but it is made with roasted cacao nibs. It has an intense chocolate aroma and flavor that enhance the chocolate flavor in recipes. Chocolate extract can be used instead of vanilla extract or along with it in recipes.

OTHER INGREDIENTS FOR WORKING WITH CHOCOLATE

BUTTER I use unsalted butter for all my desserts and highly recommend that you do the same. Unsalted butter has a clean, fresh flavor. Also, every brand of salted butter contains different amounts of salt. By using unsalted butter you are in charge of the amount of salt that goes into your desserts. I used Land O'Lakes unsalted butter to develop and test all the recipes in this book.

When a recipe calls for softened butter, it should be soft enough to hold the indentation of a finger but not so soft that it begins to become liquid.

It's not a good idea to replace unsalted butter with margarine or vegetable shortening. They react differently with other ingredients than butter does and don't have the same mouthfeel, flavor, or texture.

When a recipe calls for butter or butter and flour to prepare a baking pan, it's fine to substitute nonstick baking spray.

DAIRY PRODUCTS Several dairy products are used in these recipes including buttermilk, cream cheese, crème fraîche, heavy whipping cream, mascarpone, milk, sweetened condensed milk, and sour cream. Each of these products provides its own special flavor to desserts. All diary products have a sell-by date on their carton. Always check this date before buying, to make sure you are getting a product that is as fresh as possible. Store all dairy products in the refrigerator. The recipes in this book use full-fat dairy products, unless stated otherwise.

EGGS Eggs are one of the building blocks of desserts. They serve many roles including providing color, structure, flavor, leavening, and moisture. All the recipes in this book use large eggs. It's always a good idea to check the date on the carton and buy eggs as fresh as possible. Store eggs inside the refrigerator, not in the door, which is not as cold. Don't use egg substitutes in place of real whole eggs when making desserts.

Egg whites can be frozen for later use. I like to freeze them individually in ice cube trays and store them in freezer bags after they are frozen. This is an easy way to tell how many egg whites are in the freezer. It's also fine to use the liquid fresh egg whites available in stores. They have been pasteurized and checked for salmonella, and don't contain any preservatives.

FLOUR Flour is one of the basic ingredients used to make desserts, providing structure, texture, and color. All-purpose flour is a blend of hard and soft wheat that results in flour with a medium amount of protein (gluten), making it a good choice for most baking. Cake flour has less protein than all-purpose flour and creates a more delicate texture and crumb. All the recipes in this book were developed and tested using either all-purpose or cake flour. Don't substitute bread flour, which has much more protein than all-purpose flour. And don't substitute whole-wheat flour, because it is much denser and heavier. If you want to make a recipe that calls for cake flour but you don't have any, you can use all-purpose flour. Simply take out 2 tablespoons from each cup of all-purpose flour. The reverse is true for using cake flour in place of all-purpose flour: add 2 tablespoons of cake flour to each cup and you will have the equivalent of all-purpose flour. To measure flour, fill a dry measuring cup to the top and level it off by sweeping a straight edge across the top. Store all types of flour in tightly sealed containers at room temperature.

NUTS Nuts add great flavor and texture to desserts. These recipes use several nuts, including almonds, hazelnuts, macadamia nuts, peanuts, pecans, and walnuts. Most of the time it's fine to substitute one type of nut for another. Buy nuts in the form you need them: sliced, slivered, ground, raw, salted or unsalted. All nuts have a high content of natural oil that can go rancid, so buy in small quantities that you will use quickly.

SALT Salt enhances the flavor of other ingredients in desserts. I prefer to use coarse kosher salt or fine-grained sea salt in my desserts. Either of these can be used in the recipes in this book because they are equivalent by volume. These types of salt are less salty by volume than table salt and have a more delicate flavor. There are many types of sea salt available, so it's important to choose one with a neutral flavor for use in desserts.

SPICES Spices have wonderful flavor and aroma that they impart to desserts. The recipes in this book use cardamom, cinnamon, cloves, ginger, nutmeg, and vanilla. Whenever possible I buy whole spices and grind them as needed, because once spices are ground they lose their flavor rapidly. I always grate nutmeg fresh because it's so easy to do and makes such a noticeable difference in flavor. Vanilla is used mostly as extract, but you can always substitute vanilla bean paste in the same quantity. Buy spices in small quantities that you will use quickly. Store them in a cool, dry place away from light, which causes them to deteriorate.

SUGAR Sugar is one of the essential ingredients in desserts, providing moisture, flavor, texture, and color. The recipes in this book use granulated, superfine, confectioners', light brown, turbinado, and Demerara sugar. Store all types of sugar at room temperature in tightly sealed containers. Superfine sugar, sometimes sold as "baker's sugar," is more finely ground than granulated sugar and dissolves very easily. Although there is a difference in the sizes of their grains, in most cases it's fine to substitute one for the other.

Confectioners' sugar is also called "powdered sugar" and is used most often for decorating and garnishing. It is also used to create a delicate texture in doughs and batters. It's a good idea to sift confectioners' sugar before use because it tends to get lumpy as it sits.

Light brown sugar adds full-bodied flavor to desserts. It has more molasses and a softer texture than granulated sugar. I don't recommend substituting brown sugar for granulated entirely, but it is possible to replace up to one-third of the amount of granulated sugar with light brown sugar. Dark brown sugar has a more pronounced flavor than light brown sugar because it contains more molasses; be aware of this if you choose to substitute dark brown sugar for light brown. Because brown sugar contains more moisture and air than other sugars, it needs to be tightly packed into the measuring cup to get the correct measure.

Turbinado and Demerara are raw brown sugars with coarse crystals, used primarily for garnishing, but they can replace brown sugar in recipes.

equipment

Stocking your kitchen with good-quality equipment is well worth the investment because it will last for many, many years and make dessert making a pleasure. Storing equipment where it is easy to reach will make it more likely that you will use it.

BAKING SHEETS These are also called "jelly-roll pans." They are heavy aluminum that won't buckle in the oven and have 1-inch-high straight sides with rolled rims on all sides. They are used for baking cookies and scones, and for holding tart, tartlet, and cake pans as they bake. Baking sheets come in different sizes so be sure to buy the size that fits in your oven and leaves at least 2 inches of room around it for air to circulate.

CAKE AND BAKING PANS Several shapes and sizes of cake and baking pans are used in the recipes in this book. Round cake pans made of aluminum measure 9 inches in diameter and 2 inches deep. They have straight sides and no seams. Square pans are also made of aluminum and measure 8 inches square and 2 inches deep. A Bundt tube pan is a special, deep cake pan with a center tube and deeply grooved, rounded sides that form a pattern that is imprinted onto the cake as it bakes. I use a 10-inch round Bundt tube pan and Bundt cupcake pans to make individual cakes. These are made of heavy-gauge dark aluminum. A tube pan is also called an Angel Food Cake pan; it has straight sides with a center tube that helps conduct heat to the center of the cake as it bakes. It is 4 inches deep and made of heavy aluminum. I also use a loaf pan measuring 9 x 5 x 3 inches that is made of aluminum. Springform pans made of aluminum, measuring 9½ x 3 inches are used to make some cakes. To make Madeleines I use special pans that have 12 deeply grooved cavities, each measuring 3 inches long. The cavities transfer their designs to the cookies. A standard aluminum muffin pan with 12 cavities is used for baking muffins and cupcakes, but silicon muffin cups can be used in place of a muffin pan. They are placed onto a baking sheet.

COOKIE CUTTERS Scalloped 2½-inch-diameter metal cookie cutters are used for cutting out shapes of some cookie doughs and 3-inch round aluminum plain edge cutters are used for cutting out pastry dough to be fit into tartlet shells. The cutters should be sturdy and have sharp edges so they cut cleanly.

DOUBLE BOILER This is one of the primary tools used for melting chocolate. The bottom pan holds a shallow amount of water that is warmed to gently heat the chocolate in the top pan. It's not necessary that it be an "official" double boiler. But it is important that there be a secure fit between the top and bottom, so no water or steam escapes and mixes with the chocolate, which would cause it to seize (turn into a stiff and grainy mass). Make sure there is plenty of room in the top bowl or pan for stirring while the chocolate is melting.

I use a 3-quart heavy-duty saucepan for the bottom and a 2-quart stainless steel bowl on top. If the bottom pan is glass, it makes it easier to see the water and tell if it is getting too hot.

FOOD PROCESSOR A food processor is another one of the most important pieces of equipment in the dessert kitchen. It makes tart and cookie doughs easily and does a great job of chopping and grinding nuts. Having an extra bowl and blade is very handy if you use your food processor often. A mini food processor makes easy work of chopping and grinding small quantities.

ICE CREAM SCOOPS Ice cream scoops are very handy for portioning batters into muffin and cupcake pans, filling tartlet pans, scooping out some cookie dough and truffle mixtures. I use 1-, 1½-, and 2-inch-diameter metal ice cream scoops that have a lever on the base of the handle and a bowl on the top. When the lever is pressed the bowl of the scoop releases the mixture it holds.

MEASURING CUPS AND SPOONS Accurate measures are important for all dessert recipes. Use dry measuring cups for ingredients such as flour, sugar, coconut, and nuts. These are available in nested sets of ¼-, ⅓-, ½-, and 1-cup capacities. You can fill these to the top and level them off. Liquid measuring cups with pour spouts have extra room at the top to allow the liquids to move around, and are not good for measuring dry ingredients. Measuring spoons are used to measure both liquid and dry ingredients. Having a few sets of measuring spoons makes it easy to move through a recipe without having to stop and clean up. I find it very handy to detach measuring spoons from their ring and store the same sizes together.

MICROWAVE OVEN A microwave is very useful for softening ingredients and for melting chocolate. Become familiar with your microwave oven so you know its strength and how much time it takes for these tasks.

MIXER An electric mixer is one of the most important pieces of equipment in the dessert kitchen. Either a stand mixer or a handheld mixer can be used to make the recipes in this book. A stand mixer allows your hands to be free to add ingredients or attend to other tasks while mixing. If you have a stand mixer, keep it on the countertop so it's always available for use. Having an extra bowl, flat beater, and wire whip lets you move through a recipe without having to stop and clean up.

NONSTICK LINERS These are made of silicone and can be reused many, many times. They can't be cut to fit but come in different sizes, so buy the sizes that fit your pans.

PARCHMENT PAPER This is greaseproof and nonstick, and is used mostly to line baking sheets and cake pans to keep cookies and cakes from sticking. When parchment paper is used, the baking sheets don't need to be greased and floured. Parchment paper is also used when rolling out pastry dough.

PASTRY BAGS AND TIPS These are used for decorating and for filling tartlet shells, filling cupcake and muffin pans with batter, and filling sandwich cookies. Pastry bags are made from a variety of materials including nylon, plastic, polyester, and parchment paper. I prefer to use 12- and 14-inch pastry bags because they hold enough without over-filling and don't have to be refilled often. If a pastry bag is filled more than halfway, it becomes difficult to handle. Pastry tips are available in a wide range of sizes and shapes. The ones I find most useful are a plain ½-inch round tip, an open star tip, and a closed star tip. Both of these are 2 inches long, making them easy to keep out of the garbage disposal and easy to wash in the dishwasher. For small decorating or piping tasks parchment paper pastry cones or plastic snack-size bags can be used instead of a regular pastry bag.

PASTRY BRUSH Pastry brushes are used for a variety of tasks including brushing the tops of scones with liquid, buttering the inside of pans, brushing excess flour off of dough, and washing down the sides of the pan while sugar mixtures are cooking. I prefer natural bristle pastry brushes because the bristles are softer than other materials. One-inch-wide pastry brushes are the right size for most tasks. Pastry brushes with wooden handles should be washed by hand in hot, soapy water, not in the dishwasher. Keep pastry brushes used for brushing down pans separate from those used for butter.

RAMEKINS, CUSTARD CUPS, OR BOWLS Several recipes for custards, mousses, and puddings require ½-cup-size ramekins, custard cups, or bowls. It's important that these be heat safe because they are usually placed in the oven. I recommend ramekins, custard cups, or bowls made of ceramic or glass. There are many styles available, some flared, other with straight sides. Any of these can be used as long as they hold the correct capacity.

ROLLING PIN A rolling pin is used to roll out tart and cookie dough. There are several styles of rolling pins made from a variety of materials, such as wood, metal, and silicone covered. It's a matter of personal preference which rolling pin you use. The most important criterion is that it feels comfortable in your hands.

SCALE A reliable kitchen scale is very handy for accurately measuring chocolate and butter. There are many types of scales. I find that an electronic scale that can be set to zero when a bowl is placed on top is the most reliable. Keep a scale on your kitchen counter where it is easy to reach.

SPATULAS Both rubber and silicone spatulas are used in a variety of ways in the dessert kitchen. They are used for mixing ingredients together, folding mixtures, scraping down the sides of mixing bowls, and stirring ingredients as they cook or melt. Be sure to keep silicone spatulas, which are heat safe, separate from rubber spatulas, which are not. I like to keep a crock full of spatulas on the counter near my stovetop and mixer, so I can reach them easily. I also use offset and straight metal spatulas. A 3-inch metal blade offset spatula comes in very handy for smoothing tart fillings, brownie, and cake mixtures, and for helping release cookies from parchment paper. An 8½-inch metal blade offset spatula is useful for moving cakes and tarts to serving plates and for spreading out batters in large shallow pans. Flexible blade metal spatulas (8- and 10-inch) are helpful for spreading fillings between layers and also for moving cakes and tarts.

STRAINER AND SIFTER These are used for mixing and aerating dry ingredients, such as flour, cocoa powder, confectioners' sugar, and spices and for rinsing fruit. A variety of sizes of strainers with different size mesh is useful to have for different ingredients. I prefer strainers with plastic rims and mesh because they can easily be washed in the dishwasher.

TART AND TARTLET PANS Fluted-edge tart pans with removable bottoms imprint their design on the outside of tarts or other baked goods. They come in a wide variety of shapes and sizes. The size I use most often is a 9½-inch round, but I also like to use a 9-inch square and occasionally a 4 x 14-inch rectangular pan. The tartlet pans used for the recipes in this book are 2½ inches round without removable bottoms. Tart and tartlet pans don't need to be greased because the doughs baked in them are rich with butter and shrink slightly as they bake.

THERMOMETERS A candy thermometer, also called a sugar thermometer that reads between 100 and 400°F is important when taking the temperature of a variety of mixtures, such as custards, ice cream mixtures, and egg whites. In some cases an instant-read thermometer can also be used. Accuracy is crucial because erring a few degrees in either direction can cause problems, so it's a good idea to test the thermometer by placing it into a pan of boiling water and checking that it reads 212°F. To obtain the most precise temperature reading make sure the bulb or dimple of the thermometer is taking the temperature of the mixture and not sitting on the bottom of the pan.

TIMERS An accurate timer is an essential piece of equipment. Buy one that is reliable, easy to read, and easy to use. Set the timer for the minimum amount of time called for in a recipe; you can easily add more time if needed. When I leave the kitchen while something is in the oven I always take my timer with me so I don't miss hearing it ring.

techniques

Using the correct techniques makes time in the kitchen fun and dessert making easy. These techniques will help you make great chocolate desserts.

CHOCOLATE TECHNIQUES

CHOPPING Chocolate needs to be chopped into small pieces so it will melt evenly. Use a sharp chef's knife and a cutting board to chop chocolate into matchstick-size pieces. A tool called a chocolate chipper can also be used to chop chocolate into small pieces. Chop chocolate off of a bar or chunk that is small enough to handle.

GRINDING Some recipes call for chocolate to be finely ground. This is best accomplished in a food processor, but don't grind chocolate on its own. Add some or all of the dry ingredients from the recipe, such as flour or sugar. These will help cushion the chocolate from the heat of the machine and allow it to be ground evenly.

WEIGHING Many chocolate bars are not scored into pieces of certain weight, so it's important to weigh chocolate to make sure that you have the exact amount the recipe calls for. There are several types and brands of kitchen scales available. Find a reliable one that you like and keep it on your kitchen counter so it's always available.

MELTING Always start melting chocolate before you need it for a recipe (I usually start melting chocolate about 30 minutes before I need it). If you are in a hurry to melt chocolate, it's easy to apply too much heat and ruin it. Once chocolate is melted, it can stand at room temperature for a short while (about 15 minutes), as long as it's stirred occasionally to prevent a skin from forming on top.

There are two main ways to melt chocolate: in the top of a double boiler and in a microwave oven. If using a double boiler, make sure the top pan or bowl fits snugly so no water or steam can escape and mix with the chocolate, causing it to seize. Don't let the top pan or bowl touch the water in the bottom pan and keep the water hot but never simmering or boiling. Stir the chocolate frequently with a rubber or silicone spatula to ensure even melting. When half of the amount of chocolate is melted, turn off the heat on the burner. There will be enough residual heat to melt the rest of the chocolate.

To melt chocolate in a microwave oven, place it in a microwave-safe bowl, use the lowest power for 30-second bursts, and stir after each burst.

Because milk chocolate and white chocolate have less cacao components than dark chocolate, they are more delicate and can burn easily. Also, too much heat will coagulate the milk solids, causing them to become lumpy and grainy. Use very low heat when melting these chocolates and stir them frequently.

KEEPING CHOCOLATE FROM SEIZING Make sure all utensils that come in contact with chocolate are completely dry. A stray drop or two of liquid will cause chocolate to seize into a stiff and grainy mass. Once chocolate has seized, there is no remedy.

STORING Store all chocolate tightly wrapped at room temperature, not in the refrigerator or freezer, where it will pick up moisture that can condense on it when it's melted, causing the chocolate to seize. Chocolate is like a sponge and easily picks up other flavors and odors, so store it away from any strongly flavored foods or spices. Unsweetened, extra-bittersweet, bittersweet, and semisweet chocolate can be stored for a year or longer. Because milk chocolate and white chocolate contain milk products, they don't last as long. Store them for no longer than 8 months.

MEASURING DRY INGREDIENTS

Use dry measuring cups for measuring ingredients such as flour, sugar, and cocoa powder. These cups are designed so they can be leveled off at the top, unlike liquid measuring cups with the pour spout. Use either the "scoop and sweep" method or the "spoon and sweep" method. For the scoop and sweep method, scoop the cup into the ingredient, filling it over the top, then level it off using the back of a knife, an offset metal spatula, or other straight-edged implement. For the spoon and sweep method, spoon the ingredient into the cup and level it off at the top. All the recipes in this book also include weights for the major dry ingredients.

NUTS

TOASTING The flavor of all nuts is enhanced by toasting. Spread them in a single layer in a cake or pie pan and toast in a 350°F oven for 4 to 8 minutes. Shake the pan once or twice while the nuts are toasting. Sliced almonds begin to brown quicker than other nuts. Toast hazelnuts on a jelly-roll pan for 15 to 18 minutes, until the skins split and the nuts turn light golden brown. Remove the pan from the oven and pour the hazelnuts into a kitchen towel. Wrap the towel around them and rub the nuts together to remove most of the skins.

CHOPPING Chop nuts either by hand on a cutting board with a large chef's knife or in a food processor, pulsing until the desired chop is achieved. If it is a small amount of nuts, use a mini food processor to obtain a more even consistency.

GRINDING The food processor is the best tool for grinding nuts. For each cup of nuts I add 1 to 2 tablespoons of the sugar from the recipe to absorb the natural oil that is released when they are ground. Without the added sugar the nuts would be wet and mealy.

STORING Store all nuts in tightly covered containers in the freezer for up to a year. Be sure to label and date the containers so you know what's in them and how long they have been there.

COCONUT

To toast coconut, spread the coconut in a single layer in a cake or pie pan and toast in a 325°F oven for 5 to 7 minutes. Stir the coconut every 2 minutes until it turns light golden brown. Remove the pan from the oven and cool completely on a rack.

cakes and cupcakes

cocoa and bittersweet chocolate spiced pound cake

A BLEND OF CARDAMOM, CINNAMON, CLOVES, AND NUTMEG GIVE DISTINCTIVE FLAVOR TO THIS CAKE. BECAUSE IT'S LARGER THAN A TRADITIONAL POUND CAKE, IT'S BAKED IN A BUNDT OR PLAIN TUBE PAN, WHICH GIVES THE CAKE AN ATTRACTIVE APPEARANCE. IF YOU WANT TO EMBELLISH THIS CAKE, SERVE IT WITH A SCOOP OF BITTERSWEET CHOCOLATE ICE CREAM (PAGE 184) OR COCOA AND BITTERSWEET CHOCOLATE SORBET (PAGE 193).

MAKES one 10-inch round cake, 12 to 14 servings

SPECIAL EQUIPMENT: 10-inch round Bundt tube pan

Nonstick baking spray

½ cup (1¾ ounces) unsweetened Dutch-processed cocoa powder, sifted

⅓ cup boiling water

1 teaspoon pure vanilla extract

1 teaspoon pure chocolate extract

6 ounces (12 tablespoons, 1½ sticks) unsalted butter, softened

2 cups (13 ounces) granulated sugar

3 large eggs, at room temperature

⅓ cup sour cream

3 cups (13½ ounces) all-purpose flour

1½ teaspoons baking powder

1 teaspoon ground cardamom

1 teaspoon ground cinnamon

½ teaspoon ground cloves

¼ teaspoon freshly grated nutmeg

¼ teaspoon kosher or fine-grained sea salt

6 ounces bittersweet chocolate (66 to 72% cacao content), melted

CENTER a rack in the oven and preheat the oven to 350°F. Spray the inside of the pan with nonstick baking spray.

PLACE the cocoa powder in a small bowl and add the boiling water. Stir together with a heat-safe silicone spatula until it is a smooth paste. Add the vanilla and chocolate extracts and stir until completely blended.

BEAT the butter in the bowl of an electric stand mixer using the flat beater attachment or in a large mixing bowl using a handheld mixer until fluffy, about 2 minutes. Add the sugar and beat together until thoroughly blended.

ONE AT A TIME, add the eggs to the mixture, stopping to scrape down the sides and bottom of the bowl with a rubber spatula after each addition. At first the mixture may look curdled as the eggs are added, but as you stop and scrape down the bowl, the mixture will smooth out.

ADD the sour cream and blend thoroughly.

OVER a separate bowl, sift together the flour, baking powder, cardamom, cinnamon, and cloves. Add the nutmeg and salt and toss to blend completely.

ADD the dry ingredients to the butter mixture in 3 stages, alternately with the cocoa paste mixture and the melted chocolate. Stop occasionally and scrape down the sides and bottom of the bowl. Blend the batter thoroughly.

TRANSFER the batter to the prepared pan. Use a rubber spatula to smooth and even the top. Bake for 1 hour to 1 hour and 5 minutes, until a cake tester inserted in the center of the cake comes out clean.

REMOVE the pan from the oven and cool on a rack for 15 minutes. Invert the pan onto the rack and leave it for a few minutes so the cake will drop out of the pan. Gently remove the pan and let the cake cool completely.

keeping

Store the cake tightly wrapped in aluminum foil at room temperature up to 4 days. To freeze up to 4 months, wrap the cake tightly in several layers of plastic wrap and aluminum foil. Use a large piece of masking tape and an indelible marker to label and date the contents. If frozen, thaw overnight in the refrigerator and bring to room temperature before serving.

making a change

Replace the blend of spices with a single spice such as cinnamon, ginger, or nutmeg.

gianduia mousse cake

THIS IS A FLOURLESS CAKE, BUT IT IS NOT DENSE AS MANY OF THEM ARE. IT HAS A LIGHT QUALITY AND IS VERY DEEPLY FLAVORED WITH THE COMBINATION OF CHOCOLATE AND HAZELNUTS KNOWN AS GIANDUIA. IT CAN BE BAKED AND THEN HELD AT ROOM TEMPERATURE AS LONG AS 6 HOURS. ONCE REFRIGERATED, THE TEXTURE CHANGES AND BECOMES THICKER BUT NO LESS FLAVORFUL. I LIKE TO SERVE THIS CAKE WITH CHOCOLATE WHIPPED CREAM.

MAKES one 9½-inch round cake, 12 to 14 servings

SPECIAL EQUIPMENT: 9½-inch round springform pan; 10-inch or larger cake pan or roasting pan

CAKE

Nonstick baking spray

9 ounces bittersweet chocolate (70 to 72% cacao content)

7 ounces dark milk chocolate (38 to 42% cacao content)

1¾ cups (14½ ounces) Luscious Hazelnut Paste (page 205)

6 large eggs, at room temperature

½ cup (3½ ounces) superfine sugar

1 cup heavy whipping cream

Boiling water

GARNISH

Confectioners' sugar

CHOCOLATE WHIPPED CREAM

1 cup heavy whipping cream

3 ounces bittersweet chocolate (66 to 72% cacao content), melted

CENTER a rack in the oven and preheat the oven to 350°F. Spray the inside of the springform pan with nonstick baking spray. Line the pan with a parchment paper round and spray the round. Wrap heavy-duty foil tightly around the bottom of the pan to prevent water from seeping in as it bakes in a water bath.

PLACE the bittersweet chocolate and the dark milk chocolate together in the top of a double boiler over warm water. Melt the chocolates, stirring occasionally with a rubber spatula to ensure even melting. Or melt the chocolates in a microwave-safe bowl on low power in 30-second bursts, stirring after each burst. Remove the top pan of the double boiler, if using, and wipe the bottom and sides very dry. Stir the hazelnut paste into the chocolates until thoroughly combined.

WHIP the eggs in the bowl of an electric stand mixer using the wire whip attachment or in a large mixing bowl using a handheld mixer until frothy. Slowly sprinkle on the sugar and continue to whip until the mixture is very thick and pale yellow and holds a slowly dissolving ribbon when the beater is lifted, about 5 minutes. Combine the whipped eggs and the chocolate mixture and blend together completely.

IN a chilled bowl, whip the cream until it holds soft peaks. Gently fold the whipped cream into the batter until there are no white streaks.

POUR the batter into the prepared pan, then use a rubber spatula to smooth and even the top. Place the pan into a larger cake pan or a roasting pan. Pour boiling water into the bottom pan, until it comes halfway up the sides of the springform pan. Bake the cake for 1 hour and 10 minutes. Turn off the oven and let the cake stand in the oven for 30 minutes.

keeping

Store the cake tightly wrapped in plastic wrap up to 1 day at room temperature or up to 4 days in the refrigerator.

making a change

Replace the bittersweet chocolate and dark milk chocolate with 1 pound of gianduia chocolate.

REMOVE the pans from the oven and transfer the springform pan to a cooling rack to cool completely. Remove the aluminum foil from the bottom of the springform pan. Release the clip on the side of the springform pan and gently pull the sides away from the bottom. Lightly dust the top of the cake with confectioners' sugar.

FOR THE CHOCOLATE WHIPPED CREAM, whip the cream in a chilled bowl using the wire whip attachment or a handheld mixer on medium speed until it begins to thicken. Add the melted chocolate and continue to whip until the mixture holds soft peaks.

SERVE each slice of the cake at room temperature with a dollop of chocolate whipped cream.

bittersweet chocolate–hazelnut soufflé cake with hazelnut whipped cream

THIS UNUSUAL CAKE HAS TWO DIFFERENT TEXTURES DEPENDING ON HOW IT'S STORED. THE TEXTURE IS CREAMY WHEN SERVED AT ROOM TEMPERATURE NOT LONG AFTER BAKING. WHEN STORED IN THE REFRIGERATOR, THE TEXTURE IS DENSE AND FUDGY. LIKE A SOUFFLÉ, THIS CAKE FALLS SLIGHTLY AS IT COOLS. THE HAZELNUT WHIPPED CREAM IS AN EXCELLENT ACCOMPANIMENT FOR THIS DELECTABLE CAKE.

MAKES one 9½-inch round cake, 12 to 14 servings

SPECIAL EQUIPMENT: 9½-inch round springform pan

HAZELNUT WHIPPED CREAM

1 cup heavy whipping cream

3 tablespoons toasted and finely chopped hazelnuts (see page 10)

2 tablespoons superfine sugar

CAKE

Nonstick baking spray

1 pound bittersweet chocolate (70 to 72% cacao content), finely chopped

8 ounces (16 tablespoons, 2 sticks) unsalted butter, cut into small pieces

1 teaspoon pure vanilla extract

1 teaspoon pure chocolate extract

¼ teaspoon kosher or fine-grained sea salt

6 large eggs, at room temperature

⅔ cup (4 ounces) granulated sugar

1 cup (4 ounces) toasted and finely ground hazelnuts (see page 10)

FOR THE HAZELNUT WHIPPED CREAM, place the cream in a 1-quart heavy-duty saucepan and bring to a boil over medium-high heat. Pour the cream into a heat-safe bowl and stir in the hazelnuts. Cover the bowl tightly with plastic wrap and chill overnight.

CENTER a rack in the oven and preheat the oven to 350°F. Spray the inside of the springform pan with nonstick baking spray. Line the bottom of the pan with a parchment paper round and spray the round. Place the pan on a baking sheet.

MELT the bittersweet chocolate and butter together in the top of a double boiler over hot water, stirring frequently with a rubber spatula to ensure even melting. Or melt the chocolate and butter in a microwave-safe bowl on low power in 30-second bursts, stirring after each burst. Remove the top pan of the double boiler, if using, and wipe the bottom and sides very dry.

ADD the vanilla and chocolate extracts and the salt to the chocolate mixture and stir together to blend thoroughly.

IN the bowl of an electric stand mixer using the wire whip attachment or in a large mixing bowl using a handheld mixer, whip the eggs and granulated sugar until the mixture is very thick and pale yellow and holds a slowly dissolving ribbon when the beater is lifted, about 5 minutes.

IN 4 STAGES, gently fold the egg mixture into the chocolate mixture. Fold in the ground hazelnuts.

POUR the batter into the prepared pan then use a rubber spatula to smooth and even the top. Bake the cake for 35 to 40 minutes, until a cake tester inserted in the center of the cake comes out slightly moist.

REMOVE the pan from the oven and cool completely on a rack. Release the clip on the side of the springform pan and gently pull the sides away from the bottom.

STRAIN the hazelnuts out of the cream. In the bowl of an electric stand mixer using the wire whip attachment or in a large mixing bowl using a handheld mixer, whip the cream until frothy. Add the superfine sugar and whip until the cream holds soft peaks.

SERVE slices of the cake at room temperature with a dollop of hazelnut whipped cream.

keeping

Store the cake tightly wrapped in aluminum foil up to 3 days at room temperature or up to 4 days in the refrigerator.

making a change

Replace the hazelnuts with pecans or walnuts.

Replace the hazelnut whipped cream with Raspberry Sauce (page 31), Salted Caramel–Bittersweet Chocolate Sauce (page 203), or Hot Fudge Sauce (page 202).

flourless cocoa and bittersweet chocolate cake

THIS CAKE IS THE EPITOME OF CHOCOLATE INTENSITY. IT IS MADE WITH A COMBINATION OF UNSWEETENED CHOCOLATE AND BITTERSWEET CHOCOLATE, AS WELL AS COCOA POWDER THAT IS MIXED WITH BOILING WATER TO RELEASE ITS FULLEST FLAVOR. IT HAS A LIGHT YET DENSE TEXTURE THAT LITERALLY MELTS IN THE MOUTH. SERVE THIS LIGHTLY DUSTED WITH CONFECTIONERS' SUGAR OR WITH WHIPPED CREAM, ICE CREAM, OR THE SAUCE OF YOUR CHOICE.

MAKES one 9½-inch round cake, 12 to 14 servings

SPECIAL EQUIPMENT: 9½-inch round springform pan

CAKE

Nonstick baking spray

8 ounces bittersweet chocolate (70 to 72% cacao content), finely chopped

2 ounces unsweetened chocolate, finely chopped

5 ounces (10 tablespoons, 1¼ sticks) unsalted butter, cut into small pieces

½ cup (1¾ ounces) unsweetened cocoa powder (natural or Dutch-processed), sifted

⅓ cup boiling water

1 teaspoon pure vanilla extract

1 teaspoon pure chocolate extract

5 large eggs, at room temperature, separated

⅔ cup (4 ounces) firmly packed light brown sugar

½ cup (3½ ounces) granulated sugar

⅛ teaspoon kosher or fine-grained sea salt

¼ teaspoon cream of tartar

GARNISH

2 teaspoons confectioners' sugar, sifted

or

2 teaspoons unsweetened cocoa powder, sifted

or

1 teaspoon confectioners' sugar mixed with 1 teaspoon unsweetened cocoa powder (natural or Dutch-processed), sifted

CENTER a rack in the oven and preheat the oven to 350°F. Spray the inside of the springform pan with nonstick baking spray. Line the bottom of the pan with a parchment paper round and spray the round. Place the pan on a baking sheet.

MELT the bittersweet chocolate, unsweetened chocolate, and butter together in the top of a double boiler over hot water, stirring frequently with a rubber spatula to ensure even melting. Or melt the chocolates and butter in a microwave-safe bowl on low power in 30-second bursts, stirring after each burst. Remove the top pan of the double boiler, if using, and wipe the bottom and sides very dry.

PLACE the cocoa powder in a small mixing bowl. Add the boiling water and use a heat-safe silicone spatula to stir together until it forms a smooth paste. Add the vanilla and chocolate extracts and stir together to blend thoroughly

WHISK the egg yolks, brown sugar, and granulated sugar together until smooth in the bowl of an electric stand mixer using the wire whip attachment or in a large mixing bowl using a handheld mixer. Add the cocoa paste and chocolate mixture and blend thoroughly. Add the salt and stir to blend well.

WHIP the egg whites and cream of tartar together in the grease-free bowl of an electric stand mixer with the wire whip attachment or in a large grease-free mixing bowl with a handheld mixer until the whites hold soft peaks. In 4 stages, gently fold the whipped egg whites into the chocolate mixture until there are no white streaks.

POUR the batter into the prepared pan, then use a rubber spatula to smooth and even the top. Bake the cake for 35 minutes, or until a cake tester or toothpick inserted in the center of the cake comes out with a few crumbs clinging to it.

REMOVE the pan from the oven and cool the springform pan completely on a rack. Release the clip on the side of the springform pan and gently pull the sides away from the bottom.

LIGHTLY DUST the top of the cake with confectioners' sugar and serve at room temperature.

keeping

Store the cake tightly wrapped in aluminum foil up to 3 days at room temperature. To freeze up to 4 months, wrap the cake tightly in several layers of plastic wrap and aluminum foil. Use a large piece of masking tape and an indelible marker to label and date the contents. If frozen, thaw overnight in the refrigerator and bring to room temperature before serving.

adding style

Serve the cake with whipped cream, Raspberry Sauce (page 31), Salted Caramel–Bittersweet Chocolate Sauce (page 203), Hot Fudge Sauce (page 202), or any ice cream of your choice.

white chocolate–ginger cheesecake

THE PEPPERY FLAVOR OF GINGER IS THE PERFECT COMPLEMENT TO WHITE CHOCOLATE. IN THIS CAKE, THE GINGER IS USED IN THREE FORMS AND EACH CONTRIBUTES ITS SPECIAL NUANCE. GROUND GINGER IS USED IN BOTH THE FILLING AND THE CRUST, GINGERSNAPS MAKE UP THE CRUST, AND CRYSTALLIZED GINGER ADDS TEXTURE AND A WARM BITE TO THE FILLING. AS WITH ALL CHEESECAKES, IT'S BEST TO BAKE THIS A DAY IN ADVANCE OF WHEN YOU PLAN TO SERVE IT SO IT HAS TIME TO CHILL.

MAKES one 9½-inch round cake, 12 to 14 servings

SPECIAL EQUIPMENT: 9½-inch round springform pan; 10½-inch or larger cake pan or roasting pan

GINGERSNAP CRUST

Nonstick baking spray

13 ounces gingersnaps (about 50)

2 tablespoons granulated sugar

1 teaspoon ground ginger

3 ounces (6 tablespoons, ¾ stick) unsalted butter, melted and cooled

CHEESECAKE FILLING

1 pound white chocolate (31 to 35% cacao content), finely chopped

2 pounds cream cheese, at room temperature

¼ cup (1½ ounces) granulated sugar

4 large eggs, at room temperature

1 large egg yolk, at room temperature

1 tablespoon pure vanilla extract

1 teaspoon ground ginger

⅔ cup (2 ounces) minced crystallized ginger

GARNISH

¼ cup heavy whipping cream

2 teaspoons confectioners' sugar

12 to 20 slices of crystallized ginger

CENTER a rack in the oven and preheat the oven to 300°F. Spray the inside of the springform pan with nonstick baking spray. Wrap heavy-duty foil tightly around the bottom of the pan to prevent water from seeping in as it bakes in a water bath.

PULSE the gingersnaps, sugar, and ground ginger in the work bowl of a food processor fitted with the steel blade until the cookies are finely ground, about 1 minute. Pour the melted butter through the feed tube and pulse until the mixture begins to hold together in moist clumps. Transfer the mixture to the springform pan and press the crust evenly onto the bottom and partway up the sides of the pan.

FOR THE FILLING, melt the white chocolate in the top of a double boiler over hot water, stirring often with a rubber spatula to ensure even melting. Or melt the white chocolate in a microwave-safe bowl on low power in 30-second bursts, stirring after each burst. Remove the top pan of the double boiler, if using, and wipe the bottom and sides very dry.

BEAT the cream cheese in the bowl of an electric stand mixer with the flat beater attachment or in a mixing bowl with a handheld mixer until fluffy, about 2 minutes. Add the sugar and beat together well. One at a time, add the eggs and egg yolk, beating well after each addition. Add the vanilla and ground ginger and blend thoroughly. Stir in the crystallized ginger, then add the melted white chocolate and blend completely.

POUR the batter into the prepared pan, then use a rubber spatula to smooth and even the top. Place the pan into a larger cake pan or a roasting pan. Pour boiling water into the bottom pan until it comes halfway up the sides of the cake pan. Bake the cake for 1 hour and 30 minutes, or until the cake puffs and the top is lightly golden.

keeping

Store the cake tightly wrapped in plastic wrap up to 3 days in the refrigerator. To freeze up to 4 months, wrap the cake tightly in several layers of plastic wrap and aluminum foil. Use a large piece of masking tape and an indelible marker to label and date the contents. If frozen, thaw overnight in the refrigerator and bring to room temperature before serving.

REMOVE the pans from the oven and transfer the springform pan to a cooling rack to cool completely. Release the clip on the side of the springform pan and gently pull the sides away from the bottom.

COVER the top of the cheesecake lightly with a piece of waxed paper, then tightly wrap the pan in aluminum foil and chill in the refrigerator for at least 4 hours.

FOR THE GARNISH, whip the cream in the bowl of an electric stand mixer with the wire whip attachment or in a medium mixing bowl with a handheld mixer until fluffy. Add the confectioners' sugar and whip until the cream holds firm but not stiff peaks. Fit a 12- or 14-inch pastry bag with an open star tip and fill partway with the whipped cream. Pipe stars of whipped cream around the outside top edge of the cheesecake. Center a sliver of crystallized ginger over the top of each whipped cream star.

SERVE the cheesecake at room temperature.

bittersweet chocolate-toasted walnut bundt cake

A COMBINATION OF UNSWEETENED DUTCH-PROCESSED COCOA POWDER, BITTERSWEET CHOCOLATE CHUNKS, TOASTED WALNUTS, BUTTERMILK, AND SOUR CREAM MAKE THIS CAKE UNBELIEVABLY DELICIOUS. THE PAN IS BUTTERED AND COATED WITH A LAYER OF TURBINADO SUGAR THAT ADDS A NICE CRUNCH TO THE CAKE.

MAKES one 10-inch round cake, 12 to 14 servings

SPECIAL EQUIPMENT: 10-inch round Bundt tube pan

CAKE

1 ounce (2 tablespoons, ¼ stick) unsalted butter, melted

⅓ cup (2¼ ounces) turbinado sugar

1¼ cups (5½ ounces) walnuts, finely chopped (see page 10)

3⅓ cups (15 ounces) all-purpose flour

1 cup (3½ ounces) unsweetened Dutch-processed cocoa powder

2 teaspoons baking soda

1½ cups (9 ounces) firmly packed light brown sugar

½ teaspoon kosher or fine-grained sea salt

½ teaspoon freshly grated nutmeg

6 ounces bittersweet chocolate (66 to 72% cacao content), cut into small chunks

2¼ cups buttermilk

1½ cups sour cream

1 teaspoon pure vanilla extract

1 teaspoon pure chocolate extract

CENTER a rack in the oven and preheat the oven to 350°F. Use a pastry brush or paper towel to coat the inside and tube of the baking pan with the melted butter. Sprinkle the inside of the pan with the turbinado sugar and rotate the pan to coat all sides and the center tube.

PLACE the walnuts in a cake or pie pan and toast for 7 to 8 minutes, stirring every 3 minutes, until light golden. Remove the pan from the oven and cool on a rack.

OVER A BOWL, sift together the flour, cocoa powder, and baking soda. Add the brown sugar, salt, and nutmeg, and toss to blend completely. Add the walnuts and bittersweet chocolate chunks and stir to blend thoroughly.

PLACE the buttermilk, sour cream, and vanilla and chocolate extracts in the bowl of an electric stand mixer or a large mixing bowl. Use the flat beater attachment or a handheld mixer to blend together thoroughly. In 4 stages, add the flour mixture, blending well after each addition. Stop often to scrape down the sides and bottom of the bowl with a rubber spatula.

TRANSFER the batter to the prepared pan, then use a rubber spatula to smooth and even the top. Bake for 35 to 38 minutes, until a cake tester inserted in the center of the cake comes out clean.

REMOVE the pan from the oven and cool on a rack for 20 minutes. Invert the pan onto the rack and lift the pan off the cake. Let the cake cool completely on the rack.

SERVE the cake at room temperature.

keeping   Store the cake tightly wrapped in aluminum foil at room temperature up to 4 days. To freeze up to 3 months, wrap the cake tightly in several layers of plastic wrap and aluminum foil. Use a large piece of masking tape and an indelible marker to label and date the contents. If frozen, thaw overnight in the refrigerator and bring to room temperature before serving.

making a change   Replace the walnuts with pecans.

bittersweet chocolate and cacao nib meringue layer cake

SIMILAR TO A CLASSIC FRENCH DACQUOISE, THIS CAKE IS COMPOSED OF THREE THIN MERINGUE LAYERS WITH A FILLING IN BETWEEN EACH LAYER. THE MERINGUE LAYERS ARE MADE WITH GROUND BITTERSWEET CHOCOLATE AND CACAO NIBS RATHER THAN GROUND NUTS AS IN A TRADITIONAL DACQUOISE. THESE LAYERS ARE FILLED AND FROSTED WITH AN AIRY MIXTURE OF CRÈME FRAÎCHE, WHIPPING CREAM, AND MELTED BITTERSWEET CHOCOLATE, MAKING THIS CAKE UNIQUE. THE MERINGUE LAYERS CAN BE MADE UP TO A WEEK IN ADVANCE, THEN ASSEMBLED A FEW HOURS BEFORE SERVING.

MAKES one 8-inch round cake, 12 to 14 servings

SPECIAL EQUIPMENT (OPTIONAL): 14-inch pastry bag and ½-inch plain round tip

MERINGUES

4 ounces bittersweet chocolate (66 to 72% cacao content), chopped into small pieces

2 tablespoons granulated sugar

1 cup (4 ounces) cacao nibs

2 tablespoons cornstarch, sifted

½ teaspoon kosher or fine-grained sea salt

5 large egg whites, at room temperature

½ teaspoon cream of tartar

¾ cup (5 ounces) superfine sugar

CHOCOLATE–CRÈME FRAÎCHE FILLING

1¼ cups heavy whipping cream

1 cup crème fraîche

¼ cup (¾ ounce) confectioners' sugar, sifted

1 teaspoon pure vanilla extract

6 ounces bittersweet chocolate (66 to 72% cacao content), melted

POSITION the oven racks in the upper and lower thirds and preheat the oven to 200°F. Line two baking sheets with aluminum foil. Using an 8-inch cardboard cake circle or round cake pan as a guide, trace two 8-inch circles on each sheet of foil, then turn the foil over on the baking sheets.

IN the work bowl of a food processor fitted with the steel blade, grind the bittersweet chocolate and granulated sugar together until the mixture is a fine powder.

GRIND the cacao nibs to a fine powder in a clean coffee grinder or mini food processor. In a medium mixing bowl, combine the ground chocolate, ground cacao nibs, cornstarch, and salt and toss to blend well.

WHIP the egg whites in the grease-free bowl of an electric stand mixer using the wire whip attachment or in a large grease-free mixing bowl using a handheld mixer until frothy. Add the cream of tartar and continue to whip the egg whites. Very slowly sprinkle on the superfine sugar until the egg whites hold glossy and firm but not stiff peaks, about 5 minutes.

FOLD the chocolate mixture into the whipped egg whites in 4 stages, blending thoroughly. Fit a 14-inch pastry bag with a large pastry tube with a ½-inch round opening and fill partway with the meringue mixture. Holding the pastry bag about 1 inch above the baking sheet, pipe concentric circles of the meringue mixture onto the traced circles, filling in each completely. Or use an offset metal spatula to spread the meringue mixture evenly among the 4 traced circles.

PLACE the baking sheets in the oven and dry for 2 hours. Turn off the oven and leave the meringues in the oven until it is completely cool.

REMOVE the baking sheets from the oven and gently peel the aluminum foil off the back of the meringue layers.

FOR THE FILLING, whip the whipping cream and crème fraîche in the bowl of an electric stand mixer using the wire whisk attachment or in a large mixing bowl using a handheld mixer until thick. Add the confectioners' sugar and vanilla and continue to beat until the mixture holds soft peaks. Add the melted chocolate and blend in thoroughly.

TO ASSEMBLE THE CAKE, place 1 meringue layer on an 8-inch cardboard cake circle or on a serving plate. (First cover the plate with strips of waxed paper to keep it clean.) Spread the meringue circle evenly with one-quarter of the cream filling. Place a second meringue layer on top of the filling and spread it evenly with another quarter of the filling. Place the third meringue layer on top of the cream with the bottom of it facing up. Spread the top of the meringue layer and fill in the sides of the cake with the remaining cream mixture, smoothly and evenly.

TAKE the last meringue layer and crush it into crumbs. Press the meringue crumbs into the sides of the cake just up to the top edge. If the cake is not on a serving plate, transfer it to one. Refrigerate the cake, loosely tented in aluminum foil, until ready to serve, no longer than 6 hours.

keeping

Store the cake tented in aluminum foil up to 6 hours in the refrigerator.

streamlining

The meringue circles can be made up to 1 week in advance. Store them tightly wrapped in aluminum foil at room temperature.

making a change

Add 1 cup (4 ounces) finely ground hazelnuts to the dry ingredients.

cocoa and cacao nib angel food cake

LAYERING CHOCOLATE BY USING COCOA POWDER, FINELY GROUND CACAO NIBS, AND CHOCOLATE EXTRACT GIVE THIS CLASSIC LIGHT AND AIRY CAKE RICH, FULL CHOCOLATE FLAVOR. ALTHOUGH THE CAKE IS DELICIOUS ON ITS OWN, I LIKE TO SERVE THIS WITH SALTED CARAMEL–BITTERSWEET CHOCOLATE SAUCE (PAGE 203). MAKING THIS CAKE IS A GOOD CHANCE TO USE UP ANY EGG WHITES IN YOUR FREEZER. AS WITH ALL ANGEL FOOD CAKES, THIS IS BAKED IN AN UNGREASED PAN SO IT CAN CLING TO THE SIDES OF THE PAN AS IT RISES.

MAKES one 10-inch round cake, 12 to 14 servings

SPECIAL EQUIPMENT: 10-inch round tube or Bundt tube pan

½ cup (2 ounces) cacao nibs

¾ cup (3¼ ounces) cake flour

¼ cup (¾ ounce) unsweetened cocoa powder (natural or Dutch-processed)

⅛ teaspoon kosher or fine-grained sea salt

1½ cups (10 ounces) superfine sugar, divided

12 large egg whites, at room temperature

1 teaspoon cream of tartar

½ teaspoon pure vanilla extract

1½ teaspoons pure chocolate extract

Salted Caramel–Bittersweet Chocolate Sauce (page 203), optional

CENTER a rack in the oven and preheat the oven to 325°F.

GRIND the cacao nibs to a fine powder in a clean coffee grinder or mini food processor and place them in a large mixing bowl. Into the bowl, sift together the cake flour and cocoa powder. Add the salt and ¾ cup of the superfine sugar and stir together until thoroughly blended.

WHIP the egg whites in the grease-free bowl of an electric mixer using the wire whip attachment or in a large grease-free mixing bowl using a handheld mixer on medium speed until frothy. Add the cream of tartar and continue to whip the egg whites. Very slowly sprinkle on the remaining ¾ cup superfine sugar until the egg whites hold glossy and firm but not stiff peaks, about 5 minutes.

ADD the vanilla and chocolate extracts and blend in thoroughly. Remove the bowl from the mixer and use a long-handled rubber spatula to fold the dry ingredients into the egg whites in 4 or 5 stages.

TRANSFER the batter to the pan. Use the spatula to smooth and even the top, then gently tap the pan on the countertop to eliminate any air bubbles. Bake for 40 minutes, or until a cake tester inserted in the center of the cake comes out clean.

REMOVE the pan from the oven and invert it over a cooling rack onto its feet or hang it by the center tube over a funnel. Don't set the pan upright on the cooling rack or the cake will collapse as it cools. Leave the cake to cool completely. It should drop out of the pan on its own. If not, use a very thin long-bladed knife to run around the inner edge of the pan to help the cake release.

SERVE the cake at room temperature with the sauce, if you like.

keeping Store the cake tightly wrapped in plastic up to 3 days at room temperature. To freeze up to 4 months, wrap the cake tightly in several layers of plastic wrap and aluminum foil. Use a large piece of masking tape and an indelible marker to label and date the contents. If frozen, thaw overnight in the refrigerator and bring to room temperature before serving.

making a change Add 1 cup (4 ounces) finely ground hazelnuts to the dry ingredients.

bittersweet chocolate gingerbread

THE SPICES OF GINGER, CINNAMON, CLOVES, AND NUTMEG ADD THEIR MAGICAL FLAVORS TO BITTERSWEET CHOCOLATE AND COCOA POWDER IN THIS SOFT, CAKE-LIKE GINGERBREAD. SMALL PIECES OF CRYSTALLIZED GINGER ADD A BIT OF CHEWY TEXTURE. TRY SERVING THIS WITH WHIPPED CREAM OR ICE CREAM.

MAKES twenty-five 1½-inch squares

SPECIAL EQUIPMENT: 8-inch square baking pan

GINGERBREAD

1 tablespoon unsalted butter, softened (for the pan) or nonstick baking spray

2½ cups (11¼ ounces) all-purpose flour

2 tablespoons unsweetened cocoa powder (natural or Dutch-processed)

2 teaspoons baking soda

1 tablespoon ground ginger

1 teaspoon ground cinnamon

½ teaspoon ground cloves

¼ teaspoon freshly grated nutmeg

¼ teaspoon kosher or fine-grained sea salt

½ cup (2½ ounces) minced crystallized ginger

4 ounces (8 tablespoons, 1 stick) unsalted butter, softened

½ cup (3 ounces) firmly packed light brown sugar

3 ounces bittersweet chocolate (66 to 72% cacao content), melted

2 large eggs, at room temperature

1 teaspoon pure vanilla extract

1 cup unsulfured molasses

1 cup boiling water

GARNISH

Confectioners' sugar

CENTER a rack in the oven and preheat the oven to 350°F. Line an 8-inch square baking pan with aluminum foil, letting it hang about 2 inches over the sides. Use a paper towel or your fingers to coat the inside of the foil with the 1 tablespoon butter or spray the foil with nonstick baking spray.

OVER A BOWL, sift together the flour, cocoa powder, baking soda, ginger, cinnamon, and cloves. Add the nutmeg, salt, and crystallized ginger and toss to blend well.

BEAT the butter in the bowl of an electric stand mixer using the flat beater attachment or in a large mixing bowl using a handheld mixer until light and fluffy, about 2 minutes. Add the brown sugar and beat together until smooth. Stop and scrape down the sides and bottom of the bowl with a rubber spatula.

USE a fork to lightly beat the eggs and vanilla in a small bowl. Add the beaten eggs and the molasses to the butter mixture. Stop and scrape down the sides and bottom of the bowl with a rubber spatula. Add the boiling water to the mixture and beat to blend thoroughly.

ADJUST the mixer speed to low and add the dry ingredients in 4 stages, blending thoroughly after each edition. Stop often and scrape down the sides and bottom of the bowl with a rubber spatula.

POUR the batter into the prepared pan and use a rubber spatula to spread it evenly. Bake for 45 to 50 minutes, until a cake tester or toothpick inserted in the center of the gingerbread comes out with only a few crumbs clinging to it.

REMOVE the pan from the oven and cool completely on a rack.

DUST the top of the gingerbread lightly with confectioners' sugar. Lift the gingerbread from the pan with the aluminum foil. Carefully peel the foil away from the sides. Cut the gingerbread into 5 rows in each direction and serve at room temperature.

keeping

Store the cut or uncut gingerbread tightly wrapped in aluminum foil at room temperature up to 4 days. To freeze up to 4 months, place the gingerbread (cut or uncut) into an airtight container. Wrap the container tightly in several layers of plastic wrap and aluminum foil. Use a large piece of masking tape and an indelible marker to label the contents. If frozen, thaw overnight in the refrigerator and bring to room temperature before serving.

adding style

Serve squares of gingerbread with a dollop of lightly sweetened whipped cream or a scoop of ice cream.

cocoa and chocolate bouchons

BOUCHON IS THE FRENCH WORD FOR CORK, WHICH IS THE SHAPE OF THESE INDIVIDUAL CAKES. THEY ARE BURSTING WITH FULL-BODIED CHOCOLATE FLAVOR FROM DUTCH-PROCESSED COCOA POWDER MIXED WITH BOILING WATER TO BRING OUT ITS DEEPEST FLAVOR NOTES, MELTED BITTERSWEET CHOCOLATE AND UNSWEETENED CHOCOLATE, AND MORE BITTERSWEET CHOCOLATE ADDED TO THE BATTER AS CHUNKS. I LIKE TO SERVE THEM WITH RASPBERRY SAUCE AND FRESH RASPBERRIES, BUT THEY ARE EQUALLY DIVINE SERVED WITH SALTED CARAMEL–BITTERSWEET CHOCOLATE SAUCE (PAGE 203), HOT FUDGE SAUCE (PAGE 202), OR WHIPPED CREAM.

MAKES *twelve 1½ x 1½-inch cakes*

SPECIAL EQUIPMENT: *one 12-cavity 1½ x 1½-inch silicone bouchon pan; 1-inch-diameter ice cream scoop*

BOUCHONS

2 tablespoons unsweetened Dutch-processed cocoa powder, sifted

2 tablespoons boiling water

1 teaspoon pure vanilla extract

2 ounces bittersweet chocolate (70 to 72% cacao content), finely chopped

1 ounce unsweetened chocolate, finely chopped

3 ounces (6 tablespoons, ¾ stick) unsalted butter, cut into small pieces

1 large egg, at room temperature

¼ cup (1½ ounces) firmly packed light brown sugar

¼ cup (1½ ounces) granulated sugar

⅓ cup (1½ ounces) cake flour

½ teaspoon baking powder

⅛ teaspoon kosher or fine-grained sea salt

1½ ounces bittersweet chocolate (70 to 72% cacao content), chopped into small chunks

GARNISH

1 tablespoon confectioners' sugar, sifted

Fresh raspberries

RASPBERRY SAUCE

1 cup (4½ ounces) fresh or fresh-frozen raspberries, thawed

1 tablespoon superfine sugar

1 teaspoon freshly squeezed lemon juice

1 tablespoon framboise, Chambord, Kirsch, or Grand Marnier

CENTER a rack in the oven and preheat the oven to 325°F. Place the bouchon pan on a baking sheet.

PLACE the cocoa powder in a small mixing bowl. Add the boiling water and use a heat-safe silicone spatula to stir until it forms a smooth paste. Add the vanilla and stir together to blend thoroughly.

MELT the finely chopped bittersweet and unsweetened chocolates and the butter together in the top of a double boiler over hot water, stirring frequently with a rubber spatula to ensure even melting. Or melt the chocolates and butter in a microwave-safe bowl on low power in 30-second bursts, stirring after each burst. Remove the top pan of the double boiler, if using, and wipe the bottom and sides very dry.

IN a large mixing bowl, whisk the egg briefly to break up the yolk. Add the brown sugar and granulated sugar and whisk together until smooth. Add the cocoa paste and chocolate mixture and blend thoroughly.

OVER a bowl, sift together the cake flour and baking powder. Add the salt and toss to blend. Add this mixture to the chocolate mixture in 2 stages, blending thoroughly after each addition. Stir in the chocolate chunks.

USE a 1-inch-diameter ice cream scoop or a spoon to divide the batter evenly among the cavities of the bouchon pan. Bake the cakes for 20 to 23 minutes, until a cake tester or toothpick inserted in the center of a couple of the cakes comes out with a few crumbs clinging to it.

TRANSFER the bouchon pan to a rack to cool completely. Invert the pan over the cooling rack to release the cakes, then turn them right side up.

LIGHTLY DUST the tops of the bouchons with confectioners' sugar.

FOR THE RASPBERRY SAUCE, pulse 1 cup raspberries in the work bowl of a food processor fitted with the steel blade until they are pureed into liquid, about 1 minute. Using a rubber spatula or wooden spoon and a fine-mesh strainer, strain the raspberry puree into a medium bowl. Push through the strainer as much of the liquid as possible without the seeds. Add the superfine sugar, lemon juice, and liqueur to the raspberry puree and blend thoroughly.

SERVE each bouchon at room temperature with a spoonful of the raspberry sauce and garnish with a few fresh raspberries.

keeping

Store the bouchons tightly wrapped in aluminum foil up to 3 days at room temperature. To freeze up to 4 months, place the cakes in an airtight plastic container. Wrap the container tightly in several layers of plastic wrap and aluminum foil. Use a large piece of masking tape and an indelible marker to label and date the contents. If frozen, thaw overnight in the refrigerator and bring to room temperature before serving.

streamlining

The raspberry sauce can be made up to 5 days in advance and kept in a tightly sealed container in the refrigerator.

making a change

Serve the bouchons with Salted Caramel–Bittersweet Chocolate Sauce (page 203), Hot Fudge Sauce (page 202), or whipped cream.

adding style

Drizzle the tops of the bouchons with melted white or bittersweet chocolate in close lines.

individual chocolate bundt cakes with white chocolate–passion fruit frosting

UNSWEETENED CHOCOLATE GIVES THESE INDIVIDUAL CAKES A POWERFUL FLAVOR, WHICH IS ENHANCED BY THE FROSTING MADE WITH WHITE CHOCOLATE, CREAM CHEESE, AND PASSION FRUIT CONCENTRATE (SEE SOURCES, PAGE 209). THE CAKES AND THE ICING CAN BE MADE A COUPLE OF DAYS IN ADVANCE AND ASSEMBLED SHORTLY BEFORE SERVING.

MAKES 1½ dozen 2½-inch round Bundt cakes

SPECIAL EQUIPMENT: two 12-cavity Bundt cupcake pans; 2-inch-diameter ice cream scoop; 12- or 14-inch pastry bag and large open star tip

CAKES

Nonstick baking spray

6 ounces unsweetened chocolate, finely chopped

1¾ cups (7¾ ounces) cake flour

1 teaspoon baking soda

½ teaspoon kosher or fine-grained sea salt

4 ounces (8 tablespoons, 1 stick) unsalted butter, softened

1 cup (6½ ounces) superfine sugar

⅔ cup (4 ounces) firmly packed light brown sugar

2 large eggs, at room temperature

1 teaspoon pure vanilla extract

2 teaspoons pure chocolate extract

1 cup sour cream

WHITE CHOCOLATE–PASSION FRUIT FROSTING

⅓ cup passion fruit concentrate (see Sources, page 209)

4 ounces cream cheese, softened

4 ounces white chocolate, melted

¾ cup (2½ ounces) confectioners' sugar, sifted

POSITION the oven racks in the upper and lower thirds and preheat the oven to 350°F. Coat 18 cavities of the Bundt pans with nonstick baking spray and place each pan on a baking sheet.

MELT the unsweetened chocolate in the top of a double boiler over low heat, stirring often with a rubber spatula to ensure even melting. Or melt the chocolate in a micro-wave-safe bowl on low power in 30-second bursts, stirring after each burst. Remove the top pan of the double boiler, if using, and wipe the bottom and sides very dry.

OVER a bowl, sift together the cake flour and baking soda. Add the salt and toss to blend.

BEAT the butter in the bowl of an electric stand mixer using the flat beater attachment or in a mixing bowl using a handheld mixer until soft and fluffy, about 2 minutes. Add the superfine sugar and brown sugar and beat together well. Stop occasionally and scrape down the sides and bottom of the bowl with a rubber spatula.

USE a fork to lightly beat the eggs with the vanilla and chocolate extracts in a small bowl. Add to the butter mixture. Mix together, stopping a few times to scrape down the sides and bottom of the mixing bowl with a rubber spatula. At first the mixture may look curdled as the eggs are added, but as you stop and scrape down the bowl, the mixture will smooth out.

ADD the dry ingredients alternately with the sour cream in 4 or 5 stages, mixing thoroughly after each addition. Add the melted chocolate and blend completely. Use a 2-inch-diameter ice cream scoop to divide the batter evenly among the 18 prepared cavities of the Bundt pans. Fill the remaining cavities of the pans with water.

BAKE the cakes for 25 to 30 minutes, until a cake tester or toothpick inserted in the center of a couple of the cakes comes out with no crumbs clinging to it.

TRANSFER the Bundt pans to racks to cool completely. Pour the water out of the Bundt pan cavities taking care not to wet the cakes, then invert the pans over the cooling racks to release the cakes. Leave them bottom side up.

FOR THE FROSTING, place the passion fruit concentrate in a small saucepan. Cook over medium heat about 5 minutes to reduce it to half the original amount. This intensifies the flavor. Let the concentrate cool slightly.

BEAT the cream cheese in the bowl of an electric stand mixer using the flat beater attachment or in a mixing bowl using a handheld mixer until fluffy, about 2 minutes. Add the melted white chocolate and passion fruit concentrate and blend thoroughly. Beat in the confectioners' sugar in 2 stages, blending well after each addition. If the mixture is too soft, beat in another ¼ cup sifted confectioners' sugar.

TO DECORATE THE CAKES, fit a 12- or 14-inch pastry bag with a large open star tip. Fill the pastry bag partway with the frosting. Pipe a rosette in the center of each cake. Serve the cakes at room temperature.

keeping

Store the unfrosted cakes tightly wrapped in aluminum foil up to 3 days at room temperature. To freeze up to 4 months, place the unfrosted cakes in an airtight container and wrap it tightly in several layers of plastic wrap and aluminum foil. Use a large piece of masking tape and an indelible marker to label and date the contents. If frozen, thaw overnight in the refrigerator and bring to room temperature before serving.

streamlining

The frosting can be made up to 3 days in advance and kept in a tightly covered container in the refrigerator. Bring it to room temperature and beat until fluffy before decorating the cakes.

making a change

Add 1 cup (4 ounces) finely ground toasted hazelnuts or cacao nibs to the dry ingredients.

individual molten mocha cakes

THESE LITTLE CAKES HAVE DEEP CHOCOLATE FLAVOR THAT IS ENHANCED WITH ESPRESSO. IT'S FUN TO ANTICIPATE THE GREAT FLAVOR WHEN THE SOFT CENTER OOZES OUT AS THESE ARE CUT INTO. SERVE THEM WITH FRESH RASPBERRIES OR STRAWBERRIES AND A LIGHT DUSTING OF CONFECTIONERS' SUGAR.

MAKES 1 dozen 3-inch round cakes

SPECIAL EQUIPMENT: 1 dozen ½-cup heat-safe ramekins, custard cups, or bowls

CAKE

1 tablespoon unsalted butter, melted

8 ounces bittersweet chocolate (70 to 72% cacao content), finely chopped

4 ounces (8 tablespoons, 1 stick) unsalted butter, cut into small dice

1½ teaspoons instant espresso powder

Pinch of kosher or fine-grained sea salt

6 large egg yolks, at room temperature

⅓ cup (2 ounces) superfine sugar

1 teaspoon pure vanilla extract

½ teaspoon pure chocolate extract

2 large egg whites, at room temperature

⅛ teaspoon cream of tartar

GARNISH

2 teaspoons confectioners' sugar

1 cup (4½ ounces) fresh raspberries

USE a pastry brush or paper towel to coat the insides of the ramekins with the melted butter. Place them on a baking sheet or in a large roasting pan.

MELT the chocolate and diced butter together in the top of a double boiler over hot water, stirring frequently with a rubber spatula to ensure even melting. Or melt them in a microwave-safe bowl on low power in 30-second bursts, stirring after each burst. Remove the top pan of the double boiler, if using, and wipe the bottom and sides very dry. Stir in the espresso powder and salt and blend thoroughly.

WHIP the egg yolks and sugar together in the bowl of an electric stand mixer using the wire whip attachment or in a large mixing bowl using a handheld mixer until the mixture is thick and pale yellow and holds a slowly dissolving ribbon when the beater is lifted, about 5 minutes. Blend in the vanilla and chocolate extracts. Fold one-quarter of this mixture into the chocolate mixture, then fold the chocolate mixture into the egg yolk mixture.

WHIP the egg whites and cream of tartar together in the grease-free bowl of an electric stand mixer with the wire whip attachment or in a large grease-free mixing bowl with a handheld mixer until the whites hold soft peaks. Gently fold the whipped egg whites into the chocolate mixture until there are no white streaks.

EVENLY DIVIDE the mixture among the ramekins, filling each about two-thirds full. Cover the ramekins tightly with plastic wrap and chill at least 1 hour.

CENTER a rack in the oven and preheat the oven to 400°F. Bake for 11 to 13 minutes, until the edges look set and the centers are still soft and jiggle slightly.

REMOVE the pan from the oven and place on a rack to cool for 2 minutes. Run a thin-bladed knife around the rims inside the ramekins and invert the cakes onto individual plates. Dust the tops lightly with confectioners' sugar and scatter fresh raspberries around each plate. Serve immediately.

keeping	Store the cakes tightly wrapped in plastic wrap in the refrigerator up to 2 days. The texture will become dense.
streamlining	The unbaked cakes can be stored tightly covered in the refrigerator up to 4 hours before baking.
adding style	Serve the cakes with whipped cream, Chocolate Whipped Cream (page 14), or Raspberry Sauce (page 31).

mocha-walnut cupcakes with dulce de leche frosting

UNSWEETENED CHOCOLATE, BITTERSWEET CHOCOLATE, AND INSTANT ESPRESSO POWDER GIVE THESE CUPCAKES A DEEP, RICH FLAVOR THAT IS COMPLEMENTED PERFECTLY BY THE DULCE DE LECHE FROSTING. DULCE DE LECHE IS A CARAMEL FLAVOR WIDELY USED IN LATIN AMERICAN CUISINE. BOTH THE CUPCAKES AND THE FROSTING CAN BE MADE A COUPLE OF DAYS IN ADVANCE AND ASSEMBLED SHORTLY BEFORE SERVING.

MAKES 2 dozen cupcakes

SPECIAL EQUIPMENT: two 12-cavity muffin pans and 24 cupcake papers, or 24 silicone muffin cups; 2-inch-diameter ice cream scoop; 14-inch pastry bag and open star tip

CUPCAKES

1⅓ cups (6 ounces) walnuts

2 ounces unsweetened chocolate, finely chopped

8 ounces bittersweet chocolate (66 to 72% cacao content), finely chopped

8 ounces (16 tablespoons, 2 sticks) unsalted butter, cut into small pieces

1 tablespoon instant espresso powder

1 teaspoon pure vanilla extract

1 teaspoon pure chocolate extract

6 large eggs, at room temperature

¾ cup (5 ounces) superfine sugar

¾ cup (4½ ounces) firmly packed light brown sugar

¾ cup (3¼ ounces) all-purpose flour

¼ teaspoon kosher or fine-grained sea salt

DULCE DE LECHE FROSTING

8 ounces (16 tablespoons, 2 sticks) unsalted butter, softened

1 recipe (1 cup) Dulce de Leche (page 165)

CENTER a rack in the oven and preheat the oven to 350°F. Place the walnuts in a cake or pie pan and toast until lightly golden, about 8 minutes. Remove the pan from the oven and cool on a rack, then finely chop the walnuts. Position the oven racks in the upper and lower thirds and line the cavities of two muffin pans with cupcake papers, or place 24 silicone muffin cups on two baking sheets.

MELT the unsweetened chocolate, bittersweet chocolate, and butter together in the top of a double boiler over low heat, stirring often with a rubber spatula to ensure even melting. Or melt the chocolates and butter in a microwave-safe bowl on low power in 30-second bursts, stirring after each burst. Remove the top pan of the double boiler, if using, and wipe the bottom and sides very dry.

ADD the instant espresso powder and vanilla and chocolate extracts, and stir to blend thoroughly.

WHIP the eggs in the bowl of an electric stand mixer using the wire whip attachment or in a large mixing bowl using a handheld mixer on medium speed until they are frothy. Add the superfine sugar and brown sugar and whip together until the mixture is very thick and pale yellow and holds a slowly dissolving ribbon when the beater is lifted, about 5 minutes. Add the melted chocolate mixture and blend completely on low speed.

OVER a bowl, sift the flour, then add the salt and toss to blend. Add this mixture to the chocolate mixture in 2 stages, blending well after each addition. Stop and scrape down the sides and bottom of the bowl with a rubber spatula.

ADD the walnuts and stir to blend thoroughly. Use a 2-inch-diameter ice cream scoop to divide the batter evenly among the cavities of the cupcake pans.

BAKE the cupcakes for 18 minutes, until a cake tester or toothpick inserted in the center of a cupcake comes out slightly moist.

REMOVE the pans from the oven and cool on a rack for 15 minutes. Lift the cupcakes from the pan and cool completely on racks.

FOR THE FROSTING, beat the butter in the bowl of an electric stand mixer using the flat beater attachment or in a large mixing bowl using a handheld mixer until soft and fluffy, about 2 minutes. Add the dulce de leche and blend together thoroughly.

FIT a 14-inch pastry bag with an open star tip and fill partway with the frosting. Pipe a large rosette in the center of each cupcake. Or use a small offset metal spatula to spread the top of each cupcake with the frosting. If the frosting is soft, chill the cupcakes for 15 minutes to set the frosting. Serve the cupcakes at room temperature.

keeping

Store the unfrosted cupcakes tightly wrapped in aluminum foil up to 3 days at room temperature. Store the frosted cupcakes in a single layer in an airtight plastic container in the refrigerator up to 4 days. To freeze the frosted or unfrosted cupcakes up to 4 months place them in an airtight container and wrap the container tightly in several layers of plastic wrap and aluminum foil. Use a large piece of masking tape and an indelible marker to label and date the contents. If frozen, thaw overnight in the refrigerator and bring to room temperature before serving.

streamlining

The frosting can be made up to 3 days in advance and kept in a tightly covered container in the refrigerator. Bring it to room temperature before using.

making a change

Replace the walnuts with 1 cup (4 ounces) toasted and finely ground hazelnuts or with 1 cup (4 ounces) cacao nibs.

white chocolate–peanut cupcakes with white chocolate–peanut butter frosting

FINELY CHOPPED TOASTED PEANUTS MIXED WITH WHITE CHOCOLATE MAKE THESE DELECTABLE CUPCAKES. THEY ARE DECORATED WITH FROSTING MADE WITH A COMBINATION OF WHITE CHOCOLATE GANACHE AND SMOOTH, CREAMY PEANUT BUTTER. USE A NATURAL-STYLE PEANUT BUTTER AND BE SURE TO STIR IT WELL BEFORE ADDING TO THE GANACHE SO IT IS WELL MIXED.

MAKES 1½ dozen cupcakes

SPECIAL EQUIPMENT: Two 12-cavity muffin pans, 18 cupcake papers; 12- or 14-inch pastry bag and ½-inch plain round tip

CUPCAKES

4 ounces white chocolate (31 to 35% cacao content), finely chopped

1½ cups (6¾ ounces) all-purpose flour

2 teaspoons baking powder

Pinch of kosher or fine-grained sea salt

4 ounces (8 tablespoons, 1 stick) unsalted butter, softened

½ cup (3½ ounces) granulated sugar

2 large eggs, at room temperature

1 teaspoon pure vanilla extract

¾ cup heavy whipping cream

½ cup (2¾ ounces) toasted salted peanuts, finely chopped (see page 10)

WHITE CHOCOLATE–PEANUT BUTTER FROSTING

12 ounces white chocolate (31 to 35% cacao content), finely chopped

⅔ cup heavy whipping cream

1 cup smooth peanut butter, at room temperature

POSITION the oven racks in the upper and lower thirds and preheat the oven to 350°F. Line 18 cavities of the muffin pans with cupcake papers. Fill the remaining cavities of the muffin pans halfway with water.

MELT the white chocolate in the top of a double boiler over low heat, stirring often with a rubber spatula to ensure even melting. Or melt it in a microwave-safe bowl on low power in 30-second bursts, stirring after each burst. Remove the top pan of the double boiler, if using, and wipe the bottom and sides very dry.

OVER a bowl, sift together the flour and baking powder. Add the salt and toss to blend.

BEAT the butter in the bowl of an electric stand mixer with the flat beater attachment or in a large mixing bowl using a handheld mixer on medium speed until fluffy, about 1 minute. Add the sugar and beat the mixture until creamy, about 1 minute.

IN a small bowl whisk the eggs and vanilla together. Add to the butter mixture. Mix together, stopping a few times to scrape down the sides and bottom of the mixing bowl with a rubber spatula. At first the mixture may look curdled as the eggs are added, but as you stop and scrape down the bowl, the mixture will smooth out.

ADD the flour mixture alternately with the cream in 3 stages, blending well after each addition. Add the melted white chocolate and peanuts and stir to blend thoroughly.

USE a 2-inch-diameter ice cream scoop to fill each cupcake paper half full. Bake the cupcakes for 10 minutes. Switch the pans and bake another ten minutes, until a cake tester or toothpick inserted in the center of a cupcake comes out dry and the cupcakes are light golden.

REMOVE the pans from the oven and cool on a rack for 15 minutes. Lift the cupcakes from the pans and cool completely on racks.

FOR THE FROSTING, place the white chocolate in a large heat-safe bowl. Bring the cream to a boil in a 1-quart saucepan over medium-high heat. Pour the cream over the white chocolate and let it stand for 30 seconds. Use a heat-safe silicone spatula to stir the mixture together until smooth. Cover the bowl with plastic wrap and chill until thick but not stiff, 30 minutes to 1 hour.

BEAT the white chocolate ganache in the bowl of an electric stand mixer using the flat beater attachment or in a mixing bowl using a handheld mixer on medium speed until it holds soft peaks, about 1 minute. Add the peanut butter and blend together thoroughly.

FIT a 12- or14-inch pastry bag with a large tip with a ½-inch plain round opening and fill partway with the frosting. Hold the pastry bag about 1 inch above the center of each cupcake and pipe concentric circles of icing to cover the top of each cupcake. Or use a small offset metal spatula to spread the top of each cupcake with icing. If the icing is soft, chill the cupcakes for 15 minutes to set the icing. Serve the cupcakes at room temperature.

keeping

Store the unfrosted cupcakes tightly wrapped in aluminum foil up to 3 days at room temperature. Store the frosted cupcakes in a single layer in an airtight plastic container in the refrigerator up to 4 days. To freeze the frosted or unfrosted cupcakes up to 4 months,place them in an airtight container and wrap it tightly in several layers of plastic wrap and aluminum foil. Use a large piece of masking tape and an indelible marker to label and date the contents. If frozen, thaw overnight in the refrigerator and bring to room temperature before serving.

streamlining

The white chocolate ganache can be made up to 2 weeks in advance and kept in a tightly covered container in the refrigerator. Bring it to room temperature before using.

chocolate cupcakes with salted caramel buttercream

THESE SCRUMPTIOUS CUPCAKES ARE MADE WITH UNSWEETENED CHOCOLATE AND ARE FROSTED WITH CARAMEL BUTTERCREAM MADE WITH FLEUR DE SEL SEA SALT. THE CARAMEL SAUCE USED TO FLAVOR THE BUTTERCREAM CAN BE MADE AS LONG AS A WEEK IN ADVANCE.

MAKES 2 dozen cupcakes

SPECIAL EQUIPMENT: two 12-cavity muffin pans and 24 cupcake papers, or 24 silicone muffin cups; candy or sugar thermometer; 2-inch-diameter ice cream scoop

CUPCAKES

6 ounces unsweetened chocolate, finely chopped

1¾ cups (7¾ ounces) cake flour

1 teaspoon baking soda

½ teaspoon kosher or fine-grained sea salt

4 ounces (8 tablespoons, 1 stick) unsalted butter, softened

1 cup (6½ ounces) superfine sugar

⅔ cup (4 ounces) firmly packed light brown sugar

2 large eggs, at room temperature

1 teaspoon pure vanilla extract.

2 teaspoons pure chocolate extract

1 cup sour cream

SALTED CARAMEL SAUCE

¾ cup heavy whipping cream

1 cup (6½ ounces) granulated sugar

¼ cup water

1 tablespoon light corn syrup

2 ounces (4 tablespoons, ½ stick) unsalted butter, softened

1½ teaspoons pure vanilla extract

1 teaspoon fleur de sel

SALTED CARAMEL BUTTERCREAM

2 large eggs, at room temperature

2 large egg yolks, at room temperature

1½ cups (10 ounces) granulated sugar

½ cup water

¼ teaspoon cream of tartar

8 ounces (16 tablespoons, 2 sticks) unsalted butter, softened

GARNISH

2 teaspoons fleur de sel or other fine finishing salt

POSITION the oven racks in the upper and lower thirds and preheat the oven to 350°F. Line the cavities of 2 muffin pans with cupcake papers or place 24 silicone muffin cups on 2 baking sheets.

MELT the unsweetened chocolate in the top of a double boiler over low heat, stirring often with a rubber spatula to ensure even melting. Or melt the chocolate in a micro-wave-safe bowl on low power in 30-second bursts, stirring after each burst. Remove the top pan of the double boiler, if using, and wipe the bottom and sides very dry.

OVER a bowl, sift together the cake flour and baking soda. Add the salt and toss to blend.

BEAT the butter in the bowl of an electric stand mixer using the flat beater attachment or in a large mixing bowl using a handheld mixer on medium speed until light and fluffy, about 2 minutes. Add the superfine sugar and the brown sugar and beat together well on medium speed. Stop occasionally and scrape down the sides and bottom of the mixing bowl with a rubber spatula.

USING a fork, lightly beat the eggs with the vanilla and chocolate extracts in a small bowl. Add to the butter mixture. Mix together, stopping a few times to scrape down the sides and bottom of the mixing bowl. At first the mixture may look curdled as

Store the unfrosted cupcakes tightly wrapped in aluminum foil up to 3 days at room temperature. Store the frosted cupcakes in a single layer in an airtight plastic container in the refrigerator up to 4 days. To freeze up to 4 months, place the frosted or unfrosted cupcakes in an airtight container and wrap it tightly in several layers of plastic wrap and aluminum foil. Use a large piece of masking tape and an indelible marker to label and date the contents. If frozen, thaw overnight in the refrigerator and bring to room temperature before serving.

streamlining

The caramel sauce for the buttercream can be prepared up to a week in advance and kept in a tightly covered plastic container in the refrigerator. If it is too firm, soften it on low power in a microwave oven for 20-second bursts.

The buttercream can be prepared up to 3 days in advance and kept in an airtight plastic container in the refrigerator or up to 4 months in the freezer. If frozen, thaw overnight in the refrigerator. To rebeat the buttercream, break it up into chunks and place in a mixing bowl. Place the bowl in a saucepan of warm water and let the buttercream begin to melt around the bottom. Wipe the bottom of the bowl dry and beat the buttercream with an electric mixer until it is fluffy and smooth.

the eggs are added, but as you stop and scrape down the bowl, the mixture will smooth out.

Add the flour mixture alternately with the sour cream in 4 or 5 stages, mixing well after each addition. Stop after each addition and scrape down the sides and bottom of the bowl with a rubber spatula. Add the melted chocolate to the mixture and blend together thoroughly.

USE a 2-inch-diameter ice cream scoop to divide the batter evenly among the cavities in the muffin pans.

BAKE the cupcakes for 8 minutes, switch the pans, and bake another 8 minutes, until a cake tester or toothpick inserted in the center of a cupcake comes clean.

REMOVE the pans from the oven and cool completely on racks.

FOR THE SALTED CARAMEL SAUCE, place the cream in a small saucepan and warm over medium heat until bubbles form at the edges.

WHILE the cream is heating, combine the sugar, water, and corn syrup in a 2-quart heavy-duty saucepan. Cook over high heat without stirring until the mixture begins to boil. Place a wet pastry brush at the point where the sugar syrup meets the sides of the pan and sweep it around completely. Repeat this once to prevent the sugar from crystallizing. Cook the mixture over high heat without stirring until it turns amber, about 10 minutes.

STIR in the hot cream using a long-handled heat-safe silicone spatula. Be very careful because it will bubble and splatter. Stir to dissolve any lumps. Add the butter to the caramel mixture and stir until it is melted. Remove the saucepan from the heat and stir in the vanilla and fleur de sel. Transfer the caramel sauce to another container and cover tightly. Let the caramel sauce cool, then chill in the refrigerator until it is thick, about 2 hours.

FOR THE BUTTERCREAM, whip the eggs, egg yolks, and ¼ cup of the granulated sugar in the bowl of an electric stand mixer using the wire whip attachment or in a large mixing bowl using a handheld mixer until the mixture is very thick and pale yellow and holds a slowly dissolving ribbon when the beater is lifted, about 5 minutes.

WHILE the eggs are whipping, place the remaining 1¼ cups of sugar, the water, and cream of tartar in a 2-quart heavy-bottomed saucepan. Bring the mixture to a boil without stirring. Place a wet pastry brush at the point where the sugar syrup meets the sides of the pan and sweep it around completely. Repeat this once to prevent sugar crystallization. Cook over high heat without stirring until the mixture registers 242°F on a candy or sugar thermometer (soft ball stage). Immediately remove the thermometer and place it in a glass of warm water, then remove the pan from the heat so the caramel won't continue to cook.

ADJUST the mixer speed to low and pour the sugar syrup into the whipped eggs in a slow, steady stream. Aim the sugar syrup between the beater and the side of the bowl, so it doesn't get caught up in the beater or thrown against the sides of the bowl. Turn the mixer speed up to medium-high and whip until the bowl is cool to the touch, about 8 minutes.

ADJUST the mixer speed to medium and add the butter, two tablespoons at a time. Continue to beat until the buttercream is thoroughly blended and fluffy. Add the cooled caramel sauce and stir until it is thoroughly blended.

USE a small offset metal spatula to frost the top of each cupcake with about 2 tablespoons of the buttercream. Sprinkle the top of each cupcake with a few grains of fleur de sel or other fine finishing salt. Serve the cupcakes at room temperature.

brownies, scones, and muffins

fudgy pecan brownies

THESE BROWNIES BRING TOGETHER UNSWEETENED CHOCOLATE, BITTERSWEET CHOCOLATE, AND UNSWEETENED COCOA POWDER, WHICH MAKES THEM VERY POTENT. THEY HAVE A DENSE, FUDGY TEXTURE UNLIKE MOST OTHER BROWNIES. BECAUSE THEIR FLAVOR IS SO INTENSE I CUT THESE SMALLER THAN OTHER BROWNIES.

MAKES twenty-five 1½-inch square brownies

SPECIAL EQUIPMENT: 8-inch square baking pan

1 tablespoon unsalted butter, softened

4 ounces unsweetened chocolate, finely chopped

4 ounces bittersweet chocolate (70 to 72% cacao content), finely chopped

6 ounces (12 tablespoons, 1½ sticks) unsalted butter, cut into small dice

3 large eggs, at room temperature

1 cup (5½ ounces) firmly packed light brown sugar

½ cup (3½ ounces) granulated sugar

1 teaspoon instant espresso powder dissolved in 1 teaspoon water

1 teaspoon pure vanilla extract

½ cup (2¼ ounces) all-purpose flour

3 tablespoons (¾ ounce) unsweetened cocoa powder (natural or Dutch-processed)

¼ teaspoon kosher or fine-grained sea salt

1 cup (3¾ ounces) toasted pecans, coarsely chopped (see page 10)

CENTER a rack in the oven and preheat the oven to 350°F. Line an 8-inch square baking pan with aluminum foil, letting it hang about 2 inches over the sides. Use a paper towel or your fingers to coat the inside of the foil with the softened butter.

PLACE the unsweetened chocolate, bittersweet chocolate, and the diced butter together in the top of a double boiler over low heat. Stir often with a rubber spatula to ensure even melting. Or place the chocolates and butter in a microwave-safe bowl and melt on low power in 30-second bursts, stirring after each burst. Remove the top pan of the double boiler, if using, and wipe the bottom and sides very dry. Let the mixture cool while mixing the rest of the brownie batter, stirring occasionally with a rubber spatula to prevent a skin from forming on top.

WHIP the eggs in the bowl of an electric stand mixer with the wire whip attachment or in a large mixing bowl using a handheld mixer until they are frothy. Add the brown sugar and granulated sugar and whip together until the mixture is very thick and pale yellow and holds a slowly dissolving ribbon when the beater is lifted, about 5 minutes.

IN A SMALL BOWL, mix the espresso and vanilla together. Add to the egg mixture and stir to blend well. Add the melted chocolate mixture and blend completely on low speed. Stop and scrape down the sides and bottom of the bowl with a rubber spatula.

OVER a bowl, sift together the flour and cocoa powder. Add the salt and stir to combine. In 3 stages, add this mixture to the chocolate mixture, blending well after each addition. Stop and scrape down the sides and bottom of the bowl with the rubber spatula to make sure the mixture is blending evenly. Add the pecans and blend in completely.

POUR the batter into the prepared pan and use the rubber spatula to spread it evenly. Bake the brownies for 30 to 32 minutes, until a cake tester or toothpick inserted in the center of the brownies comes out with moist crumbs clinging to it.

REMOVE the pan from the oven and cool completely on a rack.

LIFT the brownies from the pan with the aluminum foil. Carefully peel the foil away from the sides of the brownies. Cut into 5 equal size rows in each direction. Serve at room temperature.

keeping

Store the brownies between layers of waxed paper in an airtight plastic container at room temperature up to 4 days. To freeze up to 4 months, wrap the container tightly in several layers of plastic wrap and aluminum foil. Use a large piece of masking tape and an indelible marker to label and date the contents. If frozen, thaw overnight in the refrigerator and bring to room temperature before serving.

making a change

Replace the pecans with 1 cup coarsely chopped toasted walnuts, coarsely chopped whole unblanched toasted almonds, or toasted, chopped hazelnuts.

Replace ½ teaspoon of the vanilla extract with chocolate extract.

adding style

Serve the cooled brownies with a dollop of lightly sweetened whipped cream or Chocolate Crème Fraîche (page 24).

Drizzle the top of the cooled brownies with melted white chocolate or melted milk chocolate in close lines.

triple chocolate-toasted coconut brownie wedges

THE INCREDIBLE FLAVOR IN THESE BROWNIES, MADE IN THE SHAPE OF A TART THAT IS SLICED INTO WEDGES, COMES FROM UNSWEETENED CHOCOLATE, BITTERSWEET CHOCOLATE, AND COCOA POWDER. THE TOASTED COCONUT ADDS EXTRA TEXTURE AND DISTINCTIVE FLAVOR. THE SIZE OF THE WEDGES CAN BE VARIED DEPENDING ON HOW MANY PEOPLE YOU WOULD LIKE TO SERVE.

MAKES one 9½-inch round tart, 12 to 14 servings

SPECIAL EQUIPMENT: 9½-inch round fluted-edge removable-bottom tart pan

1¼ cups (2½ ounces) sweetened shredded coconut, divided

3 ounces unsweetened chocolate, finely chopped

3 ounces bittersweet chocolate (66 to 72% cacao content), finely chopped

4 ounces (8 tablespoons, 1 stick) unsalted butter, cut into small pieces

2 large eggs, at room temperature

⅔ cup (4 ounces) granulated sugar

⅔ cup (4 ounces) firmly packed light brown sugar

1 teaspoon pure vanilla extract

½ cup (2¼ ounces) all-purpose flour

2 tablespoons unsweetened cocoa powder (natural or Dutch-processed)

¼ teaspoon kosher or fine-grained sea salt

CENTER a rack in the oven and preheat the oven to 350°F. Place the tart pan on a baking sheet. Place the coconut in a cake or pie pan and toast for 6 to 8 minutes, stirring every 2 minutes, until lightly golden. Remove the pan from the oven and cool on a rack. Set aside ¼ cup of the toasted coconut for garnish.

PLACE the unsweetened chocolate, bittersweet chocolate, and the butter in the top of a double boiler over low heat. Stir often with a rubber spatula to ensure even melting. Or place the chocolates and butter in a microwave-safe bowl and melt on low power in 30-second bursts, stirring after each burst. Remove the top pan of the double boiler, if using, and wipe the bottom and sides very dry. Let the mixture cool while mixing the rest of the batter, stirring with the rubber spatula occasionally to prevent a skin from forming on top.

WHIP the eggs in the bowl of an electric stand mixer using the wire whip attachment or in a large mixing bowl using a handheld mixer until they are frothy. Add the granulated sugar and brown sugar and whip together until the mixture is very thick and pale yellow and holds a slowly dissolving ribbon when the beater is lifted, about 5 minutes.

ADD the vanilla and stir to blend well, then add the chocolate mixture and blend completely on low speed. Stop and scrape down the sides and bottom of the bowl with the rubber spatula.

OVER a bowl, sift together the flour and cocoa powder. Add the salt and stir to combine.

IN 3 STAGES, add the flour mixture to the batter, blending well after each addition. Stop and scrape down the sides and bottom of the bowl with the rubber spatula, to help mix evenly.

ADD the cup of toasted coconut and stir to blend evenly. Transfer the mixture to the tart pan, using a rubber spatula to spread it evenly in the pan.

BAKE for 35 to 38 minutes, until puffed and set and a cake tester or toothpick inserted in the center comes out slightly moist.

REMOVE the tart pan from the oven and transfer to a rack to cool completely.

TO REMOVE the sides of the tart pan, place the pan on the top of an upside-down small bowl. Gently manipulate the edge of the pan so it falls away. Carefully lift up the tart by the bottom of the pan and place it on a serving plate. Cut the brownies into thin wedges. Sprinkle the top of each wedge with some of the remaining toasted coconut and serve at room temperature.

keeping

Store the brownie wedges up to 3 days at room temperature on a baking sheet with an inch of space between them. Tightly wrap the baking sheet in aluminum foil.

making a change

Add 1 cup (4½ ounces) toasted, chopped walnuts to the batter when adding the toasted coconut.

bittersweet chocolate– peanut butter brownies

I FIRST DEVELOPED THIS RECIPE FOR *BON APPÉTIT* MAGAZINE IN 1995. SINCE THEN I'VE TINKERED WITH IT TO CREATE BROWNIES USING BOTH BITTERSWEET AND UNSWEETENED CHOCOLATE COMBINED WITH A CRUNCHY NATURAL-STYLE PEANUT BUTTER THAT IS MADE WITH ONLY PEANUTS AND SALT. THIS COMBINATION CREATES DEEP CHOCOLATE FLAVOR WITH A NUTTY TEXTURE THAT MAKES THESE BROWNIES EXTRAORDINARY. BAKING THESE IN A 9-INCH ROUND CAKE PAN GIVES THEM A DIFFERENT LOOK.

MAKES 16 brownies

SPECIAL EQUIPMENT: 9 x 2-inch round cake pan

BROWNIES

Nonstick baking spray

3 ounces (6 tablespoons, ¾ stick) unsalted butter, softened

½ cup (5 ounces) crunchy natural-style peanut butter, at room temperature

1½ cups (9 ounces) firmly packed light brown sugar

2 large eggs, at room temperature

1 teaspoon pure vanilla extract

1 teaspoon pure chocolate extract

¾ cup (3¼ ounces) all-purpose flour

1 teaspoon baking powder

¼ teaspoon kosher or fine-grained sea salt

3 ounces bittersweet chocolate (70 to 72% cacao content), finely chopped

2 ounces unsweetened chocolate, finely chopped

GARNISH

¼ teaspoon unsweetened cocoa powder (natural or Dutch-processed)

¼ teaspoon confectioners' sugar

CENTER a rack in the oven and preheat the oven to 350°F. Spray the inside of the cake pan with nonstick baking spray. Place a 9-inch parchment paper round on the bottom of the pan and spray it with the nonstick baking spray.

BEAT the butter in the bowl of an electric stand mixer with the flat beater attachment or in a mixing bowl using a handheld mixer until light and fluffy, about 2 minutes. Add the peanut butter and blend together well. Add the brown sugar and beat the mixture until fluffy and light in color, 2 to 3 minutes.

ONE AT A TIME, add the eggs, mixing well after each addition. Use a rubber spatula to scrape down the bottom and sides of the bowl. Add the vanilla and chocolate extracts and blend well.

OVER a bowl, sift together the flour and baking powder. Add the salt and stir to combine. In 2 stages add this mixture to the peanut butter mixture, blending well after each addition. Stop and scrape down the sides and bottom of the bowl with the rubber spatula, to make sure the mixture is blending evenly. Add the bittersweet and unsweetened chocolates and blend in completely.

POUR the batter into the prepared pan and use a rubber spatula to spread it evenly. Bake the brownies for 30 to 35 minutes, until a cake tester or toothpick inserted in the center comes out with moist crumbs clinging to it.

REMOVE the pan from the oven and cool completely on a rack.

INVERT the pan onto a plate to remove the brownies. Peel the parchment paper round off the bottom, then reinvert so the top side is up.

FOR THE GARNISH, combine the cocoa powder and confectioners' sugar in a small bowl. Stir together until thoroughly blended. Sift this mixture evenly over the top of the brownies. Cut the brownies into thin wedges and serve at room temperature.

keeping

Store the brownies between layers of waxed paper in an airtight plastic container at room temperature up to 4 days. To freeze up to 4 months, wrap the container tightly in several layers of plastic wrap and aluminum foil. Use a large piece of masking tape and an indelible marker to label and date the contents. If frozen, thaw overnight in the refrigerator and bring to room temperature before serving.

making a change adding style

Add ½ cup (2 ounces) cacao nibs when adding the chopped chocolate.

Serve the cooled brownies with a dollop of lightly sweetened whipped cream or crème fraîche.

Drizzle the top of the cooled brownies with melted white chocolate or melted milk chocolate in concentric circles.

bittersweet chocolate-caramel swirl brownies

IT'S HARD TO BEAT THE TASTE OF BITTERSWEET CHOCOLATE AND CARAMEL. FOR THESE BROWNIES, RICH AND CREAMY CARAMEL IS SWIRLED THROUGH THE BATTER, CREATING NOT ONLY INCREDIBLE FLAVOR BUT AN EYE-CATCHING DESIGN.

MAKES sixteen 2-inch square brownies

SPECIAL EQUIPMENT: 8-inch square baking pan

CARAMEL SWIRL

¼ cup heavy whipping cream

¼ cup (1½ ounces) granulated sugar

1 tablespoon water

1 teaspoon light corn syrup

1 tablespoon (½ ounce) unsalted butter, softened

½ teaspoon pure vanilla extract

BROWNIES

1 tablespoon (½ ounce) unsalted butter, softened

4 ounces bittersweet chocolate (66 to 72% cacao content), finely chopped

2 ounces unsweetened chocolate, finely chopped

4 ounces (8 tablespoons, 1 stick) unsalted butter, cut into small dice

1 teaspoon pure vanilla extract

¼ teaspoon kosher or fine-grained sea salt

2 large eggs, at room temperature

½ cup (3½ ounces) granulated sugar

½ cup (3½ ounces) firmly packed light brown sugar

½ cup (2¼ ounces) all-purpose flour

FOR THE CARAMEL, warm the cream in a small saucepan over medium-low heat until it forms bubbles around the edges. At the same time combine the granulated sugar, water, and corn syrup in a 1-quart heavy-duty saucepan and cook over high heat, without stirring, until it boils. Dip a clean pastry brush in warm water and run it around the inside edges of the pan to prevent sugar crystallization. Do this once more as the sugar cooks. Cook the mixture until it turns amber, about 5 minutes.

STIR the hot cream into the caramel using a long-handled heat-safe silicone spatula. Be careful because the mixture will bubble and foam.

REMOVE the pan from the heat and stir in the butter until it is completely melted. Stir in the vanilla. Transfer the caramel to a bowl, cover tightly, and cool at room temperature while preparing the brownie batter.

CENTER a rack in the oven and preheat the oven to 350°F. Line an 8-inch square baking pan with aluminum foil, letting it hang about 2 inches over the sides. Use a paper towel or your fingers to coat the inside of the foil with the softened butter.

PLACE the bittersweet chocolate, unsweetened chocolate, and the diced butter in the top of a double boiler over low heat. Stir often with a rubber spatula to ensure even melting. Or place the chocolates and butter in a microwave-safe bowl and melt on low power in 30-second bursts, stirring after each burst. Remove the top pan of the double boiler, if using, and wipe the bottom and sides very dry. Stir in the vanilla and salt thoroughly. Let the mixture cool while mixing the rest of the batter, stirring with a rubber spatula occasionally to prevent a skin from forming on top.

PLACE the eggs in the bowl of an electric stand mixer or in a large mixing bowl. Using the wire whip attachment or a handheld mixer, whip the eggs until they are frothy. Add the granulated sugar and brown sugar and whip together until the mixture is very thick and pale yellow and holds a slowly dissolving ribbon when the beater is lifted, about 5 minutes.

ADD the melted chocolate mixture and blend completely on low speed. Stop and scrape down the sides and bottom of the bowl with the rubber spatula.

OVER a bowl, sift flour and in 3 stages add it to the batter, blending well after each addition. Stop and scrape down the sides and bottom of the bowl with the rubber spatula, to help mix evenly.

POUR the batter into the prepared pan and use the rubber spatula to spread it evenly. Drizzle the caramel mixture over the top of the brownies in a random pattern. Use the point of a knife or a toothpick to draw through the caramel, creating a swirl design. Don't mix the caramel and the batter together completely or the brownies will lose the design as they bake.

BAKE the brownies for 30 minutes, until a cake tester or toothpick inserted in the center comes out with moist crumbs clinging to it.

REMOVE the pan from the oven and cool completely on a rack.

LIFT the brownies from the pan by holding the edges of the foil. Peel the foil away from the sides of the pan and cut into 4 rows in each direction. Serve the brownies at room temperature.

keeping

Store the brownies between layers of waxed paper in an airtight plastic container at room temperature up to 4 days. To freeze up to 4 months, wrap the container tightly in several layers of plastic wrap and aluminum foil. Use a large piece of masking tape and an indelible marker to label and date the contents. If frozen, thaw overnight in the refrigerator and bring to room temperature before serving.

adding style

Serve the brownies with Bittersweet Chocolate Ice Cream (page 184).

gianduia brownie cake

A BLEND OF BITTERSWEET CHOCOLATE, DARK MILK CHOCOLATE, AND TOASTED HAZELNUTS CREATES THE LUSCIOUS FLAVOR OF GIANDUIA. THIS CAKE STARTED LIFE AS A BROWNIE RECIPE THAT I DECIDED TO BAKE AS A ROUND CAKE. IT IS RICH AND SATISFYING, NEEDING ONLY A DRIZZLE OF BITTERSWEET CHOCOLATE OR A LIGHT DUSTING OF CONFECTIONERS' SUGAR FOR GARNISH.

MAKES one 9-inch round cake

SPECIAL EQUIPMENT: 9 x 2-inch round cake pan

BROWNIE CAKE

Nonstick baking spray

6 ounces bittersweet chocolate (70 to 72% cacao content), finely chopped

4 ounces dark milk chocolate (38 to 42% cacao content), finely chopped

4 ounces (8 tablespoons, 1 stick) unsalted butter, cut into small pieces

¼ cup (1½ ounces) granulated sugar

⅓ cup (2 ounces) firmly packed light brown sugar

2 large eggs, at room temperature

1 teaspoon pure vanilla extract

1½ cups (7½ ounces) toasted and partially skinned hazelnuts (see page 10)

1 tablespoon all-purpose flour

½ cup (2¼ ounces) cake flour

½ teaspoon baking powder

¼ teaspoon kosher or fine-grained sea salt

GARNISH

1 ounce bittersweet chocolate (70 to 72% cacao content), finely chopped

CENTER a rack in the oven and preheat the oven to 350°F. Spray the inside of the cake pan with nonstick baking spray. Line the bottom of the pan with a parchment paper round and spray the round with the nonstick spray.

MELT the bittersweet chocolate, dark milk chocolate, and butter together in the top of a double boiler over hot water, stirring frequently with a rubber spatula to ensure even melting. Or melt the chocolates and butter in a microwave-safe bowl on low power in 30-second bursts, stirring after each burst. Remove the top pan of the double boiler, if using, and wipe the bottom and sides very dry. Add the granulated sugar and brown sugar to the chocolate mixture and blend thoroughly.

USING a fork, lightly beat the eggs and vanilla together in a small bowl. Add to the chocolate mixture and blend thoroughly.

PLACE the hazelnuts and the 1 tablespoon all-purpose flour in the work bowl of a food processor fitted with the steel blade. Pulse until the hazelnuts are finely ground, about 1 minute. Stir this into the chocolate mixture, blending completely.

OVER a bowl, sift together the ½ cup cake flour and the baking powder. Add the salt and toss to blend. Fold this mixture into the chocolate mixture thoroughly.

POUR the batter into the prepared pan. Bake for 35 to 40 minutes, until a cake tester or toothpick inserted in the center comes out slightly moist.

REMOVE the pan from the oven and cool completely on a rack.

PLACE a 9-inch cardboard cake round or a serving plate over the top of the cake pan. Invert the cake pan and pull it away from the cake. Peel the parchment paper off the back of the cake. Leave the cake bottom side up.

FOR THE GARNISH, melt the bittersweet chocolate in a microwave-safe bowl on low power in 30-second bursts, stirring after each burst. Pour the melted chocolate into a parchment paper pastry cone or a plastic snack bag. Fold down or seal the top and snip off a tiny piece of the pointed end. Hold the cone about 1 inch above the surface of the cake. Starting in the center of the cake, pipe thin lines of chocolate in a spiral design, working toward the outer edges. Take a toothpick or the tip of a knife and draw it from the center outward in several places around the cake to create a spider web design. Let the chocolate set for 20 to 30 minutes before serving.

CUT the cake into wedges and serve at room temperature.

keeping Store the brownie cake tightly wrapped in aluminum foil up to 3 days at room temperature. To freeze up to 4 months, wrap the cake tightly in several layers of plastic wrap and aluminum foil. Use a large piece of masking tape and an indelible marker to label and date the contents. If frozen, thaw overnight in the refrigerator and bring to room temperature before serving.

making a change Replace the bittersweet chocolate and dark milk chocolate with an equal amount of gianduia chocolate.

An alternative to the chocolate spider web design is to lightly dust the top of the cake with confectioners' sugar.

adding style Serve the cake with whipped cream, Salted Caramel–Bittersweet Chocolate Sauce (page 203), Hot Fudge Sauce (page 202), or any ice cream of your choice.

white chocolate—macadamia nut brownies

THESE UNUSUAL BROWNIES ARE MADE WITH WHITE CHOCOLATE RATHER THAN DARK CHOCOLATE. THE ADDITION OF MACADAMIA NUTS ADDS EXTRA SPECIAL FLAVOR AND TEXTURE.

MAKES sixteen 2-inch square brownies

SPECIAL EQUIPMENT: 8-inch square baking pan

1 tablespoon unsalted butter, softened

8 ounces white chocolate (31 to 35% cacao content), cut into small chunks

3 ounces (6 tablespoons, ¾ stick) unsalted butter, cut into small dice

2 large eggs, at room temperature

⅓ cup (2 ounces) granulated sugar

2 teaspoons pure vanilla extract

1 cup (4½ ounces) all-purpose flour

Pinch of kosher or fine-grained sea salt

1 cup (5½ ounces) toasted macadamia nuts, coarsely chopped (see page 10)

CENTER a rack in the oven and preheat the oven to 350°F. Line an 8-inch square baking pan with aluminum foil, letting it hang about 2 inches over the sides. Use a paper towel or your fingers to coat the inside of the foil with the softened butter.

PLACE 6 ounces of the white chocolate and the diced butter together in the top of a double boiler over low heat. Stir often with a rubber spatula to ensure even melting. Or place the white chocolate and butter in a microwave-safe bowl and melt on low power in 30-second bursts, stirring after each burst. Remove the top pan of the double boiler, if using, and wipe the bottom and sides very dry. Let the mixture cool while mixing the rest of the batter, stirring with the rubber spatula occasionally to prevent a skin from forming on top.

WHIP the eggs in the bowl of an electric stand mixer with the wire whip attachment or in a large mixing bowl using a handheld mixer, until they are frothy. Add the sugar and whip together until the mixture is very thick and pale yellow and holds a slowly dissolving ribbon when the beater is lifted, about 5 minutes.

ADD the white chocolate mixture and blend together thoroughly. Add the vanilla, flour, and salt and beat until smooth. Add the macadamia nuts and the remaining 2 ounces white chocolate chunks.

POUR the batter into the prepared pan and use the rubber spatula to spread it evenly. Bake the brownies for 35 minutes, until a cake tester or toothpick inserted in the center comes out with slightly moist crumbs clinging to it.

REMOVE the pan from the oven and cool completely on a rack.

LIFT the brownies from the pan with the aluminum foil. Carefully peel the foil away from the sides of the brownies. Cut into 4 equal size rows in each direction. Serve at room temperature.

Store the brownies between layers of waxed paper in an airtight plastic container at room temperature up to 4 days. To freeze up to 4 months, wrap the container tightly in several layers of plastic wrap and aluminum foil. Use a large piece of masking tape and an indelible marker to label and date the contents. If frozen, thaw overnight in the refrigerator and bring to room temperature before serving.

making a change
adding style

Replace the macadamia nuts with pecans.

Drizzle the top of the cooled brownies with melted white chocolate in close lines.

white chocolate—sour cream—blueberry scones

SOUR CREAM GIVES THESE SCONES A BIT OF A TANGY TASTE AND LIGHT TEXTURE. IT IS A BEAUTIFUL FLAVOR ACCENT FOR THE WHITE CHOCOLATE AND FRESH BLUEBERRIES. THESE ARE LOVELY FOR BREAKFAST, AS A SNACK, OR FOR AFTERNOON TEA. THEY ARE BEST SERVED WARM AND CAN BE REHEATED IN A 350°F OVEN FOR 10 TO 15 MINUTES.

MAKES sixteen 3-inch round scones

SPECIAL EQUIPMENT: 2½-inch round plain-edge cutter

SCONES

3 cups (13½ ounces) all-purpose flour

½ cup (1¾ ounces) sliced or slivered almonds, blanched or unblanched

3 tablespoons (1¼ ounces) granulated sugar

1 tablespoon baking powder

¼ teaspoon kosher or fine-grained sea salt

4 ounces (8 tablespoons, 1 stick) unsalted butter, chilled

6 ounces white chocolate (31 to 35% cacao content), chopped into small chunks

1 cup sour cream

1 large egg, at room temperature

1 cup (5 ounces) fresh or fresh-frozen blueberries

GARNISH

1 tablespoon heavy whipping cream

1 tablespoon Demerara or turbinado sugar

POSITION the oven racks in the upper and lower thirds and preheat the oven to 375°F. Line two baking sheets with parchment paper or nonstick liners.

BRIEFLY pulse together the flour, almonds, granulated sugar, baking powder, and salt in the work bowl of a food processor fitted with a steel blade. Cut the butter into small pieces and add to the mixture. Pulse until the butter is cut into very tiny pieces, about 30 seconds. The texture should be sandy with very tiny lumps throughout. Add the white chocolate chunks and pulse a few times to mix.

USING a fork, lightly beat the sour cream and egg together in a small bowl. Add this mixture to the food processor along with the blueberries and process until the dough forms itself into a ball, about 30 seconds.

DUST a large piece of waxed or parchment paper with flour and turn the dough out onto it. Pat the dough into a round or rectangle about 1 inch high. Use a 2½-inch round plain-edge cutter dipped in flour to cut out the scones. Cut straight down without twisting, which seals the edges and keeps the scones from rising. Transfer the scones to the baking sheets, leaving at least an inch of space between them so they have room to expand as they bake.

FOR THE GARNISH, use a pastry brush to coat the top of each scone with cream, taking care that it doesn't run down the sides and under the scones. If it does, wipe it up because it can cause the bottom of the scones to burn. Lightly sprinkle the top of each scone with Demerara sugar.

BAKE the scones for 9 minutes, switch the baking sheets, and bake another 9 to 10 minutes, until light golden.

REMOVE the baking sheets from the oven and transfer them to racks to cool.

SERVE the scones warm or at room temperature.

keeping

Store the scones in an airtight plastic container between layers of waxed paper or on a lined baking sheet tightly covered with aluminum foil at room temperature up to 4 days. To freeze up to 4 months, wrap the container tightly in several layers of plastic wrap and aluminum foil. Use a large piece of masking tape and an indelible marker to label and date the contents. If frozen, thaw overnight in the refrigerator and bring to room temperature before serving.

making a change

Replace the blueberries with raspberries. Replace the almonds with coarsely chopped walnuts, pecans, or macadamia nuts.

milk chocolate–oatmeal–pecan scones

DARK MILK CHOCOLATE, OLD-FASHIONED ROLLED OATS, AND TOASTED PECANS ARE MIXED TOGETHER TO MAKE THESE DELICATE-TEXTURED YUMMY SCONES. BE SURE TO USE OLD-FASHIONED ROLLED OATS, NOT QUICK-COOKING, FOR THE RIGHT TEXTURE. AS WITH ALL SCONES THESE ARE GREAT FOR BREAKFAST AND FOR AFTERNOON TEA. THEY CAN BE REHEATED IN A 350°F OVEN FOR 10 TO 15 MINUTES.

MAKES *sixteen 3-inch round scones*

SPECIAL EQUIPMENT: *2½-inch round plain-edge cutter*

SCONES

1¾ cups (7¾ ounces) all-purpose flour

1 cup (3¼ ounces) old-fashioned rolled oats

¼ cup (1½ ounces) firmly packed light brown sugar

1 teaspoon baking powder

¼ teaspoon baking soda

¼ teaspoon kosher or fine-grained sea salt

4 ounces (8 tablespoons, 1 stick) unsalted butter, chilled

6 ounces dark milk chocolate (38 to 42% cacao content), chopped into small chunks

⅔ cup (2½ ounces) toasted pecans, coarsely chopped (see page 10)

½ cup heavy whipping cream

GARNISH

1 tablespoon heavy whipping cream

1 tablespoon Demerara or turbinado sugar

POSITION the oven racks in the upper and lower thirds and preheat the oven to 375°F. Line two baking sheets with parchment paper or nonstick liners.

BRIEFLY pulse together the flour, rolled oats, brown sugar, baking powder, baking soda, and salt in the work bowl of a food processor fitted with a steel blade. Cut the butter into small pieces and add to the mixture. Pulse until the butter is cut into very tiny pieces, about 30 seconds. The texture should be sandy with very tiny lumps throughout. Add the milk chocolate chunks and pecans and pulse a few times to mix.

WITH the food processor running add the cream through the feed tube and process until the dough forms itself into a ball, about 30 seconds.

DUST a large piece of waxed or parchment paper with flour and turn the dough out onto it. Pat the dough into a round or rectangle about 1 inch high. Use a 2½-inch round plain-edge cutter dipped in flour to cut out the scones. Cut straight down without twisting, which seals the edges and keeps the scones from rising. Transfer the scones to the baking sheets, leaving at least an inch of space between them so they have room to expand as they bake.

FOR THE GARNISH, use a pastry brush to coat the top of each scone with cream, taking care that it doesn't run down the sides and under the scones. If it does, wipe it up because it can cause the bottom of the scones to burn. Lightly sprinkle the top of each scone with Demerara sugar.

BAKE the scones for 8 minutes, switch the baking sheets and bake another 7 minutes, until light golden and set.

REMOVE the baking sheets from the oven and transfer them to racks to cool. Serve the scones warm or at room temperature.

keeping   Store the scones in an airtight plastic container between layers of waxed paper or on a lined baking sheet tightly covered with aluminum foil at room temperature up to 4 days. To freeze up to 4 months, wrap the container tightly in several layers of plastic wrap and aluminum foil. Use a large piece of masking tape and an indelible marker to label and date the contents. If frozen, thaw overnight in the refrigerator and bring to room temperature before serving.

making a change   Replace the pecans with walnuts.

semisweet chocolate, almond, and dried cherry scones

THIS VARIATION ON THE CLASSIC ENGLISH TEATIME TREAT USES ALMONDS, DRIED CHERRIES, AND SEMISWEET CHOCOLATE. THE DRIED CHERRIES ADD A TARTNESS THAT MAKES THESE SCONES UNIQUE. BECAUSE THESE ARE NOT OVERLY SWEET THEY ARE GREAT FOR BREAKFAST. SCONES ARE BEST SERVED WARM AND CAN BE REHEATED IN A 350°F OVEN FOR 10 TO 15 MINUTES.

MAKES *2 dozen 3-inch triangular scones*

SCONES

1½ cups (6¾ ounces) all-purpose flour

1¼ cups (5½ ounces) cake flour

½ cup (1¾ ounces) sliced or slivered almonds, blanched or unblanched

3 tablespoons (1¼ ounces) granulated sugar

1 tablespoon baking powder

¼ teaspoon kosher or fine-grained sea salt

4 ounces (8 tablespoons, 1 stick) unsalted butter, chilled

½ cup (2½ ounces) dried tart cherries

3 ounces semisweet chocolate (62 to 64% cacao content), chopped into small chunks

¾ cup heavy whipping cream

1 large egg, at room temperature

GARNISH

1 tablespoon heavy whipping cream

1 to 2 tablespoons Demerara or turbinado sugar

CENTER a rack in the oven and preheat the oven to 375°F. Line a baking sheet with parchment paper or a nonstick liner.

BRIEFLY pulse together the all-purpose flour, cake flour, almonds, granulated sugar, baking powder, and salt in the work bowl of a food processor fitted with a steel blade. Cut the butter into small pieces and add. Pulse until the butter is cut into very tiny pieces, about 30 seconds. The texture should be sandy with very tiny lumps throughout. Add the dried cherries and chocolate chunks and pulse a few times to mix.

USING a fork, lightly beat the cream and egg together in a liquid measuring cup. With the food processor running, pour this mixture through the feed tube and process until the dough forms itself into a ball, about 30 seconds.

DUST a large piece of waxed or parchment paper with flour and turn the dough out onto it. Divide the dough into 3 equal pieces and shape each into a round about 6 inches in diameter and 1 inch high. Use a sharp knife dipped in flour to cut each round into quarters, then cut each quarter in half, forming 8 triangular scones. Separate the scones and transfer them to the baking sheet, leaving at least an inch of space between them so they have room to expand as they bake.

FOR THE GARNISH, use a pastry brush to coat the top of each scone with cream, taking care that it doesn't run down the sides and under the scones. If it does, wipe it up because it can cause the bottom of the scones to burn. Lightly sprinkle the top of each scone with Demerara sugar.

BAKE the scones for 18 to 20 minutes, until light golden.

REMOVE the baking sheet from the oven and transfer it to a rack to cool. Serve the scones warm or at room temperature.

keeping   Store the scones in an airtight plastic container between layers of waxed paper or on a lined baking sheet tightly covered with aluminum foil at room temperature up to 4 days. To freeze up to 4 months, wrap the container tightly in several layers of plastic wrap and aluminum foil. Use a large piece of masking tape and an indelible marker to label and date the contents. If frozen, thaw overnight in the refrigerator and bring to room temperature before serving.

making a change   Replace the dried cherries with raisins or dried cranberries, or chopped dried apricots, figs, or pitted dates.
Replace the almonds with chopped walnuts, pecans, or macadamia nuts.
Replace the semisweet chocolate with white or milk chocolate.

cocoa scones

EVEN THOUGH THESE SCONES ARE MADE USING ONLY COCOA POWDER, THEY HAVE GREAT DEPTH OF FLAVOR. LIKE OTHER SCONES SERVE THESE WARM WITH BUTTER AND JAM. OR FOR A TRULY DECADENT TREAT SERVE THEM WITH A CHOCOLATE-HAZELNUT SPREAD, LIKE CHOCOLATE HAZELNUT PASTE (PAGE 205). THEY CAN BE REHEATED IN A 350°F OVEN FOR 10 TO 15 MINUTES.

MAKES *2 dozen 2-inch round scones*

SPECIAL EQUIPMENT: *1¾-inch round plain-edge cutter*

SCONES

6 ounces (12 tablespoons, 1½ sticks) unsalted butter, chilled

2 cups (9 ounces) all-purpose flour

½ cup (1¾ ounces) unsweetened Dutch-processed cocoa powder

3 tablespoons (1¼ ounces) granulated sugar

2 tablespoons light brown sugar

2½ teaspoons baking powder

½ teaspoon baking soda

½ teaspoon kosher or fine-grained sea salt

½ cup (2¼ ounces) lightly toasted walnuts, finely chopped (see page 10)

1 cup heavy whipping cream

GARNISH

1 tablespoon heavy whipping cream

1 to 2 tablespoons Demerara or turbinado sugar

POSITION the oven racks in the upper and lower thirds and preheat the oven to 400°F. Line 2 baking sheets with parchment paper or nonstick liners. Cut the butter into small pieces and chill in the freezer for 8 to 10 minutes.

BRIEFLY pulse together the flour, cocoa powder, granulated sugar, brown sugar, baking powder, baking soda, and salt in the work bowl of a food processor fitted with a steel blade. Add the frozen butter and pulse until it is cut into very tiny pieces, about 30 seconds. The texture should be sandy with very tiny lumps throughout. Add the walnuts and pulse to distribute evenly.

WITH the food processor running, pour the cream through the feed tube and process until the dough forms itself into a ball, about 30 seconds.

DUST a large piece of waxed or parchment paper with flour and turn the dough out onto it. Knead the dough briefly, then shape it into a round or rectangle about 1 inch high. Use the round cutter dipped in flour to cut out the scones. Separate the scones and transfer them to the baking sheet, leaving at least an inch of space between them so they have room to expand as they bake. Gather together the scraps, knead briefly, and cut out more scones.

FOR THE GARNISH, use a pastry brush to coat the top of each scone with cream, taking care that it doesn't run down the sides and under the scones. If it does, wipe it up because it can cause the bottom of the scones to burn. Lightly sprinkle the top of each scone with Demerara sugar.

BAKE the scones for 6 minutes, switch the baking sheets and bake another 6 to 8 minutes until set and a cake tester or toothpick inserted in the center of a scone comes out clean.

REMOVE the baking sheets from the oven and transfer them to racks to cool. Serve the scones warm or at room temperature.

keeping

Store the scones in an airtight plastic container between layers of waxed paper or on a lined baking sheet tightly covered with aluminum foil at room temperature up to 4 days. To freeze up to 4 months, wrap the container tightly in several layers of plastic wrap and aluminum foil. Use a large piece of masking tape and an indelible marker to label and date the contents. If frozen, thaw overnight in the refrigerator and bring to room temperature before serving.

making a change

Replace the walnuts with almonds, pecans, or hazelnuts.

cocoa-banana muffins

THESE MUFFINS ARE MADE BY MIXING BOILING WATER WITH COCOA POWDER, WHICH BRINGS OUT THE MOST INTENSE CHOCOLATE NOTES. THE ADDITION OF BANANAS AND MACADAMIA NUTS MAKES THESE MUFFINS EXCEPTIONALLY FLAVORFUL. THEY ARE GREAT FOR BREAKFAST AND SNACKS. I LIKE THEM EITHER AT ROOM TEMPERATURE OR WARM. THEY CAN BE WARMED IN A 350°F OVEN FOR 10 TO 15 MINUTES.

MAKES 1 dozen muffins

SPECIAL EQUIPMENT: 12-cavity muffin pan; 12 cupcake papers; 2-inch-diameter ice cream scoop

4 ounces (8 tablespoons, 1 stick) unsalted butter, softened

⅔ cup (4 ounces) firmly packed light brown sugar

2 large eggs, at room temperature

¼ cup (¾ ounce) unsweetened Dutch-processed cocoa powder, sifted

3 tablespoons boiling water

3 medium ripe bananas

¼ cup plain lowfat yogurt

½ teaspoon pure vanilla extract

½ teaspoon pure chocolate extract

2 cups (9 ounces) all-purpose flour

2 teaspoons baking powder

½ teaspoon baking soda

¼ teaspoon kosher or fine-grained sea salt

¾ cup (3¾ ounces) coarsely chopped toasted, unsalted macadamia nuts (see page 10)

CENTER a rack in the oven and preheat the oven to 375°F. Line each cavity of the muffin pan with a cupcake paper. Or cut parchment paper into twelve 5-inch squares and line each cavity with one of these squares. They will naturally form pleats as they line the cavities of the pan.

PLACE the butter in the bowl of an electric stand mixer or a large mixing bowl. Use the flat beater attachment or a handheld mixer to beat the butter until light and fluffy, about 2 minutes. Add the brown sugar and cream the mixture together well.

ONE AT A TIME, add the eggs, stopping to scrape down the sides and bottom of the bowl with a long-handled rubber spatula after each addition.

PLACE the cocoa powder in a small bowl and add the boiling water. Stir together with a heat-safe silicone spatula until it forms a smooth paste. Add this paste to the butter mixture and blend together well.

USE a fork to mash the bananas in a medium bowl. Add the yogurt and vanilla and chocolate extracts and blend together. Add this mixture to the chocolate mixture and blend completely.

IN a large bowl, sift together the flour, baking powder, and baking soda. Add the salt and toss to blend. Add this mixture to the chocolate-banana mixture in 3 stages, stopping after each to scrape down the sides and bottom of the bowl to promote even blending. Add the macadamia nuts and stir to distribute evenly.

USE a 2-inch-diameter ice cream scoop to divide the batter evenly among the cavities of the muffin pan. Bake the muffins for 25 minutes, until a cake tester or toothpick inserted in the center comes out clean.

REMOVE the muffin pan from the oven and transfer it to a rack to cool. Carefully lift the muffins from the pan and serve them warm or at room temperature.

keeping Store the muffins in an airtight plastic container between layers of waxed paper or on a lined baking sheet tightly covered with aluminum foil at room temperature up to 4 days. To freeze up to 4 months, wrap the container tightly in several layers of plastic wrap and aluminum foil. Use a large piece of masking tape and an indelible marker to label and date the contents. If frozen, thaw overnight in the refrigerator and bring to room temperature before serving.

making a change Replace the macadamia nuts with walnuts, pecans, or toasted hazelnuts.

To make Mini Cocoa Banana Muffins, divide the batter evenly among two 12-cavity 2-inch silicone mini muffin pans. Bake 18 to 20 minutes, until a tester or toothpick inserted in the center comes out clean.

white chocolate–mixed berry muffins

ALMOST CAKE-LIKE, THESE WHITE CHOCOLATE MUFFINS HAVE A LIGHT TEXTURE ENHANCED WITH A MIXTURE OF BLUEBERRIES AND RASPBERRIES. YOU CAN USE EITHER FRESH OR FROZEN BERRIES. IF USING FROZEN BERRIES, BE SURE TO USE ONES THAT ARE NOT IN SYRUP AND DON'T BOTHER TO THAW THEM. SERVE THE MUFFINS WARM OR AT ROOM TEMPERATURE. THEY CAN EASILY BE WARMED IN A 350°F OVEN FOR 10 TO 15 MINUTES.

MAKES 1½ dozen muffins

SPECIAL EQUIPMENT: two 12-cavity muffin pans; 18 cupcake papers; 2-inch-diameter ice cream scoop

2 cups (9 ounces) all-purpose flour

1 tablespoon baking powder

Pinch of kosher or fine-grained sea salt

⅔ cup (4 ounces) superfine sugar

1 cup half-and-half

2 ounces (4 tablespoons, ½ stick) unsalted butter, melted

1 large egg, at room temperature

5 ounces white chocolate (31 to 35% cacao content), cut into small chunks

1 cup (4½ ounces) fresh or fresh-frozen raspberries

1 cup (5 ounces) fresh or fresh-frozen blueberries

½ cup (1¾ ounces) sliced almonds, blanched or unblanched

POSITION the oven racks in the upper and lower thirds and preheat the oven to 375°F. Line 18 cavities of the muffin pans with cupcake papers. Or cut parchment paper into 5-inch squares and line 18 cavities of the pans with one each of these squares. They will naturally form pleats as they line the cavities of the pan.

SIFT together the flour and baking powder into a large mixing bowl. Add the salt and sugar and stir to blend.

IN a liquid measuring cup, combine the half-and-half, melted butter, and egg. Use a fork to stir together to break up the egg. Add this mixture to the flour mixture and stir together with a rubber spatula until combined. Stir in the white chocolate chunks, raspberries and blueberries.

USE a 2-inch-diameter ice cream scoop to divide the batter evenly among the 18 cavities of the muffin pans. Fill the remaining 6 cavities with water. Sprinkle the top of each muffin with sliced almonds, distributing them evenly.

BAKE the muffins for 12 minutes, switch the pans and bake another 10 to 12 minutes, until the tops are lightly golden and set.

REMOVE the muffin pans from the oven and transfer them to racks to cool. Carefully lift the muffins from the pans and serve them warm or at room temperature.

keeping

Store the muffins in an airtight plastic container between layers of waxed paper or on a lined baking sheet tightly covered with aluminum foil at room temperature up to 4 days. To freeze up to 4 months, wrap the container tightly in several layers of plastic wrap and aluminum foil. Use a large piece of masking tape and an indelible marker to label and date the contents. If frozen, thaw overnight in the refrigerator and bring to room temperature before serving.

making a change

Use one type of berry instead of blending them.

cocoa shortcakes with semisweet chocolate whipped cream

DELICATE, DEEPLY FLAVORED COCOA SHORTCAKES ARE SPLIT AND FILLED WITH SEMISWEET CHOCOLATE WHIPPED CREAM AND FRESH RASPBERRIES. IT'S FINE TO BAKE THE SHORTCAKES IN ADVANCE, BUT ASSEMBLE THEM RIGHT BEFORE SERVING.

MAKES ten 3-inch round shortcakes

SPECIAL EQUIPMENT: 2½-inch round plain-edge cutter

BISCUITS

4 ounces (8 tablespoons, 1 stick) unsalted butter, chilled

1⅔ cups (7½ ounces) all-purpose flour

⅓ cup (1¼ ounces) unsweetened natural cocoa powder

⅓ cup (2 ounces) granulated sugar

1 teaspoon baking soda

¼ teaspoon kosher or fine-grained sea salt

¼ teaspoon freshly grated nutmeg

2 extra large eggs, at room temperature

1 cup milk (whole or 2%)

1 teaspoon pure vanilla extract

1 teaspoon pure chocolate extract

BISCUIT GARNISH

1 tablespoon milk, (whole or 2%)

1 tablespoon Demerara or turbinado sugar

SEMISWEET CHOCOLATE WHIPPED CREAM

1 cup heavy whipping cream

2 teaspoons confectioners' sugar

2 ounces semisweet chocolate (50 to 62% cacao content), melted

SHORTCAKE GARNISH

2 cups (9 ounces) fresh raspberries

CENTER a rack in the oven and preheat the oven to 400°F. Line a baking sheet with parchment paper or a nonstick liner. Cut the butter into small pieces and chill in the freezer for 8 to 10 minutes.

FOR THE BISCUITS, pulse together the flour, cocoa powder, granulated sugar, baking soda, salt, and nutmeg in the work bowl of a food processor fitted with a steel blade. Add the frozen butter and pulse until the butter is cut into pea-size pieces, about 30 seconds. The mixture should be crumbly. Don't cut the butter too small or the shortcakes will lose their flaky quality.

USING a fork, lightly beat the eggs in a small bowl. Pour the milk into a liquid measuring cup and add the beaten eggs and the vanilla and chocolate extracts . With the food processor running, pour this mixture through the feed tube and process until all the ingredients are combined and the dough is moist, about 30 seconds.

TURN the dough out onto a large piece of waxed or parchment paper dusted with flour. Dust your hands with flour and shape the dough into a circle or rectangle about ½ inch thick. Use a 2½-inch round plain-edge cutter to cut out the biscuits. Place them on the lined baking sheet, leaving at least two inches of space between them so they have room to expand as they bake. Gather the scraps together and knead slightly. Pat them into a ½-inch-thick circle or rectangle and proceed as above. Brush any excess flour off the biscuits.

BRUSH the top of the biscuits with milk, being careful that it doesn't run down the sides and underneath. If it does, wipe it up because it can cause the bottom of the biscuits to burn. Lightly sprinkle the top of the biscuits with Demerara sugar.

BAKE the biscuits for 12 to15 minutes, until set and a cake tester or toothpick inserted in the center comes out dry.

REMOVE the baking sheet from the oven and cool completely on a rack.

FOR THE WHIPPED CREAM, whip the cream in the chilled bowl of an electric stand mixer using the wire whip attachment or in a medium mixing bowl using a handheld mixer on medium speed until it is frothy. Add the confectioners' sugar and continue to whip the cream on medium speed until it holds soft peaks. Remove the bowl from the mixer and fold in the melted chocolate.

SLICE the biscuits in half horizontally. Place the bottom of one on each serving plate and cover with a scoop of whipped cream. Place about a tablespoon of raspberries on top of the cream and cover them with another small scoop of whipped cream. Lightly place the top of the shortcake on top of the raspberries or arrange it at an angle to the bottom of the shortcake. Scatter a few raspberries around the plate. Serve immediately.

keeping

Store the unassembled shortcakes in an airtight plastic container between layers of waxed paper or on a lined baking sheet tightly covered with aluminum foil at room temperature up to 4 days. To freeze up to 4 months, wrap the container tightly in several layers of plastic wrap and aluminum foil. Use a large piece of masking tape and an indelible marker to label and date the contents. If frozen, thaw overnight in the refrigerator and bring to room temperature before serving.

making a change

Replace the raspberries with blueberries or sliced strawberries, or use a combination of berries.

Add 2 ounces finely chopped semisweet chocolate (50 to 62% cacao content) to the shortcake batter after adding the liquid ingredients.

tarts and tartlets

semisweet chocolate truffle tart

A SYMPHONY OF MAGNIFICENT FLAVORS AND TEXTURES MAKE UP THE HEART OF THIS TART. A CRUST OF GROUND TOASTED WALNUTS AND A SEMISWEET CHOCOLATE TRUFFLE-LIKE FILLING ARE BAKED TOGETHER. WHEN COOLED, THE TART IS FINISHED WITH A SHINY SEMISWEET CHOCOLATE GLAZE AND GARNISHED WITH A VERY LIGHT DUSTING OF COCOA POWDER. A THIN SLICE OF THIS TART WILL GO A LONG WAY WITH CHOCOLATE LOVERS.

MAKES one 9½-inch round tart, 12 to 14 servings

SPECIAL EQUIPMENT: 9½-inch round fluted-edge removable-bottom tart pan

WALNUT CRUST

2 cups (9 ounces) walnuts

½ cup (3½ ounces) granulated sugar

4 ounces (8 tablespoons, 1 stick) unsalted butter, melted

SEMISWEET CHOCOLATE FILLING

9 ounces semisweet chocolate (60 to 62% cacao content), finely chopped

1¼ cups heavy whipping cream

2 large eggs, at room temperature

1½ teaspoons pure vanilla extract

½ teaspoon pure chocolate extract

¼ teaspoon kosher or fine-grained sea salt

SEMISWEET CHOCOLATE GLAZE

2 ounces semisweet chocolate (60 to 62% cacao content), finely chopped

3 tablespoons heavy whipping cream

1 teaspoon light corn syrup

1 teaspoon pure vanilla extract

1 teaspoon pure chocolate extract

GARNISH

2 teaspoons cocoa powder (natural or Dutch-processed)

CENTER a rack in the oven and preheat the oven to 350°F. Place the walnuts in a cake or pie pan and toast in the oven for 6 to 8 minutes, until lightly colored. Remove the pan from the oven and cool on a rack.

PLACE the walnuts and sugar in the work bowl of a food processor fitted with a steel blade and pulse together to finely grind the walnuts. Add the melted butter and process until the mixture is fully combined. Transfer the mixture to the tart pan and press it into the bottom and up the sides. Place the tart pan on a baking sheet and bake for 15 minutes, until the crust is lightly colored. Remove the baking sheet from the oven and place the tart pan on a rack to cool.

FOR THE FILLING, place the semisweet chocolate in a large heat-safe mixing bowl. Heat the cream in a small saucepan until bubbles form around the edges. Pour the cream over the chocolate and let stand for 30 seconds. Whisk together until smooth and all the chocolate is melted.

USE a fork to stir the eggs, vanilla and chocolate extracts, and salt together in a small bowl. Add to the chocolate mixture and stir together until smooth. Transfer the filling to the crust in the tart pan. Bake for 20 to 25 minutes, until the filling is set around the edges but still jiggles in the center.

REMOVE the pan from the oven and cool completely on a rack.

FOR THE GLAZE, place the semisweet chocolate in a medium heat-safe mixing bowl. Heat the cream in a small saucepan until bubbles form around the edges. Pour the cream over the chocolate and let stand for 30 seconds. Whisk together until smooth and all the chocolate is melted. Stir in the corn syrup and vanilla and chocolate extracts until completely blended. Pour the glaze over the top of the tart and spread it to the edges with a rubber spatula. Lightly tap the tart pan on the countertop to eliminate any bubbles. Let the glaze set up at room temperature, at least 1 hour.

FOR THE GARNISH, Lightly dust the top of the tart with the cocoa powder.

TO REMOVE the sides of the tart pan, place the pan on the top of an upside-down small bowl. Gently manipulate the edge of the pan so it falls away. Carefully lift up the tart by the bottom of the pan and place it on a serving plate. Serve the tart at room temperature.

keeping

Store the tart on a plate lightly covered with waxed paper, then tightly wrapped in aluminum foil at room temperature up to 3 days.

streamlining

The walnut crust can be made up to 4 days in advance and pressed into the tart pan, then kept tightly wrapped with plastic wrap in the refrigerator.

making a change

Replace the walnuts with pecans, almonds, or hazelnuts.

semisweet chocolate-passion fruit ganache tart

CLASSIC SWEET PASTRY DOUGH ENCLOSES A VELVETY SMOOTH SEMISWEET CHOCOLATE AND PASSION FRUIT GANACHE FILLING TO CREATE A FABULOUS TASTE EXPERIENCE. A SIMPLE GARNISH OF WHIPPED CREAM FLAVORED WITH PASSION FRUIT IS ALL THIS TART NEEDS. I USE PASSION FRUIT CONCENTRATE AVAILABLE FROM PERFECT PURÉE OF NAPA VALLEY (SEE SOURCES, PAGE 209).

MAKES one 4 x 14-inch tart, 12 to 14 servings

SPECIAL EQUIPMENT: 4 x 14-inch rectangular fluted-edge removable-bottom tart pan

PASTRY DOUGH

1¼ cups (5½ ounces) all-purpose flour

3 tablespoons (1¼ ounces) granulated sugar

⅛ teaspoon kosher or fine-grained sea salt

4 ounces (8 tablespoons, 1 stick) unsalted butter, chilled

1 large egg yolk, at room temperature

½ teaspoon pure vanilla extract

1 tablespoon heavy whipping cream

PASSION FRUIT GANACHE FILLING

8 ounces semisweet chocolate (60 to 62% cacao content), finely chopped

⅔ cup heavy whipping cream

⅓ cup passion fruit concentrate

GARNISH

⅓ cup heavy whipping cream

2 teaspoons confectioners' sugar, sifted

2 tablespoons passion fruit concentrate

FOR THE PASTRY DOUGH, briefly pulse together the flour, sugar, and salt in the work bowl of a food processor fitted with a steel blade. Cut the chilled butter into small pieces and add. Pulse until the butter is cut into very tiny pieces, about 30 seconds. The texture will be sandy with very tiny lumps.

IN a small bowl or liquid measuring cup, beat the egg yolk, vanilla, and cream together. With the food processor running, pour this mixture through the feed tube. Process until the dough wraps itself around the blade, about 1 minute. Shape the dough into a flat disk and wrap tightly in a double layer of plastic wrap. Chill in the refrigerator until firm before using, about 2 hours.

CENTER a rack in the oven and preheat the oven to 375°F. On a smooth, flat surface, roll out the pastry dough between sheets of lightly floured waxed or parchment paper to a large rectangle ¼ inch thick. Peel off the top piece of paper, brush off any excess flour, and gently roll the pastry dough around the rolling pin. Place the tart pan directly under the rolling pin and carefully unroll the dough into the pan. Gently lift up the edges and fit the pastry dough against the bottom and sides of the tart pan, pushing it lightly into the fluted edges. Trim off any excess pastry dough at the top edge of the pan and patch any places that have holes or tears. Place the pan on a baking sheet and freeze for 15 minutes.

LINE the shell with a large piece of aluminum foil that fits well against the bottom and sides and fill with tart weights. Bake the shell for 10 minutes, then remove the foil and weights. Lightly pierce the bottom of the shell with a fork to release air and prevent it from puffing up. Bake another 12 to 15 minutes, until lightly golden and set. Remove the baking sheet from the oven and transfer the tart pan to a rack to cool completely.

FOR THE FILLING, place the semisweet chocolate in a 2-quart heat-safe mixing bowl. Bring the cream to a boil in a small saucepan over medium heat. Immediately pour the hot cream over the chopped chocolate and let stand for 30 seconds. Stir together with a heat-safe silicone spatula until completely smooth and all the chocolate is melted. Stir in the passion fruit concentrate and blend thoroughly.

POUR the filling into the cooled tart shell, making sure it fills the corners. Chill the tart for 1 to 2 hours, until set.

TO REMOVE the sides of the tart pan, place the pan on the top of an upside-down small bowl. Gently manipulate the sides of the pan so it falls away. Carefully lift up the tart by the bottom of the pan and place it on a serving plate.

FOR THE GARNISH, whip the cream in the bowl of an electric stand mixer using the wire whip attachment or in a mixing bowl using a handheld mixer on medium speed until frothy. Add the confectioners' sugar and whip until the cream holds soft peaks. Add the passion fruit concentrate and blend thoroughly.

CUT slices of the tart across the width. Serve each slice at room temperature with a dollop of whipped cream on top.

keeping

Store the tart on a baking sheet tightly wrapped in aluminum foil at room temperature up to 3 days.

streamlining

The pastry dough can be made up to 4 days in advance and kept tightly wrapped in the refrigerator. To freeze up to 3 months, place it in a plastic freezer bag. Use a large piece of masking tape and an indelible marker to label and date the contents. If frozen, thaw overnight in the refrigerator and bring to room temperature before using.

making a change

To make Semisweet Chocolate–Guava Ganache Tart, replace the passion fruit concentrate with guava puree.

bittersweet chocolate-caramel-walnut tart

LUSCIOUS IS THE BEST WORD TO DESCRIBE THIS TART. TWO LAYERS OF GANACHE ENVELOP A MIXTURE OF CARAMEL AND TOASTED WALNUTS, ALL NESTLED INSIDE A SWEET PASTRY SHELL. THERE ARE A FEW STEPS INVOLVED IN PREPARING THIS TART, BUT THEY CAN BE SPREAD OUT OVER A COUPLE OF DAYS.

MAKES one 9½-inch round tart, 12 to 14 servings

SPECIAL EQUIPMENT: 9½-inch round fluted-edge removable-bottom tart pan

PASTRY DOUGH

1¼ cups (5½ ounces) all-purpose flour

½ cup (1¾ ounces) confectioners' sugar

⅛ teaspoon kosher or fine-grained sea salt

4 ounces (8 tablespoons, 1 stick) unsalted butter, chilled

1 large egg yolk, at room temperature

½ teaspoon pure vanilla extract

BITTERSWEET CHOCOLATE GANACHE FILLING

6 ounces bittersweet chocolate (66 to 72% cacao content), finely chopped

¾ cup heavy whipping cream

CARAMEL-WALNUT FILLING

¾ cup (5 ounces) granulated sugar

¼ cup water

1 tablespoon light corn syrup

⅓ cup heavy whipping cream

3 ounces (6 tablespoons, ¾ stick) unsalted butter, softened

½ teaspoon pure vanilla extract

Pinch of kosher or fine-grained sea salt

1½ cups (6¾ ounces) toasted walnuts, coarsely chopped (see page 10)

GARNISH

18 to 20 walnut halves, toasted

FOR THE PASTRY DOUGH, briefly pulse together the flour, confectioners' sugar, and salt in the work bowl of a food processor fitted with the steel blade. Cut the chilled butter into small pieces and add. Pulse until the butter is cut into very tiny pieces, about 30 seconds. The texture will be sandy with very tiny lumps.

IN a small bowl or liquid measuring cup, use a fork to beat the egg yolk and vanilla together. With the food processor running, pour this mixture through the feed tube. Process until the dough wraps itself around the blade, about 1 minute. Shape the dough into a flat disk and wrap tightly in a double layer of plastic wrap. Chill in the refrigerator until firm before using, about 2 hours.

CENTER a rack in the oven and preheat the oven to 375°F. On a smooth, flat surface, roll out the pastry dough between sheets of lightly floured waxed or parchment paper to a large rectangle ¼ inch thick. Peel off the top piece of paper, brush off any excess flour, and gently roll the pastry dough around the rolling pin. Place the tart pan directly under the rolling pin and carefully unroll the dough into the pan. Gently lift up the edges and fit the pastry dough against the bottom and sides of the tart pan, pushing it lightly into the fluted edges. Trim off any excess pastry dough at the top edge of the pan and patch any places that have holes or tears. Place the pan on a baking sheet and freeze for 15 minutes.

LINE the shell with a large piece of aluminum foil that fits well against the bottom and sides and fill with tart weights. Bake the shell for 10 minutes, then remove the foil and weights. Lightly pierce the bottom of the shell with a fork to release air and prevent it from puffing up. Bake another 12 to 15 minutes, until light golden and set. Remove the baking sheet from the oven and transfer the tart pan to a rack to cool completely.

FOR THE CHOCOLATE GANACHE FILLING, place the bittersweet chocolate in a large heat-safe mixing bowl. Heat the cream in a small saucepan until bubbles form around the edges. Pour the cream over the chocolate and let stand for 30 seconds. Whisk the cream and chocolate together with a heat-safe silicone spatula until completely melted and smooth. Pour half of this mixture into the cooled tart shell. Cover the bowl of the remaining ganache tightly with plastic wrap and hold at room temperature. Place the tart shell in the refrigerator to set the filling for 30 to 45 minutes.

FOR THE CARAMEL-WALNUT FILLING, combine the sugar, water, and corn syrup in a 3-quart heavy-duty saucepan. Stir over medium-high heat to dissolve the sugar. Place a wet pastry brush at the point where the sugar syrup meets the sides of the pan and sweep it around completely. Cook the mixture without stirring until it turns amber, about 8 minutes. At the same time, heat the cream to a boil in a small saucepan.

WHEN the caramel mixture turns amber, add the hot cream, the butter, vanilla, and salt and stir constantly with a long-handled heat-safe silicone spatula. Be careful, because the mixture will bubble and foam. When the butter is completely melted, add the walnuts and stir to coat them completely with the caramel mixture. Turn the mixture into a 2-quart heat-safe bowl and chill in the refrigerator until cool and spreadable, about 15 minutes.

POUR the caramel-walnut filling over the chocolate ganache in the tart shell, spreading it evenly.

WARM the remaining chocolate ganache filling in a small saucepan over low heat or in a microwave-safe bowl on low power in 30-second bursts, stirring often, until the mixture is fluid. Pour the ganache over the walnut caramel filling and spread it out evenly.

FOR THE GARNISH, place the walnut halves close together around the outer edges of the tart. Chill the tart for 45 minutes to 1 hour, until firm but not hard.

TO REMOVE the sides of the tart pan, place the pan on the top of an upside-down small bowl. Gently manipulate the edge of the pan so it falls away. Carefully lift up the tart by the bottom of the pan and place it on a serving plate. Serve slices of the tart at room temperature.

keeping

Store the tart on a plate lightly covered with waxed paper, then tightly wrapped in aluminum foil in the refrigerator up to 3 days.

streamlining   The pastry dough can be made up to 4 days in advance and kept tightly wrapped in plastic wrap in the refrigerator. To freeze up to 3 months, place it in a plastic freezer bag. Use a large piece of masking tape and an indelible marker to label and date the contents. If frozen, thaw overnight in the refrigerator and bring to room temperature before using.

The pastry dough can be baked up to 2 days in advance and kept tightly wrapped in aluminum foil at room temperature.

making a change   Replace the walnuts with pecans.

cocoa and bittersweet chocolate frangipane tart

COCOA PASTRY DOUGH HOLDS A FRAGRANT AND TASTY ALMOND AND BITTERSWEET CHOCOLATE FILLING THAT BAKES WITH A SPRINKLING OF SLICED ALMONDS ON TOP. BOTH THE PASTRY DOUGH AND THE FILLING CAN BE MADE A FEW DAYS IN ADVANCE, THEN ASSEMBLED AND BAKED THE DAY YOU WANT TO SERVE THE TART.

MAKES one 9½-inch round tart, 12 to 14 servings

SPECIAL EQUIPMENT: 9½-inch round fluted-edge removable-bottom tart pan

COCOA PASTRY DOUGH

1 cup (4¼ ounces) all-purpose flour

¼ cup (¾ ounce) unsweetened cocoa powder (natural or Dutch-processed)

⅓ cup (2 ounces) superfine sugar

⅛ teaspoon kosher or fine-grained sea salt

3 ounces (6 tablespoons, ¾ stick) unsalted butter, chilled

1 large egg, at room temperature

1 teaspoon pure chocolate extract

BITTERSWEET CHOCOLATE FRANGIPANE FILLING

4 ounces bittersweet chocolate (66 to 72% cacao content), finely chopped

1 cup (3 ounces) sliced almonds

½ cup (3½ ounces) granulated sugar

1 large egg, at room temperature

½ teaspoon pure vanilla extract

½ teaspoon pure almond extract

2½ ounces (5 tablespoons, ⅝ stick) unsalted butter, softened

2 tablespoons all-purpose flour

TOPPING

½ cup (1½ ounces) sliced almonds, blanched or unblanched

FOR THE PASTRY DOUGH, briefly pulse together the flour, cocoa powder, superfine sugar, and salt in the work bowl of a food processor fitted with a steel blade. Cut the chilled butter into small pieces and add. Pulse until the butter is cut into very tiny pieces, about 30 seconds. The texture will be sandy with very tiny lumps.

IN a small bowl or liquid measuring cup, beat the egg and chocolate extract together. With the food processor running, pour this mixture through the feed tube. Process until the dough wraps itself around the blade, about 1 minute. Shape the dough into a flat disk and wrap tightly in a double layer of plastic wrap. Chill in the refrigerator until firm before using, about 2 hours.

CENTER a rack in the oven and preheat the oven to 375°F. On a smooth, flat surface, roll out the pastry dough between sheets of lightly floured waxed or parchment paper to a large rectangle ¼ inch thick. Peel off the top piece of paper, brush off any excess flour, and gently roll the pastry dough around the rolling pin. Place the tart pan directly under the rolling pin and carefully unroll the dough into the pan. Gently lift up the edges and fit the pastry dough against the bottom and sides of the tart pan, pushing it lightly into the fluted edges. Trim off any excess pastry dough at the top edge of the pan and patch any places that have holes or tears. Place the pan on a baking sheet and chill for 15 minutes.

FOR THE FILLING, melt the bittersweet chocolate in the top of a double boiler over hot water, stirring frequently with a rubber spatula to ensure even melting. Or melt the chocolate in a microwave-safe bowl on low power in 30-second bursts, stirring after each burst. Remove the top pan of the double boiler, if using, and wipe the bottom and sides very dry.

PLACE the almonds and granulated sugar in the work bowl of a food processor fitted with a steel blade. Pulse until the almonds are finely ground, about 1 minute. In a small bowl beat together the egg and vanilla and almond extracts. And add this mixture through the feed tube while the food processor is running.

CUT the butter into small pieces and add to the mixture. Pulse several times to blend. Add the flour and pulse until the mixture is smooth, about 15 seconds. Add the melted chocolate to the mixture and pulse to blend thoroughly.

TRANSFER the filling to the tart shell and spread it out evenly. Sprinkle the topping of sliced almonds evenly over the tart. Bake the tart for 25 minutes, until the filling is puffed and set.

REMOVE the pan from the oven and transfer the tart pan to a cooling rack to cool completely.

TO REMOVE the sides of the tart pan, place the pan on the top of an upside-down small bowl. Gently manipulate the edges of the pan so it falls away. Carefully lift up the tart by the bottom of the pan and place it on a serving plate. Serve the tart at room temperature.

keeping

Store the tart on a baking sheet tightly wrapped in aluminum foil at room temperature up to 3 days.

streamlining

The pastry dough can be made up to 4 days in advance and kept tightly wrapped in the refrigerator. To freeze up to 3 months, place it in a plastic freezer bag. Use a large piece of masking tape and an indelible marker to label and date the contents. If frozen, thaw overnight in the refrigerator and bring to room temperature before using.

The frangipane filling can be made up to 4 days in advance and kept in a tightly sealed container in the refrigerator. To freeze up to 3 months, place the container in a plastic freezer bag. Use a large piece of masking tape and an indelible marker to label and date the contents. If frozen, thaw overnight in the refrigerator and bring to room temperature before using.

making a change

Replace the almonds with toasted and skinned hazelnuts, or toasted pecans, macadamia nuts, or walnuts.

adding style

Serve slices of the tart with Bittersweet Chocolate Ice Cream (page 184) or Cocoa and Bittersweet Chocolate Sorbet (page 193).

bittersweet chocolate ganache pizza

THIS IS A CHOCOLATE TART SHAPED TO LOOK LIKE A PIZZA AND MADE IN A PIZZA PAN. A THIN LAYER OF SWEET PASTRY DOUGH IS BAKED BLIND, THEN SPREAD WITH A LAYER OF WHIPPED BITTERSWEET CHOCOLATE GANACHE, AND TOPPED WITH WHITE CHOCOLATE SHAVINGS. THIS TART IS A GOOD CHOICE TO SERVE FOR A LARGE GROUP BECAUSE IT YIELDS MANY SERVINGS.

MAKES one 12-inch round tart, 12 to 18 servings

SPECIAL EQUIPMENT: 12-inch round pizza pan

PASTRY DOUGH

2 cups (9 ounces) all-purpose flour

¾ cup (2¼ ounces) confectioners' sugar

⅛ teaspoon kosher or fine-grained sea salt

8 ounces (16 tablespoons, 2 sticks) unsalted butter, chilled

2 large egg yolks, at room temperature

1 teaspoon pure vanilla extract

BITTERSWEET CHOCOLATE GANACHE FILLING

1 pound bittersweet chocolate (66 to 72% cacao content), finely chopped

1½ cups heavy whipping cream

2 teaspoons pure vanilla extract

GARNISH

3 ounces white chocolate (31 to 35% cacao content), shaved

FOR THE PASTRY DOUGH, briefly pulse the flour, sugar, and salt in the work bowl of a food processor fitted with a steel blade. Cut the chilled butter into small pieces and add. Pulse until the butter is cut into very tiny pieces, about 30 seconds. The texture will be sandy with very tiny lumps.

IN a small bowl, use a fork to beat the egg yolks and vanilla together. With the food processor running, pour this mixture through the feed tube. Process until the dough wraps itself around the blade, about 1 minute. Shape the dough into a flat disk and wrap tightly in a double layer of plastic wrap. Chill in the refrigerator until firm before using, about 2 hours.

ON a smooth, flat surface, roll out the pastry dough between sheets of waxed or parchment paper to a large circle ¼ inch thick. Peel off the top piece of paper and gently roll the pastry dough around the rolling pin. Place the pizza pan directly under the rolling pin and carefully unroll the dough onto the pan. Trim off any excess pastry dough at the outer edge of the pan. Use the tines of a fork to press around the outer edges of the pastry dough, forming a design and creating the outer border. Freeze the dough for 15 minutes. Center a rack in the oven and preheat the oven to 375°F.

LINE the pastry dough with a large piece of aluminum foil that fits well against the bottom and border and fill with tart weights. Bake for 10 minutes. Remove the foil and weights, lightly pierce the dough with a fork in several places to release air and prevent it from puffing up, and bake another 12 to 15 minutes, until lightly golden and set. Remove the pan from the oven and transfer to a rack to cool completely.

FOR THE FILLING, place the bittersweet chocolate in a 2-quart heat-safe mixing bowl. Bring the cream to a boil in a 1-quart saucepan over medium heat. Immediately

Store the pizza lightly covered with waxed paper and tightly wrapped in aluminum foil in the refrigerator up to 3 days.

streamlining

The pastry dough can be made up to 4 days in advance and kept tightly wrapped in the refrigerator. To freeze up to 3 months, place it in a plastic freezer bag. Use a large piece of masking tape and an indelible marker to label and date the contents. If frozen, thaw overnight in the refrigerator and bring to room temperature before using.

The pastry shell can be baked and held at room temperature tightly wrapped in aluminum foil up to 2 days before adding the filling.

The ganache filling can be made up to 4 days in advance and kept in a tightly sealed container in the refrigerator. To freeze up to 3 months, place the container in a plastic freezer bag. Use a large piece of masking tape and an indelible marker to label and date the contents. If frozen, thaw overnight in the refrigerator and bring to room temperature before using.

pour the hot cream over the chopped chocolate and let stand for 30 seconds. Stir together with a heat-safe silicone spatula until completely melted and smooth. Stir in the vanilla and blend thoroughly. Cover the top of the bowl tightly with plastic wrap and chill until thick but not stiff, about 1 hour.

BEAT the ganache filling in the bowl of an electric stand mixer using the flat beater attachment or in a large mixing bowl using a handheld mixer on medium speed until it holds soft peaks, no longer than 1 minute.

TRANSFER the filling to the cooled pizza shell and spread it out evenly with a rubber spatula or small offset metal spatula, leaving a 1-inch border of the dough all around. Sprinkle the white chocolate shavings evenly over the top of the pizza.

CUT wedge-shaped slices of the pizza and serve at room temperature.

bittersweet chocolate–caramelized banana tart

CHOCOLATE AND BANANAS ARE A GREAT FLAVOR COMBINATION AND THE FILLING OF CARAMELIZED BANANAS MAKES THIS A SENSATIONAL DESSERT. IN THIS TART, COCOA PASTRY DOUGH IS BAKED BLIND, THEN PAINTED WITH BITTERSWEET CHOCOLATE WHEN COOL. THE TART SHELL HOLDS THE FILLING OF CARAMELIZED BANANAS THAT ARE DECORATED BY DRIZZLING BITTERSWEET CHOCOLATE ON TOP.

MAKES one 9½-inch round tart, 12 to 14 servings

SPECIAL EQUIPMENT: 9½-inch round fluted-edge removable-bottom tart pan

COCOA PASTRY DOUGH

1 cup (4¼ ounces) all-purpose flour

¼ cup unsweetened cocoa powder (natural or Dutch-processed)

⅓ cup (2 ounces) superfine sugar

⅛ teaspoon kosher or fine-grained sea salt

3 ounces (6 tablespoons, ¾ stick) unsalted butter, chilled

1 large egg, at room temperature

1 teaspoon pure chocolate extract

CHOCOLATE FILLING

2 ounces bittersweet chocolate (66 to 72% cacao content), finely chopped

CARAMELIZED BANANA FILLING

2 ounces (4 tablespoons, ½ stick) unsalted butter, softened

4 large, firm, ripe bananas cut into ½-inch-thick diagonal slices

⅓ cup (2 ounces) firmly packed light brown sugar

½ teaspoon kosher or fine-grained sea salt

CHOCOLATE DRIZZLE GARNISH

1 ounce bittersweet chocolate (66 to 72% cacao content), finely chopped

FOR THE PASTRY DOUGH, briefly pulse together the flour, cocoa powder, superfine sugar, and salt in the work bowl of a food processor fitted with a steel blade. Cut the chilled butter into small pieces and add. Pulse until the butter is cut into very tiny pieces, about 30 seconds. The mixture will be sandy with very tiny lumps.

IN a small bowl or liquid measuring cup, beat the egg and chocolate extract together. With the food processor running, pour this mixture through the feed tube. Process until the dough wraps itself around the blade, about 1 minute. Shape the dough into a flat disk and wrap tightly in a double layer of plastic wrap. Chill in the refrigerator until firm before using, about 2 hours.

CENTER a rack in the oven and preheat the oven to 375°F. On a smooth, flat surface, roll out the pastry dough between sheets of lightly floured waxed or parchment paper to a large rectangle ¼ inch thick. Peel off the top piece of paper, brush off any excess flour, and gently roll the pastry dough around the rolling pin. Place the tart pan directly under the rolling pin and carefully unroll the dough into the pan. Gently lift up the edges and fit the pastry dough against the bottom and sides of the tart pan, pushing it lightly into the fluted edges. Trim off any excess pastry dough at the top edge of the pan and patch any places that have holes or tears. Place the pan on a baking sheet and chill for 15 minutes.

LINE the pastry shell with a large piece of aluminum foil and fill with tart weights. Bake the tart for 10 minutes. Remove the foil and tart weights, lightly pierce the pastry shell with a fork in several places to release air and prevent it from puffing up, and bake the pastry shell another 10 to 12 minutes, until firm and completely baked. Remove the baking sheet from the oven and transfer the tart pan to a rack to cool completely.

FOR THE CHOCOLATE FILLING, melt the chocolate in the top of a double boiler over hot water, stirring frequently with a rubber spatula to ensure even melting. Or melt the chocolate in a microwave-safe bowl on low power in 30-second bursts, stirring after each burst. Remove the top pan of the double boiler, if using, and wipe the bottom and sides very dry. Use a pastry brush or the back of a spoon to paint the inside of the tart shell with the melted chocolate. Let the chocolate set at room temperature.

FOR THE CARAMELIZED BANANA FILLING, melt the butter in a large saucepan or skillet. Add the sliced bananas and sprinkle with the light brown sugar. Stir the mixture and cook over medium heat to caramelize the sugar, about 5 minutes. Sprinkle the mixture with the salt and stir to distribute evenly. Transfer the bananas to the tart shell and spread them out evenly.

FOR THE CHOCOLATE DRIZZLE GARNISH, melt the bittersweet chocolate in a microwave-safe bowl on low power in 30-second bursts, stirring after each burst. Pour the melted chocolate into a parchment paper pastry cone or a plastic snack bag. Fold down or seal the top and snip off a tiny piece of the pointed end. Hold the cone about 1 inch above the surface of the cake. Drizzle the chocolate over the top of the bananas in a random pattern. Let the chocolate set at room temperature, about 15 minutes.

TO REMOVE the sides of the tart pan place the pan on the top of an upside-down small bowl. Gently manipulate the edges of the pan so it falls away. Carefully lift up the tart by the bottom of the pan and place it on a serving plate. Serve the tart at room temperature.

keeping

Store the tart on a baking sheet tightly wrapped in aluminum foil at room temperature up to 2 days.

streamlining

The pastry dough can be made up to 4 days in advance and kept tightly wrapped in the refrigerator. To freeze up to 3 months, place it in a plastic freezer bag. Use a large piece of masking tape and an indelible marker to label and date the contents. If frozen, thaw overnight in the refrigerator and bring to room temperature before using.

The pastry shell can be baked and held at room temperature tightly wrapped in aluminum foil up to 2 days before filling.

making a change

To make White Chocolate Mousse Tart, replace the caramelized banana filling with White Chocolate Mousse (page 156).

bittersweet chocolate, apple, and pecan strudel

A BLEND OF BITTERSWEET CHOCOLATE CHUNKS, GRANNY SMITH APPLES, AND TOASTED PECANS MAKE A TANTALIZING FILLING ENVELOPED IN LAYERS OF FILO DOUGH. IT CAN BE SERVED EITHER WARM OR AT ROOM TEMPERATURE AND CAN BE REHEATED IN A 350°F OVEN FOR ABOUT 8 MINUTES. BE SURE TO THAW THE FILO DOUGH IN THE REFRIGERATOR AT LEAST A DAY IN ADVANCE OF WHEN YOU PLAN TO MAKE THIS.

MAKES three 8 x 3-inch strudels, 12 to 15 servings

STRUDEL

⅔ cup (2½ ounces) pecans

2 large or 3 medium Granny Smith apples (1 to 1¼ pounds)

1 teaspoon freshly squeezed lemon juice

1 teaspoon pure vanilla bean paste

2 tablespoons firmly packed light brown sugar

6 ounces bittersweet chocolate (66 to 72% cacao content), chopped into small chunks

18 half-size (9 x 12-inch) sheets filo dough, thawed

3 ounces (6 tablespoons, ¾ stick) unsalted butter, melted

GARNISH

1 ounce bittersweet chocolate, finely chopped

CENTER a rack in the oven and preheat the oven to 350°F. Place the pecans in a cake or pie pan and toast in the oven for 8 minutes. Remove the pan from the oven and cool then chop the pecans fine. Line a baking sheet with parchment paper or a nonstick liner.

PEEL, quarter, and core the apples, then cut them into 1-inch-thick chunks. Put them in a large mixing bowl and add the lemon juice, vanilla bean paste, and brown sugar. Toss to coat the apples completely and let the mixture stand for 10 minutes. Add the chocolate chunks and stir to blend well.

KEEP the filo dough covered with a damp paper towel so it doesn't dry out. Take one sheet of filo dough and lay it across the width of the baking sheet at one short end. Use a pastry brush to lightly brush the filo dough with melted butter. Repeat with 5 more sheets of the filo.

TAKE one-third of the apple mixture and spread it along the center of the filo, lengthwise. Leave 2 inches at the short ends and 3 inches at the long ends. Fold the short ends of the filo dough into the center and brush lightly with butter, then fold the long ends in and brush them lightly with butter. Use a long-bladed offset metal spatula to turn the strudel over so the seam is on the bottom.

REPEAT with the remaining sheets of filo dough, butter, and filling, making two more strudels.

BAKE the strudels for 20 to 25 minutes, until light golden brown. Remove the pan from the oven and cool on a rack.

FOR THE GARNISH, melt the chocolate in a microwave-safe bowl on low power in 30-second bursts, stirring after each burst. Pour the melted chocolate into a parchment paper pastry cone or a plastic snack bag. Fold down or seal the top and snip off a tiny piece of the pointed end. Hold the cone about 1 inch above the surface of the cake. Drizzle the chocolate over the strudels, moving from side to side, forming thin lines across the tops. Let the chocolate set at room temperature, about 15 minutes.

CUT 2-inch slices of strudel across the width and serve warm or at room temperature.

keeping
making a change
adding style

Store the strudel tightly covered with aluminum foil at room temperature for 2 days.

Replace the pecans with walnuts.

Serve the strudel with scoops of Bittersweet Chocolate Ice Cream (page 184) or White Chocolate Ice Cream (page 190).

bittersweet chocolate tart with candied orange peel and almonds

BITTERSWEET CHOCOLATE GANACHE IS POURED OVER A MIXTURE OF CANDIED ORANGE PEEL, TOASTED ALMONDS, SUGAR, AND CINNAMON IN A PREBAKED COCOA PASTRY SHELL. WHEN THE FILLING IS ALMOST SET, A LITTLE OF THE CANDIED ORANGE PEEL MIXTURE IS SPRINKLED ON TOP OF THE GANACHE ADDING COLOR AND TEXTURE. THIS IS A GREAT CHOICE FOR SPECIAL OCCASIONS.

MAKES one 9½-inch round tart, 12 to 14 servings

SPECIAL EQUIPMENT: 9½-inch round fluted-edge removable-bottom tart pan

COCOA PASTRY DOUGH

¾ cup (3¼ ounces) all-purpose flour

⅓ cup (1¼ ounces) unsweetened cocoa powder (natural or Dutch-processed)

½ cup (3½ ounces) superfine sugar

½ teaspoon ground cinnamon

⅛ teaspoon kosher or fine-grained sea salt

4 ounces (8 tablespoons, 1 stick) unsalted butter, chilled

2 tablespoons heavy whipping cream

½ teaspoon pure vanilla extract

CANDIED ORANGE PEEL

1 large orange

¾ cup (5 ounces) granulated sugar

½ cup water

ALMOND, ORANGE, AND CINNAMON FILLING

1¼ cups (3¾ ounces) sliced almonds, blanched or unblanched, toasted and finely chopped (see page 10)

1 cup (4¾ ounces) finely chopped candied orange peel

1 tablespoon superfine sugar

1½ teaspoons ground cinnamon

BITTERSWEET CHOCOLATE GANACHE FILLING

8 ounces bittersweet chocolate (66 to 72% cacao content), finely chopped

1 cup heavy whipping cream

1 tablespoon Grand Marnier or other orange-flavored liqueur

FOR THE PASTRY DOUGH, briefly pulse together the flour, cocoa powder, superfine sugar, cinnamon, and salt in the work bowl of a food processor fitted with a steel blade. Cut the chilled butter into small pieces and add. Pulse until the butter is cut into very tiny pieces, about 30 seconds. The texture will be sandy with very tiny lumps.

IN a small bowl or liquid measuring cup, combine the cream and vanilla. With the food processor running, pour this mixture through the feed tube. Process until the dough wraps itself around the blade, about 1 minute. Shape the dough into a flat disk and wrap tightly in a double layer of plastic wrap. Chill in the refrigerator until firm before using, about 2 hours.

CENTER a rack in the oven and preheat the oven to 375°F. On a smooth, flat surface, roll out the pastry dough between sheets of lightly floured waxed or parchment paper to a large circle about ¼ inch thick. Peel off the top piece of paper, brush off any excess flour, and gently roll the pastry dough around the rolling pin. Place the tart pan directly under the rolling pin and carefully unroll the dough into the pan. Gently lift up the edges and fit the pastry dough against the bottom and sides of the tart pan, pushing it lightly into the fluted edges. Trim off any excess pastry dough at the top edge of the pan and patch any places that have holes or tears. Place the pan on a baking sheet and freeze for 15 minutes.

LINE the shell with a large piece of aluminum foil that fits well against the bottom and sides and fill with tart weights. Bake the tart shell for 10 minutes. Remove the foil and tart weights, lightly pierce the tart shell in several places with a fork to release air and prevent it from puffing up, and bake another 8 to 10 minutes, until firm and completely baked. Remove the baking sheet from the oven and transfer the tart pan to a rack to cool completely.

FOR THE CANDIED ORANGE PEEL, slice both ends off the orange, then cut the orange into quarters. Cut off most of the pulp and cut each quarter into thin slices. Place the slices in a 2-quart heavy-duty saucepan, cover with cold water, bring to a boil, and boil for 10 minutes. Drain off the water and repeat this process with fresh cold water two more times. After the third boil, drain the orange slices, rinse them in cold water, and remove any remaining pulp.

COMBINE the sugar and water in the saucepan and bring to a boil. Cook the mixture until the sugar is completely dissolved. Add the orange slices and simmer the mixture for 20 minutes, stirring occasionally. Use a fork or tongs to transfer the orange peel to a cooling rack set over waxed or parchment paper. Let the orange peel air dry for at least 1 hour or as long as overnight. Using a chef's knife dice the orange peel into ¼-inch pieces.

FOR THE ALMOND, ORANGE, AND CINNAMON FILLING, combine all the ingredients in a mixing bowl and stir together until thoroughly blended. Reserve 3 tablespoons of the mixture for the garnish and transfer the remaining mixture to the cooled tart shell, spreading it out evenly.

FOR THE CHOCOLATE GANACHE FILLING, place the bittersweet chocolate in a 2-quart heat-safe mixing bowl. Heat the cream in a 1-quart saucepan over medium-high heat until it boils. Immediately pour the cream over the chocolate. Let it stand for 30 seconds, then stir together with a heat-safe silicone spatula until completely smooth. Add the Grand Marnier and stir until well blended. Pour this mixture over the almond, orange, and cinnamon filling in the tart shell. Gently shake the tart to eliminate any air bubbles.

CHILL the tart for 30 minutes, then sprinkle the remaining almond mixture evenly over the top. Continue to chill until the filling is set, about 1 hour.

TO REMOVE the sides of the tart pan place the pan on the top of an upside-down small bowl. Gently manipulate the edges of the pan so it falls away. Carefully lift up the tart by the bottom of the pan and place it on a serving plate. Serve the tart at room temperature.

keeping streamlining

Store the tart on a serving plate tightly wrapped in aluminum foil in the refrigerator up to 3 days.

The pastry dough can be made up to 4 days in advance and kept tightly wrapped in the refrigerator. To freeze up to 3 months, place it in a plastic freezer bag. Use a large piece of masking tape and an indelible marker to label and date the contents. If frozen, thaw overnight in the refrigerator and bring to room temperature before using.

The pastry shell can be baked and held at room temperature tightly wrapped in aluminum foil up to 2 days before filling.

The candied orange peel can be made up to 2 weeks in advance and kept in a tightly sealed container in the refrigerator.

cocoa pavlova with cacao nib whipped cream

THIS CLASSIC PASTRY TAKES ON A NEW AND EXTRAORDINARY FLAVOR BY USING COCOA POWDER IN THE MERINGUE SHELL. TO FURTHER ENHANCE THE CHOCOLATE FLAVOR, THE SHELL IS FILLED WITH CACAO NIB WHIPPED CREAM, THEN DECORATED WITH TROPICAL FRUIT, SUCH AS RASPBERRIES, BANANAS, AND KIWIFRUIT. THE CACAO NIBS NEED TO STEEP IN THE CREAM OVERNIGHT SO BE SURE TO DO THAT THE DAY BEFORE ASSEMBLING THE PAVLOVA. ASSEMBLE NO MORE THAN 3 HOURS BEFORE SERVING, BECAUSE THE CREAM SOFTENS THE MERINGUE SHELL.

MAKES one 9-inch round pastry, 12 to 14 servings

SPECIAL EQUIPMENT: 12- or 14-inch pastry bag and large closed star tip

CACAO NIB WHIPPED CREAM

2 cups heavy whipping cream

⅓ cup (1½ ounces) cacao nibs

3 tablespoons confectioners' sugar

MERINGUE SHELL

4 large egg whites, at room temperature

¼ teaspoon cream of tartar

1 cup (6½ ounces) superfine sugar

1 tablespoon plus 1 teaspoon cornstarch, sifted

2 tablespoons unsweetened cocoa powder (natural or Dutch-processed), sifted

½ teaspoon distilled white vinegar

½ teaspoon pure vanilla extract

ASSEMBLY

1 cup (4½ ounces) fresh raspberries, strawberries, or blackberries

1 medium banana, thinly sliced

2 or 3 kiwifruit, peeled and thinly sliced

BRING the cream to a boil in a 1-quart saucepan over medium heat. Turn off the heat and add the cacao nibs. Transfer the mixture to a bowl and cover tightly. Chill overnight.

CENTER a rack in the oven and preheat the oven to 400°F. Line a baking sheet with aluminum foil. Using a 9-inch cardboard cake circle or cake pan as a guide, trace a 9-inch circle onto the dull side of the foil, then turn the foil over on the baking sheet.

WHIP the egg whites and cream of tartar in the grease-free bowl of an electric stand mixer using the wire whip attachment or in a large grease-free mixing bowl using a handheld mixer on medium-high speed until frothy. Slowly sprinkle on the superfine sugar and continue whipping the egg whites until they hold firm peaks, about 3 minutes. Turn the mixer speed to low and sprinkle on the cornstarch and cocoa powder. Blend together well, then add the white vinegar and vanilla and blend thoroughly.

USING a rubber spatula, spread the meringue mixture onto the foil on the baking sheet, using the circle as a guide. Mound the mixture around the edges so they are slightly thicker than the center, creating a shallow bowl. Place the baking sheet in the oven, lower the oven temperature to 250°F, and dry the meringue for 1½ hours.

TURN OFF the oven, prop open the oven door, and leave the meringue in the oven until it is cool. Remove the baking sheet from the oven and carefully peel the foil off the back of the meringue shell. Place the meringue shell onto a 9-inch cardboard cake circle or a serving plate.

STRAIN the cream to remove the cacao nibs. Whip the chilled cream in the bowl of an electric stand mixer using the wire whip attachment or in a large mixing bowl using a handheld mixer on medium speed until frothy. Add the confectioners' sugar and whip the cream until it holds soft peaks. Reserve one-quarter of the cream for decoration, and use a rubber spatula to spread the cream in the meringue shell, mounding it slightly in the center.

ARRANGE the fruit in concentric circles over the cream. Fit a 12- or 14-inch pastry bag with a large closed star tip and fill with the remaining whipped cream. Pipe a decorative border around the outer edge of the fruit. Refrigerate the Pavlova until ready to serve, no more than 3 hours.

keeping

Store the Pavlova loosely covered with waxed paper, then tightly wrapped with aluminum foil in the refrigerator up to 2 days.

streamlining

The meringue shell can be made up to 2 days in advance. Store it at room temperature tightly wrapped in aluminum foil to protect it from moisture, which will make it soft.

making a change

Use other fruit such as star fruit and pineapple.

milk chocolate cheesecake tart

THIS IS AN UNUSUAL TART WITH
A DISTINCTIVE COMBINATION OF
TEXTURES. A SOFT, CREAMY DARK
MILK CHOCOLATE CHEESECAKE
FILLING IS BAKED IN A CLASSIC SWEET
PASTRY SHELL. THERE IS NO NEED FOR
A WATER BATH OR A SPRINGFORM
PAN TO MAKE THIS.

MAKES one 9½-inch round
tart, 12 to 14 servings

SPECIAL EQUIPMENT: 9½-inch round
fluted-edge removable-bottom tart pan;
10- or 12-inch pastry bag and open star tip

PASTRY DOUGH

1¼ cups (5½ ounces) all-purpose flour

½ cup (1¾ ounces) confectioners' sugar

⅛ teaspoon kosher or fine-grained sea salt

4 ounces (8 tablespoons, 1 stick) unsalted butter, chilled

1 large egg yolk, at room temperature

½ teaspoon pure vanilla extract

MILK CHOCOLATE CHEESECAKE FILLING

8 ounces dark milk chocolate (38 to 42% cacao content), finely chopped

1 pound cream cheese, at room temperature

¼ cup (1½ ounces) granulated sugar

2 large eggs, at room temperature

¼ cup sour cream

GARNISH

¼ cup heavy whipping cream

3 tablespoons finely shaved dark milk chocolate (38 to 42% cacao content)

FOR THE PASTRY DOUGH, briefly pulse together the flour, confectioners' sugar, and salt in the work bowl of a food processor fitted with the steel blade. Cut the chilled butter into small pieces and add. Pulse until the butter is cut into very tiny pieces, about 30 seconds. The texture will be sandy with very tiny lumps.

IN a small bowl or liquid measuring cup, use a fork to beat the egg yolk and vanilla together. With the food processor running, pour this mixture through the feed tube. Process until the dough wraps itself around the blade, about 1 minute. Shape the dough into a flat disk and wrap tightly in a double layer of plastic wrap. Chill in the refrigerator until firm before using, about 2 hours.

CENTER a rack in the oven and preheat the oven to 375°F. On a smooth, flat surface, roll out the pastry dough between sheets of lightly floured waxed or parchment paper to a large rectangle ¼ inch thick. Peel off the top piece of paper, brush off any excess flour, and gently roll the pastry dough around the rolling pin. Place the tart pan directly under the rolling pin and carefully unroll the dough into the pan. Gently lift up the edges and fit the pastry dough against the bottom and sides of the tart pan, pushing it lightly into the fluted edges. Trim off any excess pastry dough at the top edge of the pan and patch any places that have holes or tears. Place the pan on a baking sheet and freeze for 15 minutes.

LINE the shell with a large piece of aluminum foil that fits well against the bottom and sides and fill with tart weights. Bake the shell for 10 minutes, then remove the foil and weights. Lightly pierce the bottom of the shell with a fork to release air and prevent it from puffing up. Bake another 12 to 15 minutes, until light golden and set. Remove the baking sheet from the oven and transfer the tart pan to a rack to cool completely.

FOR THE FILLING, melt the dark milk chocolate in the top of a double boiler over hot water, stirring often with a rubber spatula to ensure even melting. Or melt the chocolate in a microwave-safe bowl on low power in 30-second bursts, stirring after each burst. Remove the top pan of the double boiler, if using, and wipe the bottom and sides very dry.

BEAT the cream cheese in the bowl of an electric stand mixer using the flat beater attachment or in a large mixing bowl using a handheld mixer until fluffy, about 2 minutes. Add the granulated sugar and beat together thoroughly. One at a time, add the eggs, beating well after each addition. Stir in the sour cream and the melted dark milk chocolate.

POUR the batter into the baked tart shell and place the tart shell on a baking sheet. Bake the tart for 45 minutes, until the filling is slightly puffed over the top of the tart shell and is set when the tart pan is jiggled. Remove the baking sheet from the oven and transfer the tart pan to a rack to cool completely.

TO REMOVE the sides of the tart pan, place the pan on the top of an upside-down small bowl. Gently manipulate the edge of the pan so it falls away. Carefully lift up the tart by the bottom of the pan and place it on a serving plate.

FOR THE GARNISH, whip the cream in the bowl of an electric stand mixer using the wire whip attachment or in a large mixing bowl using a handheld mixer on medium speed until it holds soft peaks. Fit a 10- or 12-inch pastry bag with a large, open star tip and fill partway with the whipped cream. Pipe rosettes or stars around the outer edges of the tart and sprinkle them with the shaved dark milk chocolate. Once garnished, serve the tart immediately.

keeping

Store the ungarnished tart on a plate lightly covered with waxed paper, then tightly wrapped in aluminum foil in the refrigerator up to 3 days.

streamlining

The pastry dough can be made up to 4 days in advance and kept tightly wrapped in plastic wrap in the refrigerator. To freeze up to 3 months, place it in a plastic freezer bag. Use a large piece of masking tape and an indelible marker to label and date the contents. If frozen, thaw overnight in the refrigerator and bring to room temperature before using.

The pastry shell can be baked up to 2 days in advance and kept tightly wrapped in aluminum foil at room temperature.

white chocolate–caramel tart

THIS TART LOOKS LIKE A BEAUTIFUL PIECE OF VENETIAN ENDPAPER WITH A SWIRL OF AMBER-COLORED CARAMEL SAUCE DRAWN THROUGH THE PURE IVORY OF THE WHITE CHOCOLATE GANACHE FILLING. A CLASSIC SWEET PASTRY SHELL HOLDS THIS REMARKABLE FILLING. IF YOU HAVEN'T TASTED WHITE CHOCOLATE WITH CARAMEL, YOU ARE IN FOR AN EXCEPTIONAL TASTE ADVENTURE. I LIKE TO MAKE THIS IN A SQUARE TART PAN BECAUSE IT IS UNUSUAL, BUT IT CAN ALSO BE MADE IN A STANDARD 9½-INCH ROUND TART PAN.

MAKES one 9-inch square tart, sixteen 2¼-inch square servings

SPECIAL EQUIPMENT: 9-inch square fluted-edge removable-bottom tart pan

PASTRY DOUGH
1¼ cups (5½ ounces) all-purpose flour
½ cup (1¾ ounces) confectioners' sugar
⅛ teaspoon kosher or fine-grained sea salt
4 ounces (8 tablespoons, 1 stick) unsalted butter, chilled
1 large egg yolk, at room temperature
½ teaspoon pure vanilla extract

WHITE CHOCOLATE GANACHE FILLING
10 ounces white chocolate (31 to 35% cacao content), finely chopped

⅔ cup heavy whipping cream

CARAMEL SAUCE
¼ cup heavy whipping cream
¼ cup (1½ ounces) granulated sugar
1 tablespoon water
1 teaspoon light corn syrup
1 tablespoon (½ ounce) unsalted butter, softened
½ teaspoon pure vanilla extract

FOR THE PASTRY DOUGH, briefly pulse together the flour, confectioners' sugar, and salt in the work bowl of a food processor fitted with the steel blade. Cut the chilled butter into small pieces and add. Pulse until the butter is cut into very tiny pieces, about 30 seconds. The texture will be sandy with very tiny lumps.

IN a small bowl or liquid measuring cup, use a fork to beat the egg yolk and vanilla together. With the food processor running, pour this mixture through the feed tube. Process until the dough wraps itself around the blade, about 1 minute. Shape the dough into a flat disk and wrap tightly in a double layer of plastic wrap. Chill in the refrigerator until firm before using, about 2 hours.

CENTER a rack in the oven and preheat the oven to 375°F. On a smooth, flat surface, roll out the pastry dough between sheets of lightly floured waxed or parchment paper to a large square about ¼ inch thick. Peel off the top piece of paper, brush off any excess flour, and gently roll the pastry dough around the rolling pin. Place the tart pan directly under the rolling pin and carefully unroll the dough into the pan. Gently lift up the edges and fit the pastry dough against the bottom and sides of the tart pan, pushing it lightly into the fluted edges. Trim off any excess pastry dough at the top edge of the pan and patch any places that have holes or tears. Place the pan on a baking sheet and freeze for 15 minutes.

LINE the shell with a large piece of aluminum foil that fits well against the bottom and sides and fill with tart weights. Bake the shell for 10 minutes then remove the foil and weights. Lightly pierce the bottom of the shell with a fork to release air and prevent it from puffing up. Bake another 12 to 15 minutes, until light golden and set. Remove the baking sheet from the oven and transfer the tart pan to a rack to cool completely.

FOR THE WHITE CHOCOLATE GANACHE FILLING, place the white chocolate in a 2-quart heat-safe mixing bowl. Bring the cream to a boil in a small saucepan over high heat. Immediately pour the cream over the white chocolate and let it stand for 30 seconds. Then stir together with a heat-safe silicone spatula until completely smooth. Pour the ganache into the cooled tart shell.

FOR THE CARAMEL, warm the cream in a small saucepan over medium-low heat until it forms bubbles around the edges. At the same time, combine the granulated sugar, water, and corn syrup in a 1-quart heavy-duty saucepan and cook over high heat, without stirring, until it boils. Dip a clean pastry brush in warm water and run it around the inside edges of the pan to prevent sugar crystallization. Do this once more as the sugar cooks. Cook the mixture without stirring until it turns amber, about 5 minutes.

STIR the hot cream into the caramel using a long-handled heat-safe silicone spatula. Be careful, because the mixture will bubble and foam. Remove the pan from the heat and stir in the butter until it is completely melted, then stir in the vanilla.

TRANSFER the caramel sauce to a heat-safe liquid measuring cup. Starting at the center of the tart and working toward the outer edges, drizzle half of the caramel sauce in concentric circles over the white chocolate ganache. Use the point of a sharp knife or a toothpick to pull through the caramel sauce, creating a spider web design.

CHILL the tart for 30 to 45 minutes to set the filling.

TO REMOVE the sides of the tart pan, place the pan on the top of an upside-down small bowl. Gently manipulate the edge of the pan so it falls away. Carefully lift up the tart by the bottom of the pan and place it on a serving plate.

SERVE the tart at room temperature cut into squares or wedges. Use the remaining caramel sauce as a garnish, if you wish, or save it in a tightly covered container in the refrigerator for another use.

keeping

streamlining

Store the tart on a plate lightly covered with waxed paper, then tightly wrapped in aluminum foil in the refrigerator up to 3 days.

The pastry dough can be made up to 4 days in advance and kept tightly wrapped in plastic wrap in the refrigerator. To freeze up to 3 months, place it in a plastic freezer bag. Use a large piece of masking tape and an indelible marker to label and date the contents. If frozen, thaw overnight in the refrigerator and bring to room temperature before using.

The pastry shell can be baked up to 2 days in advance and kept tightly wrapped in aluminum foil at room temperature.

The caramel sauce can be made up to a week in advance and kept in a tightly covered container in the refrigerator. Warm it in the top of a double boiler over hot water or in a microwave oven on low power before using.

double white chocolate–berry tartlets

GROUND WHITE CHOCOLATE GIVES EXTRA FLAVOR AND TEXTURE TO A CLASSIC PASTRY DOUGH IN THESE ELEGANT TARTLETS. WHITE CHOCOLATE GANACHE WHIPPED TO SOFT PEAKS MAKES THE FILLING THAT IS TOPPED WITH FRESH BLUEBERRIES OR RASPBERRIES.

MAKES eighteen 2½-inch round tartlets

SPECIAL EQUIPMENT: 3-inch round plain-edge cutter; thirty-six 2½-inch round fluted-edge tartlet pans; 12- or 14-inch pastry bag and ½-inch plain round tip

PASTRY DOUGH

1 cup (4¼ ounces) all-purpose flour

½ cup (1¾ ounces) sliced almonds, blanched or unblanched

1 ounce white chocolate (31 to 35% cacao content), finely chopped

2 teaspoons granulated sugar

¼ teaspoon kosher or fine-grained sea salt

4 ounces (8 tablespoons, 1 stick) unsalted butter, chilled

2 teaspoons freshly squeezed lemon juice

1 tablespoon cold water

WHITE CHOCOLATE GANACHE FILLING

8 ounces white chocolate (31 to 35% cacao content), finely chopped

⅓ cup heavy whipping cream

1 teaspoon freshly squeezed lemon juice

TOPPING

2 cups (10 ounces) fresh blueberries or raspberries, or a mix

FOR THE PASTRY DOUGH, combine the flour, almonds, white chocolate, sugar, and salt in the work bowl of a food processor fitted with a steel blade. Pulse until the white chocolate and almonds are finely ground, about 1 minute. Cut the chilled butter into small pieces and add. Pulse until the butter is cut into very tiny pieces, about 30 seconds. The texture will be sandy with very tiny lumps.

IN a small bowl or liquid measuring cup, combine 2 teaspoons of the lemon juice and the water. With the food processor running, pour this mixture through the feed tube. Process until the dough wraps itself around the blade, about 1 minute. Shape the dough into a flat disk and wrap tightly in a double layer of plastic wrap. Chill in the refrigerator until firm before using, about 2 hours.

CENTER a rack in the oven and preheat the oven to 350°F. On a smooth, flat surface, roll out the pastry dough between sheets of lightly floured waxed or parchment paper to a large rectangle ¼ inch thick. Peel off the top piece of paper, brush off any excess flour, and use a 3-inch round plain-edge cutter to cut out individual rounds. Gently fit the rounds into 2½-inch round fluted-edge tartlet pans, pinching off any excess dough at the top. Gather together the scraps, reroll, and cut out more rounds as needed. Place another tartlet pan on top of the dough in each tartlet pan to act as a weight as they bake. Place the tartlet pans on a baking sheet and chill for 15 minutes.

BAKE the tartlet shells for 8 minutes. Remove the top tartlet pans and lightly pierce the bottoms with a fork to release steam. Bake the tartlet shells another 8 to 10 minutes, until set and pale gold. Remove the baking sheet from the oven and place it on a rack to cool completely.

FOR THE FILLING, place the white chocolate in a heat-safe mixing bowl. Heat the cream in a small saucepan until bubbles form around the edges. Immediately pour

Store the filled tartlets on a baking sheet tightly wrapped in aluminum foil in the refrigerator up to 2 days.

streamlining

The pastry dough can be made up to 4 days in advance and kept tightly wrapped in the refrigerator. To freeze up to 3 months, place it in a plastic freezer bag. Use a large piece of masking tape and an indelible marker to label and date the contents. If frozen, thaw overnight in the refrigerator and bring to room temperature before using.
The pastry shells can be baked and held tightly covered with aluminum foil at room temperature up to 2 days in advance.
The ganache filling can be made up to 1 week in advance. Bring it to room temperature before beating.

making a change

Replace the fresh berries with other fresh fruit, such as sliced nectarines and plums or tangerine segments.

the hot cream over the chopped chocolate. Let it stand for 15 seconds, then stir together using a heat-safe silicone spatula until smooth. Add the lemon juice and stir until thoroughly blended. Cover the bowl tightly with plastic wrap, cool to room temperature, and chill until thick, 45 minutes to 1 hour.

TO REMOVE the tartlet shells from the pans, gently tap the pans on the countertop and they should slide out. Or use the tip of a sharp knife to gently nudge the shells from the pans. Place them on a baking sheet or serving plate.

BEAT the ganache in the bowl of an electric stand mixer using the flat beater attachment or in a medium mixing bowl using a handheld mixer on medium speed until it holds soft peaks. Fit a 12- or 14-inch pastry bag with a ½-inch plain round tip. Fill the pastry bag partway with the whipped ganache and pipe it into the center of the tartlet shells, filling them. Arrange the blueberries over the top of the ganache.

CHILL the tartlets, covered, up to 2 hours before serving. Bring them to room temperature to serve.

milk chocolate-toasted pecan tartlets

DARK MILK CHOCOLATE AND PECANS ARE IN BOTH THE PASTRY DOUGH AND THE FILLING, GIVING THESE TARTLETS AN EXTRA BOOST OF FLAVOR AND TEXTURE. THEY CAN BE MADE IN STAGES AND ASSEMBLED A FEW HOURS BEFORE SERVING. BECAUSE THESE ARE SMALL, THEY ARE PERFECT FINGER FOOD FOR ANY GATHERING.

MAKES *eighteen 2-inch round tartlets*

SPECIAL EQUIPMENT: *2½-inch round plain-edge cutter; thirty-six 2-inch round fluted-edge tartlet pans; 12- or 14-inch pastry bag and ½-inch plain round tip*

PASTRY DOUGH

1¼ cups (5½ ounces) all-purpose flour

⅓ cup (1¼ ounces) toasted pecans (see page 10)

¼ cup (1½ ounces) granulated sugar

Pinch of kosher or fine-grained sea salt

3 ounces (6 tablespoons, ¾ stick) unsalted butter, chilled

2 ounces dark milk chocolate (38 to 42% cacao content), finely chopped

1 large egg yolk, at room temperature

½ teaspoon pure vanilla extract

1 teaspoon heavy whipping cream

MILK CHOCOLATE–PECAN FILLING

8 ounces dark milk chocolate (38 to 42% cacao content), finely chopped

⅓ cup heavy whipping cream

2 tablespoons toasted pecans, finely chopped (see page 10)

GARNISH

1 tablespoon toasted pecans, finely chopped (see page 10)

FOR THE PASTRY DOUGH, briefly pulse together the flour, pecans, sugar, and salt in the work bowl of a food processor fitted with a steel blade. Cut the chilled butter into small pieces and add. Pulse until the butter is cut into very tiny pieces, about 30 seconds. The texture will be sandy with very tiny lumps. Add the milk chocolate and pulse briefly to blend.

IN a small bowl or liquid measuring cup, combine the egg yolk, vanilla, and cream. With the food processor running, pour this mixture through the feed tube. Process until the dough wraps itself around the blade, about 1 minute. Shape the dough into a flat disk and wrap tightly in a double layer of plastic wrap. Chill in the refrigerator until firm before using, about 2 hours.

CENTER a rack in the oven and preheat the oven to 350°F. On a smooth, flat surface, roll out the pastry dough between sheets of lightly floured waxed or parchment paper to a large rectangle ¼ inch thick. Peel off the top piece of paper, brush off any excess flour, and use a 2½-inch round plain-edge cutter to cut out individual rounds. Gently fit the rounds into the tartlet pans, pinching off any excess dough at the top. Gather together the scraps, reroll, and cut out more rounds as needed. Place another tartlet pan on top of the dough in each tartlet pan to act as a weight as they bake. Place the tartlet pans on a baking sheet and chill in the freezer for 15 minutes.

BAKE the tartlet shells for 12 minutes. Remove the top tartlet pans and pierce the bottoms with a fork to release steam. Bake the tartlet shells another 5 to 8 minutes, until set and pale gold. Remove the baking sheet from the oven and place it on a rack to cool completely.

FOR THE FILLING, place the milk chocolate in a heat-safe mixing bowl. Warm the cream in a small saucepan over medium heat until it bubbles around the edges. Immediately pour the cream over the chopped chocolate. Let it stand for 15 seconds then stir together with a heat-safe silicone spatula until smooth. Add the pecans and stir until thoroughly blended. Cover the bowl tightly with plastic wrap and let stand at room temperature until thick, 30 to 45 minutes.

TO REMOVE the tartlet shells from the pans, gently tap the pans on the countertop and they should slide out. Or use the tip of a sharp knife to gently nudge the shells from the pans, then place them on a baking sheet or serving plate.

BEAT the ganache in the bowl of an electric stand mixer using the flat beater attachment or in a medium mixing bowl using a handheld mixer on medium speed until it holds soft peaks. Fit a 12- or 14-inch pastry bag with a ½-inch plain round tip and fill the bag partway with the filling. Pipe a mound of the filling in the center of each tartlet. Garnish the tops of the tartlet with the pecans.

CHILL the tartlets, covered, up to 2 hours before serving. Bring them to room temperature to serve.

keeping

Store the tartlets on a baking sheet tightly wrapped in aluminum foil in the refrigerator up to 2 days.

streamlining

The pastry dough can be made up to 4 days in advance and kept tightly wrapped in the refrigerator. To freeze up to 3 months, place it in a plastic freezer bag. Use a large piece of masking tape and an indelible marker to label and date the contents. If frozen, thaw overnight in the refrigerator and bring to room temperature before using.

The pastry shells can be baked and held tightly covered with aluminum foil at room temperature up to 2 days in advance.

The filling can be made up to 1 week in advance. Store it in a tightly covered container in the refrigerator but bring it to room temperature before beating.

making a change

Replace the pecans with almonds or hazelnuts.

cocoa and bittersweet chocolate-hazelnut tartlets

WHAT SEPARATES THESE TARTLETS FROM OTHERS IS THAT THE PASTRY DOUGH IS MADE WITH COCOA AND TOASTED, GROUND HAZELNUTS. THESE GIVE THE DOUGH A SUPERB TASTE THAT PAIRS PERFECTLY WITH THE CREAMY BITTERSWEET CHOCOLATE AND HAZELNUT FILLING.

MAKES sixteen 2½-inch round tartlets

SPECIAL EQUIPMENT: 3-inch round plain-edge cutter, thirty-two 2½-inch round fluted-edge tartlet pans

PASTRY DOUGH

1 cup (4¼ ounces) all-purpose flour

½ cup (1¾ ounces) confectioners' sugar

¼ cup (¾ ounce) unsweetened cocoa powder (natural or Dutch-processed)

¼ cup (1 ounce) toasted and finely ground hazelnuts (see page 10)

⅛ teaspoon kosher or fine-grained sea salt

4 ounces (8 tablespoons, 1 stick) unsalted butter, chilled

1 large egg, at room temperature

½ teaspoon pure chocolate extract

BITTERSWEET CHOCOLATE–HAZELNUT FILLING

4 ounces bittersweet chocolate (70 to 72% cacao content), finely chopped

¾ cup heavy whipping cream

1 large egg yolk, at room temperature

⅓ cup (1½ ounces) toasted and finely ground hazelnuts (see page 10)

FOR THE PASTRY DOUGH, briefly pulse together the flour, confectioners' sugar, cocoa powder, hazelnuts, and salt in the work bowl of a food processor fitted with a steel blade. Cut the chilled butter into small pieces and add. Pulse until the butter is cut into very tiny pieces, about 30 seconds. The texture will be sandy with very tiny lumps.

IN a small bowl or liquid measuring cup, use a fork to lightly beat the egg and chocolate extract together. With the food processor running, pour the egg mixture through the feed tube. Process until the mixture wraps itself around the blade, about 1 minute. Shape the dough into a flat disk and wrap tightly in a double layer of plastic wrap. Chill in the refrigerator until firm before using, 3 to 4 hours.

CENTER a rack in the oven and preheat the oven to 375°F. On a smooth, flat surface, roll out the pastry dough between sheets of lightly floured waxed or parchment paper to a large rectangle about ¼ inch thick. Peel off the top piece of paper, brush off any excess flour, and use a 3-inch round plain-edge cutter to cut out 16 individual rounds. Gently fit the rounds into 2½-inch round fluted-edge tartlet pans, pinching off any excess dough at the top. Place another tartlet pan on top of the dough in each tartlet pan to act as a weight as they bake. Place the tartlet pans on a baking sheet and chill for 15 minutes.

BAKE the tartlet shells for 8 minutes. Remove the top tartlet pans and pierce the bottoms with a fork to release steam. Bake the tartlet shells another 4 to 6 minutes, until set. Remove the baking pan from the oven and place on a rack while preparing the filling.

FOR THE FILLING, place the chocolate and cream in the top of a double boiler over hot water. Stir often with a rubber spatula to ensure even melting. Or place the chocolate and cream in a microwave-safe bowl and melt on low power in 30-second bursts, stirring after each burst. Remove the top pan of the double boiler, if using, and wipe the bottom and sides very dry.

USE a whisk or heat-safe silicone spatula to stir the egg yolk and hazelnuts into the chocolate mixture and stir until very smooth.

DIVIDE the filling evenly among the tartlet shells. Bake for 15 to 18 minutes, until the filling is puffed and looks set. Remove the pan from the oven and transfer the tartlets to racks to cool.

TO REMOVE the tartlets from the pans, gently tap the pans on the countertop and the tartlets will slip out. Serve them at room temperature.

keeping

Store the tartlets on a baking sheet tightly wrapped in aluminum foil at room temperature up to 4 days. To freeze up to 3 months, place them in a tightly sealed container between layers of waxed paper. Wrap the container tightly in several layers of plastic wrap and aluminum foil. Use a large piece of masking tape and an indelible marker to label and date the contents. If frozen, thaw overnight in the refrigerator and bring to room temperature before serving.

streamlining

The pastry dough can be made up to 4 days in advance and kept tightly wrapped in the refrigerator. To freeze up to 3 months, place it in a plastic freezer bag. Use a large piece of masking tape and an indelible marker to label and date the contents. If frozen, thaw overnight in the refrigerator and bring to room temperature before using.

crème fraîche–bittersweet chocolate tartlets

IF YOU ARE A FAN OF CRÈME FRAÎCHE, THESE TARTLETS ARE FOR YOU. CRÈME FRAÎCHE IS COMBINED WITH BITTERSWEET CHOCOLATE AS A FILLING AND NESTLED IN CLASSIC SWEET PASTRY DOUGH TARTLET SHELLS. AND CHOCOLATE CRÈME FRAÎCHE TOPS OFF THESE SPECIAL TARTLETS.

MAKES twenty 2½-inch round tartlets

SPECIAL EQUIPMENT: twenty 2½-inch round fluted-edge tartlet pans; 3-inch round plain-edge cutter, 1-inch-diameter ice cream scoop (optional); 12- or 14-inch pastry bag and ½-inch plain round tip

PASTRY DOUGH

1¼ cups (5½ ounces) all-purpose flour

3 tablespoons (1¼ ounces) granulated sugar

⅛ teaspoon kosher or fine-grained sea salt

4 ounces (8 tablespoons, 1 stick) unsalted butter, chilled

1 large egg yolk, at room temperature

½ teaspoon pure vanilla extract

1 teaspoon heavy whipping cream

BITTERSWEET CHOCOLATE–CRÈME FRAÎCHE FILLING

8 ounces bittersweet chocolate (70 to 72% cacao content), finely chopped

⅔ cup heavy whipping cream

1 cup crème fraîche

1 large egg yolk, at room temperature

Pinch of kosher or fine-grained sea salt

CHOCOLATE CRÈME FRAÎCHE GARNISH

2 ounces bittersweet chocolate (70 to 72% cacao content), finely chopped

½ cup crème fraîche

FOR THE PASTRY DOUGH, briefly pulse together the flour, sugar, and salt in the work bowl of a food processor fitted with a steel blade. Cut the chilled butter into small pieces and add. Pulse until the butter is cut into very tiny pieces, about 30 seconds. The texture will be sandy with very tiny lumps.

IN a small bowl or liquid measuring cup, combine the egg yolk, vanilla, and cream. With the food processor running, pour this mixture through the feed tube. Process until the dough wraps itself around the blade, about 1 minute. Shape the dough into a flat disk and wrap tightly in a double layer of plastic wrap. Chill in the refrigerator until firm before using, about 2 hours.

CENTER a rack in the oven and preheat the oven to 325°F. On a smooth, flat surface, roll out the pastry dough between sheets of lightly floured waxed or parchment paper to a large rectangle ¼ inch thick. Peel off the top piece of paper, brush off any excess flour, and use a 3-inch round plain-edge cutter to cut out individual rounds. Gently fit the rounds into the tartlet pans, pinching off any excess dough at the top. Gather together the scraps, reroll, and cut out more rounds as needed. Place the tartlet pans on a baking sheet and chill while preparing the filling.

FOR THE FILLING, place the bittersweet chocolate in a heat-safe mixing bowl. Warm the cream in a small saucepan over medium heat until bubbles form around the edges. Immediately pour the cream over the chopped chocolate. Let it stand for 15 seconds then stir together with a heat-safe silicone spatula until smooth.

IN another bowl whisk together the crème fraîche, egg yolk, and salt until smooth and completely blended. Add this mixture to the chocolate mixture and blend thoroughly. Use a spoon or 1-inch-diameter ice cream scoop to evenly divide the filling among the tartlet shells.

BAKE the tartlets for 30 to 32 minutes, until the pastry shells are light golden brown and the filling is puffed and set.

REMOVE the baking sheet from the oven and place it on a rack to cool the tartlets. To remove the tartlet shells from the pans, gently tap the pans on the countertop and they should slide out. Or use the tip of a sharp knife to gently nudge the shells from the pans. Place the pans on a baking sheet or serving plate.

FOR THE GARNISH, melt the chocolate in a microwave-safe bowl on low power in 30-seconds bursts, stirring after each burst. Whip the crème fraîche in the bowl of an electric stand mixer using the wire whip attachment or in a mixing bowl using a handheld mixer on medium speed until it holds soft peaks. Add the melted chocolate and blend thoroughly. Fit a 12- or 14-inch pastry bag with a ½-inch plain round tip and fill the bag partway with the filling. Pipe a mound of the chocolate crème fraîche in the center of each tartlet

CHILL the tartlets, covered, up to 2 hours before serving. Bring them to room temperature to serve.

keeping

Store the ungarnished tartlets on a baking sheet tightly wrapped in aluminum foil in the refrigerator up to 2 days.

streamlining

The pastry dough can be made up to 4 days in advance and kept tightly wrapped in the refrigerator. To freeze up to 3 months, place it in a plastic freezer bag. Use a large piece of masking tape and an indelible marker to label and date the contents. If frozen, thaw overnight in the refrigerator and bring to room temperature before using.

The filling can be made up to 3 days in advance. Store it in a tightly covered container in the refrigerator.

cookies

cacao nib and cocoa shortbread

THE COCOA USED TO MAKE THESE SHORTBREAD COOKIES PROVIDES DEEP CHOCOLATE FLAVOR AND THE FINELY CRUSHED CACAO NIBS GIVES THEM A CRUNCHY TEXTURE. ALTHOUGH THESE ARE SCRUMPTIOUS ON THEIR OWN, I USE THEM TO MAKE SANDWICH COOKIES WITH BITTERSWEET CHOCOLATE–SALTED CARAMEL ICE CREAM (PAGE 185), MOCHA–CHOCOLATE CHUNK ICE CREAM (PAGE 186), BITTERSWEET CHOCOLATE GANACHE (PAGE 93), OR WHITE CHOCOLATE GANACHE (PAGE 104).

MAKES 3½ dozen cookies

SPECIAL EQUIPMENT: 2-inch round scalloped-edge cookie cutter

COOKIES

8 ounces (16 tablespoons, 2 sticks) unsalted butter, softened

1¼ cups (4¼ ounces) confectioners' sugar, sifted

1 teaspoon pure chocolate extract

1½ cups (6¾ ounces) all-purpose flour

¾ cup (2¼ ounces) unsweetened cocoa powder (natural or Dutch-processed)

¼ teaspoon kosher or fine-grained sea salt

⅓ cup (1½ ounces) cacao nibs

GARNISH

Confectioners' sugar

BEAT the butter in the bowl of an electric stand mixer with the flat beater attachment or in a large mixing bowl using a handheld mixer until fluffy, about 1 minute. Add the confectioners' sugar and beat together just until blended. Add the chocolate extract and blend well.

OVER A BOWL, sift together the flour and cocoa powder. Add the salt and toss to blend. Place the cacao nibs in a plastic freezer bag and seal it. Run a rolling pin over them several times to crush them. Add the crushed cacao nibs to the flour mixture and stir to blend.

ADD the flour mixture to the butter mixture in 3 stages, stopping to scrape down the sides and bottom of the bowl with a rubber spatula after each addition. Form the dough into a disk and wrap tightly in plastic wrap. Chill in the refrigerator until firm, at least 1 hour.

POSITION the oven racks in the upper and lower thirds and preheat the oven to 325°F. Line two baking sheets with parchment paper or nonstick liners. Roll out the shortbread between sheets of lightly floured waxed paper to a thickness of ¼ inch. Use a 2-inch round scalloped-edge cookie cutter to cut out individual cookies. Transfer the cookies to the lined baking sheets, leaving at least an inch of space between them. Gather the scraps together, reroll, and recut more cookies.

BAKE the cookies for 8 minutes. Switch the pans and bake another 8 to 10 minutes, until the cookies are firm.

REMOVE the baking sheets from the oven and transfer them to racks to cool completely.

LIGHTLY DUST the tops of the shortbread with confectioners' sugar. Serve the cookies at room temperature.

keeping — Store the cookies in an airtight plastic container between layers of waxed paper at room temperature up to 5 days. To freeze up to 3 months, wrap the container tightly in several layers of plastic wrap and aluminum foil. Use a large piece of masking tape and an indelible marker to label and date the contents. If frozen, thaw overnight in the refrigerator and bring to room temperature before serving.

streamlining — The shortbread dough can be stored tightly covered in plastic wrap in the refrigerator up to 4 days before rolling it out and baking. To freeze up to 4 months, place the wrapped dough in a freezer bag and seal tightly. Use a large piece of masking tape and an indelible marker to label and date the contents. Thaw overnight in the refrigerator and bring to room temperature before rolling.

making a change — Replace the cacao nibs with toasted and finely chopped hazelnuts, pecans, or almonds.

adding style — Use other shape cookie cutters to cut out individual cookies.

mocha shortbread wedges

FINELY GROUND BITTERSWEET CHOCOLATE AND ESPRESSO POWDER COMBINE TO MAKE THESE SHORTBREAD WEDGES. THE SHORTBREAD IS BAKED IN A FLUTED-EDGE TART PAN THAT IMPRINTS ITS DESIGN ONTO THE OUTER EDGES OF EACH WEDGE.

MAKES *16 wedges*

SPECIAL EQUIPMENT: *9-inch round fluted-edge removable-bottom tart pan*

4 ounces (8 tablespoons, 1 stick) unsalted butter, softened

¼ cup (1½ ounces) granulated sugar

1 teaspoon instant espresso powder

1 teaspoon pure chocolate extract

1 cup (4½ ounces) all-purpose flour, plus 2 teaspoons for the pan

¼ teaspoon kosher or fine-grained sea salt

4 ounces bittersweet chocolate (66 to 72% cacao content), cut into small chunks.

BEAT the butter in the bowl of an electric stand mixer with the flat beater attachment or in a large mixing bowl using a handheld mixer until fluffy, about 1 minute. Add the sugar and beat together until well blended.

IN A SMALL BOWL combine the instant espresso powder and the chocolate extract and stir until the espresso powder is completely dissolved. Add to the butter mixture and beat to blend well.

PULSE together 1 cup flour, the salt, and bittersweet chocolate in the work bowl of a food processor until the chocolate is finely ground, about 2 minutes. Add this mixture to the butter mixture in 3 stages, stopping to scrape down the sides and bottom of the bowl with a rubber spatula after each addition.

LIGHTLY DUST the bottom of a 9-inch round fluted-edge removable-bottom tart pan with flour. Press the dough into the pan evenly. Cover the pan tightly with plastic wrap and chill in the refrigerator until firm, at least 2 hours or overnight.

CENTER a rack in the oven and preheat the oven to 350°F. Use a sharp knife to score the shortbread into quarters, then score each quarter into four equal pieces. Use the tines of a fork to pierce each shortbread wedge on the diagonal in two places. Bake for 30 minutes.

REMOVE the tart pan from the oven and transfer it to a rack. Use a sharp knife to cut through the scored lines of the shortbread wedges before they set up. Leave the shortbread in the pan on the rack to cool completely.

TO REMOVE the sides of the tart pan, place the pan on the top of an upside-down small bowl. Gently manipulate the edge of the pan so it falls away. Carefully break apart the wedges along the scoring and place them on a serving plate. Serve the shortbread wedges at room temperature.

Store the shortbread wedges in an airtight plastic container at room temperature up to 5 days. To freeze up to 3 months, wrap the container tightly in several layers of plastic wrap and aluminum foil. Use a large piece of masking tape and an indelible marker to label and date the contents. If frozen, thaw overnight in the refrigerator and bring to room temperature before serving.

streamlining

The shortbread dough can be stored tightly covered in plastic wrap in the refrigerator up to 4 days before rolling it out and baking. To freeze up to 4 months, place the wrapped dough in a freezer bag and seal tightly. Use a large piece of masking tape and an indelible marker to label and date the contents. Thaw overnight in the refrigerator and bring to room temperature before rolling.

making a change
adding style

Add ½ cup (2 ounces) cacao nibs with the flour mixture.

Dip the shortbread bars partway into melted bittersweet chocolate (see page 9).

cocoa gingersnaps

THE ADDITION OF COCOA POWDER
TO CLASSIC GINGERSNAPS GIVES
THESE COOKIES AN EXTRA FLAVOR
DIMENSION THAT MAKES THEM
UNFORGETTABLE. BOTH GROUND
GINGER AND CHOPPED CRYSTALLIZED
GINGER GIVES THEM A SWEET-HOT
FLAVOR AND CHEWY TEXTURE.

MAKES *about 5 dozen cookies*

GINGERSNAPS

2 cups (9 ounces) all-purpose flour

¼ cup (¾ ounce) unsweetened Dutch-processed cocoa powder

2 teaspoons ground ginger

1 teaspoon ground cinnamon

1 teaspoon baking soda

½ teaspoon finely ground cloves

¼ teaspoon kosher or fine-grained sea salt

⅓ cup (1¾ ounces) finely chopped crystallized ginger

8 ounces (16 tablespoons, 2 sticks) unsalted butter, softened

½ cup (3 ounces) firmly packed light brown sugar

½ cup (3½ ounces) granulated sugar

1 large egg, at room temperature

⅓ cup unsulfured molasses

GARNISH

⅓ cup (2 ounces) granulated sugar

OVER A BOWL, sift together the flour, cocoa powder, ground ginger, cinnamon, and baking soda. Add the cloves, salt, and crystallized ginger and toss to blend.

BEAT the butter in the bowl of an electric stand mixer with the flat beater attachment or in a large mixing bowl using a handheld mixer until fluffy, about 1 minute. Add the brown sugar and granulated sugar and beat together until thoroughly blended.

USING A FORK, lightly beat the egg with the molasses in a small bowl or liquid measuring cup. Add this mixture to the butter mixture and blend thoroughly. Stop and scrape down the bottom and sides of the bowl with a long-handled rubber spatula to ensure even mixing.

ADD the dry ingredients to the butter mixture in 4 stages, stopping to scrape down the sides and bottom of the bowl with the rubber spatula after each addition. Add the chocolate chunks and stir to distribute evenly. Cover the bowl tightly with plastic wrap and chill for 30 minutes.

POSITION the oven racks in the upper and lower thirds and preheat the oven to 350°F. Line three baking sheets with aluminum foil or nonstick liners.

PLACE the granulated sugar garnish in a small bowl. Dampen your hands with water. Pinch off 2-tablespoon-size pieces of the dough and roll them in your hands into balls, then roll them in the sugar. Place the balls on the baking sheets, leaving at least 2 inches of space between them. Chill one sheet of the cookies while baking the other two.

BAKE the cookies for 6 minutes. Switch the pans and bake another 6 to 7 minutes, until the cookies are firm.

REMOVE the baking sheets from the oven and transfer them to racks to cool completely. Peel the foil off the back of the cookies and serve them at room temperature.

keeping

Store the cookies in an airtight plastic container between layers of waxed paper at room temperature up to 5 days. To freeze up to 3 months, wrap the container tightly in several layers of plastic wrap and aluminum foil. Use a large piece of masking tape and an indelible marker to label and date the contents. If frozen, thaw overnight in the refrigerator and bring to room temperature before serving.

streamlining

The cookie dough can be stored tightly covered in plastic wrap in the refrigerator up to 4 days before rolling it into balls and baking. To freeze up to 4 months, place the wrapped dough in a freezer bag and seal tightly. Use a large piece of masking tape and an indelible marker to label and date the contents. Thaw overnight in the refrigerator and bring to room temperature before using.

bittersweet chocolate- peanut butter cookies

THESE ARE CLASSIC PEANUT BUTTER COOKIES TAKEN TO A WHOLE NEW LEVEL WITH THE ADDITION OF BITTERSWEET CHOCOLATE AND CACAO NIBS. THEY ARE BEST WHEN MADE WITH A NATURAL-STYLE OR FRESHLY GROUND PEANUT BUTTER. BE SURE TO STIR IT WELL BEFORE ADDING.

MAKES *about 4 dozen cookies*

SPECIAL EQUIPMENT: 1¼-inch-diameter ice cream scoop

2 cups (9 ounces) all-purpose flour

1 teaspoon baking soda

¼ teaspoon kosher or fine-grained sea salt

6 ounces (12 tablespoons, 1½ sticks) unsalted butter, softened

1 cup chunky peanut butter, at room temperature

1¼ cups (7½ ounces) firmly packed light brown sugar

½ cup (3½ ounces) granulated sugar

2 large eggs, at room temperature

1 teaspoon pure vanilla extract

8 ounces bittersweet chocolate (70 to 72% cacao content), melted (see page 9)

½ cup (2¾ ounces) salted peanuts, finely chopped (see page 10)

½ cup (2 ounces) cacao nibs

POSITION the oven racks in the upper and lower thirds and preheat the oven to 350°F. Line four baking sheets with parchment paper or nonstick liners.

OVER A LARGE BOWL, sift together the flour and baking soda. Add the salt and toss to blend.

BEAT the butter in the bowl of an electric stand mixer with the flat beater attachment or in a large mixing bowl using a handheld mixer until fluffy, about 1 minute. Add the peanut butter and beat together until well blended. Add the brown sugar and granulated sugar and beat the mixture until thoroughly blended.

USING A FORK, lightly beat the eggs and vanilla together in a small bowl or liquid measuring cup. Add to the butter mixture and blend thoroughly. Stop and scrape down the bottom and sides of the bowl with a rubber spatula to ensure even mixing.

ADD the flour mixture to the butter mixture in 3 stages, stopping to scrape down the sides and bottom of the bowl with the rubber spatula after each addition.

ADD the melted chocolate, chopped peanuts, and cacao nibs to the cookie mixture, blending thoroughly.

USE a 1¼-inch-diameter ice cream scoop to scoop out small mounds. Place the mounds on the baking sheets, leaving at least 2 inches of space between them. Use the back of a damp fork to press down each mound, making a crosshatch pattern on top. Chill two sheets of the cookies while baking the other two.

BAKE the cookies for 6 minutes. Switch the pans and bake another 5 minutes, until the cookies are firm.

REMOVE the baking sheets from the oven and transfer them to racks to cool completely. Serve the cookies at room temperature.

keeping

Store the cookies in an airtight plastic container between layers of waxed paper at room temperature up to 5 days. To freeze up to 3 months, wrap the container tightly in several layers of plastic wrap and aluminum foil. Use a large piece of masking tape and an indelible marker to label and date the contents. If frozen, thaw overnight in the refrigerator and bring to room temperature before serving.

streamlining

The cookie dough can be stored tightly covered in plastic wrap in the refrigerator up to 4 days before scooping it out and baking. Bring it to room temperature before using. To freeze up to 4 months, place the wrapped dough in a freezer bag and seal tightly. Use a large piece of masking tape and an indelible marker to label and date the contents. Thaw overnight in the refrigerator and bring to room temperature before using.

making a change

Add 2 ounces bittersweet chocolate chunks to the batter when adding the melted chocolate, chopped peanuts, and cacao nibs.

chunky bittersweet chocolate wafers

THESE THIN COOKIES ARE MADE WITH COCOA POWDER AND PACKED FULL OF BITTERSWEET CHOCOLATE CHUNKS. THEY ARE PERFECT ON THEIR OWN AS A SNACK OR DESSERT AND CAN EASILY BE PAIRED WITH A HOT CUP OF ESPRESSO OR A COLD GLASS OF MILK

MAKES about 5 dozen cookies

SPECIAL EQUIPMENT: 1¼-inch-diameter ice cream scoop

COOKIES

1¾ cups (7¾ ounces) all-purpose flour

1 teaspoon ground cinnamon

1 teaspoon baking soda

¼ teaspoon kosher or fine-grained sea salt

½ cup (1¾ ounces) unsweetened Dutch-processed cocoa powder

¼ cup boiling water

6 ounces (12 tablespoons, 1½ sticks) unsalted butter, softened

½ cup (3 ounces) firmly packed light brown sugar

½ cup (3½ ounces) granulated sugar

1 large egg, at room temperature

⅓ cup unsulfured molasses

4 ounces bittersweet chocolate (66 to 72% cacao content), cut into small chunks

GARNISH

¾ cup (5 ounces) granulated sugar

OVER a bowl, sift together the flour, cinnamon, and baking soda. Add the salt and toss to blend.

PLACE the cocoa powder in a bowl and add the boiling water. Stir together with a heat-safe silicone spatula until it forms a smooth paste.

BEAT the butter in the bowl of an electric stand mixer with the flat beater attachment or in a large mixing bowl using a handheld mixer until fluffy, about 1 minute. Add the brown sugar and granulated sugar and beat together until thoroughly blended.

USING a fork, lightly beat the egg with the molasses in a small bowl or liquid measuring cup. Add this mixture to the butter mixture and blend thoroughly. Stop and scrape down the bottom and sides of the bowl with a rubber spatula to ensure even mixing. Add the cocoa paste and blend thoroughly.

ADD the flour mixture to the butter mixture in 4 stages, stopping to scrape down the sides and bottom of the bowl with the rubber spatula after each addition. Add the chocolate chunks and stir to distribute evenly. Cover the bowl tightly with plastic wrap and chill for 30 minutes.

POSITION the oven racks in the upper and lower thirds and preheat the oven to 350°F. Line three baking sheets with aluminum foil or nonstick liners.

PLACE the granulated sugar garnish in a small bowl. Use a 1¼-inch-diameter ice cream scoop to scoop out mounds of the dough. Place the mounds in the sugar and roll to cover them completely, then transfer the mounds to the lined baking sheets, leaving at least 2 inches of space between them. Chill one sheet of the cookies while baking the other two.

BAKE the cookies for 6 minutes. Switch the pans and bake another 6 to 7 minutes, until the cookies are firm.

REMOVE the baking sheets from the oven and transfer them to racks to cool completely. Peel the foil off the back of the cookies and serve them at room temperature.

keeping

Store the cookies in an airtight plastic container between layers of waxed paper at room temperature up to 4 days. To freeze up to 3 months, wrap the container tightly in several layers of plastic wrap and aluminum foil. Use a large piece of masking tape and an indelible marker to label and date the contents. If frozen, thaw overnight in the refrigerator and bring to room temperature before serving.

streamlining

The cookie dough can be stored tightly covered in plastic wrap in the refrigerator up to 4 days before scooping it out and baking. Bring it to room temperature before using. To freeze up to 4 months, place the wrapped dough in a freezer bag and seal tightly. Use a large piece of masking tape and an indelible marker to label and date the contents. Thaw overnight in the refrigerator and bring to room temperature before using.

making a change

Replace the bittersweet chocolate chunks with dark milk chocolate or white chocolate.

cocoa cookies with a trio of chocolate chunks

SIMILAR TO CHOCOLATE CHIP COOKIES, THESE ARE PACKED FULL OF CHUNKS OF WHITE CHOCOLATE, DARK MILK CHOCOLATE, AND BITTERSWEET CHOCOLATE. COCOA POWDER MIXED WITH BOILING WATER TO MAKE A PASTE GIVES THESE COOKIES A DISTINCT CHOCOLATE FLAVOR. THEY ARE PERFECT WITH A CUP OF ESPRESSO OR A COLD GLASS OF MILK.

MAKES *about 4 dozen cookies*

SPECIAL EQUIPMENT: *1¼-inch-diameter ice cream scoop*

⅔ cup (2½ ounces) coarsely chopped pecans (see page 10)

4 ounces (8 tablespoons, 1 stick) unsalted butter, softened

½ cup (3 ounces) firmly packed light brown sugar

½ cup (3½ ounces) granulated sugar

1 large egg, at room temperature

1 large egg yolk, at room temperature

1 teaspoon pure vanilla extract

1 teaspoon pure chocolate extract

⅔ cup (3 ounces) all-purpose flour

⅔ cup (3 ounces) cake flour

½ teaspoon baking soda

¼ teaspoon kosher or fine-grained sea salt

½ cup (1¾ ounces) unsweetened Dutch-processed cocoa powder, sifted

¼ cup boiling water

2 ounces white chocolate (31 to 35% cacao content), cut into small chunks

2 ounces dark milk chocolate (38 to 42% cacao content), cut into small chunks

2 ounces bittersweet chocolate (66 to 72% cacao content), cut into small chunks

POSITION the oven racks in the upper and lower thirds and preheat the oven to 350°F. Line three baking sheets with parchment paper or nonstick liners. Place the pecans in a cake or pie pan and toast in the oven for 7 to 8 minutes, until golden. Remove the pan from the oven and cool on a rack.

BEAT the butter in the bowl of an electric stand mixer with the flat beater attachment or in a large mixing bowl using a handheld mixer until fluffy, about 1 minute. Add the brown sugar and granulated sugar and beat together until thoroughly blended.

USING a fork, lightly beat the egg, egg yolk, and vanilla and chocolate extracts together in a small bowl or liquid measuring cup. Add to the butter mixture and blend thoroughly. Stop and scrape down the bottom and sides of the bowl with a rubber spatula to ensure even mixing.

OVER a bowl, sift together the flour, cake flour, and baking soda. Add the salt and toss to blend. Add this mixture to the butter mixture in 4 stages, stopping to scrape down the sides and bottom of the bowl with the rubber spatula after each addition.

PLACE the cocoa powder in a bowl and pour the boiling water over it. Stir together with a heat-safe silicone spatula until it forms a smooth paste. Add the cocoa paste to the cookie mixture, blending thoroughly.

ADD the chocolate chunks and the toasted pecans and stir to distribute evenly. Use a 1¼-inch-diameter ice cream scoop to scoop out small mounds. Place the mounds on the baking sheets, leaving at least 2 inches of space between them. Chill one sheet of the cookies while baking the other two.

BAKE the cookies for 5 minutes. Switch the pans and bake another 5 to 6 minutes, until the cookies are firm.

REMOVE the baking sheets from the oven and transfer them to racks to cool completely. Serve the cookies at room temperature.

keeping

Store the cookies in an airtight plastic container between sheets of waxed paper at room temperature up to 5 days. To freeze up to 3 months, wrap the container tightly in several layers of plastic wrap and aluminum foil. Use a large piece of masking tape and an indelible marker to label and date the contents. If frozen, thaw overnight in the refrigerator and bring to room temperature before serving.

streamlining

The cookie dough can be stored tightly covered in plastic wrap in the refrigerator up to 4 days before scooping it out and baking. Bring it to room temperature before using. To freeze up to 4 months, place the wrapped dough in a freezer bag and seal tightly. Use a large piece of masking tape and an indelible marker to label and date the contents. Thaw overnight in the refrigerator and bring to room temperature before using.

making a change

Replace the pecans with walnuts.
Use one or two types of chocolate chunks instead of all three.

diamond-studded mocha-cinnamon rounds

THESE COOKIES HAVE DEEP CHOCOLATE FLAVOR FROM COCOA POWDER, UNSWEETENED CHOCOLATE, AND BITTERSWEET CHOCOLATE THAT IS ENHANCED EVEN MORE BY INSTANT ESPRESSO POWDER. CRYSTAL SUGAR ON THE OUTSIDE MAKES THEM LOOK LIKE THEY ARE STUDDED WITH DIAMONDS. THESE ARE CLASSIC REFRIGERATOR COOKIES: THE DOUGH NEEDS TO BE MADE AHEAD SO IT HAS PLENTY OF TIME TO CHILL BEFORE IT IS CUT AND BAKED.

MAKES *about 3½ dozen cookies*

2¼ cups (5½ ounces) all-purpose flour

1 cup (6½ ounces) granulated sugar

⅓ cup (1¼ ounces) unsweetened Dutch-processed cocoa powder

2 teaspoons instant espresso powder

1½ teaspoons ground cinnamon

½ teaspoon baking powder

⅛ teaspoon kosher or fine-grained sea salt

8 ounces (16 tablespoons, 2 sticks) unsalted butter, chilled

1 large egg, at room temperature

1 teaspoon pure vanilla extract

1 teaspoon pure chocolate extract

2 ounces unsweetened chocolate, finely chopped

2 ounces bittersweet chocolate (70 to 72% cacao content), finely chopped

1 large egg yolk, at room temperature

¼ cup (2 ounces) crystal sugar

BRIEFLY pulse together the flour, sugar, cocoa powder, espresso powder, cinnamon, baking powder, and salt in the work bowl of a food processor fitted with a steel blade.

CUT the butter into small pieces and add. Pulse until the butter is cut into very tiny pieces, about 1 minute. The texture should be sandy with tiny lumps throughout.

USE a fork to lightly beat the egg and vanilla and chocolate extracts together in a small bowl or liquid measuring cup. Add to the mixture. Pulse until blended, about 30 seconds. Add the unsweetened and bittersweet chocolates and pulse to blend thoroughly, 30 seconds to 1 minute. The mixture will be smooth with very tiny chocolate pieces embedded within and will feel like soft pie or tart dough.

PLACE two large sheets of waxed paper on a flat surface and divide the dough evenly between them. Use the waxed paper to shape and roll the dough into cylinders about 11 inches long and 1 inch in diameter. Wrap the cylinders tightly with the waxed paper, then wrap each in plastic wrap. Chill in the freezer for 45 minutes or in the refrigerator for at least 4 hours, until firm enough to slice.

POSITION the oven racks in the upper and lower thirds and preheat the oven to 350°F. Line two baking sheets with parchment paper or nonstick liners.

USING a fork, lightly beat the egg yolk in a small bowl. Divide the crystal sugar evenly between two sheets of waxed or parchment paper. Use one portion for one cylinder and the rest for the other. Using a pastry brush or a spoon, coat the outside of each dough cylinder with egg yolk, then roll in the crystal sugar, coating each completely.

PLACE a dough cylinder on a cutting board. Use a sharp knife to cut each cylinder into ½-inch-thick slices. Cut straight down, and rotate the cylinder a quarter-turn after every six slices so it will keep its round shape. If the dough becomes soft while working with it, rewrap it, chill for another 10 to 15 minutes, then continue slicing.

PLACE the slices onto the lined baking sheets, leaving at least an inch of space between them. Bake for 5 minutes. Switch the pans and bake another 5 to 6 minutes, until set.

REMOVE the baking sheets from the oven and cool the cookies on the baking sheets on racks.

keeping

Store the cookies in an airtight plastic container between layers of waxed paper at room temperature up to a week. To freeze up to 3 months, wrap the container in several layers of plastic wrap and aluminum foil. Use a large piece of masking tape and an indelible marker to label and date the contents. If frozen, thaw overnight in the refrigerator and bring to room temperature before serving.

streamlining

The dough cylinders can be made and kept in the refrigerator up to 3 days before baking. They can also be kept in the freezer up to 3 months. To refrigerate, wrap the cylinders tightly in several layers of plastic wrap. To freeze, wrap the same way and place each cylinder in a plastic freezer bag. You can take them directly from the freezer and slice for baking, or thaw the cylinders overnight in the refrigerator.

making a change

Add ½ teaspoon ground ginger and ½ teaspoon freshly grated nutmeg to the dry ingredients. Add ½ cup (2 ounces) cacao nibs when adding the chopped chocolate.

adding style

Make sandwich cookies using ice cream, White Chocolate Ganache (page 104) Bittersweet Chocolate Ganache (page 93), White Chocolate–Passion Fruit Frosting (page 33), or raspberry or apricot preserves.

double gianduia sandwich cookies

GIANDUIA IS AN INCOMPARABLE FLAVOR COMBINATION OF CHOCOLATE AND HAZELNUTS THAT WAS CREATED IN ITALY IN THE MID-NINETEENTH CENTURY. THE COOKIES ARE MADE WITH BOTH GIANDUIA AND HAZELNUTS AND THE FILLING CONTAINS BITTERSWEET CHOCOLATE AND HAZELNUT PASTE. GIANDUIA CHOCOLATE IS AVAILABLE (SEE SOURCES, PAGE 209), BUT YOU CAN ALSO CREATE THIS SUBLIME FLAVOR BY COMBINING CHOCOLATE WITH LUSCIOUS HAZELNUT PASTE (PAGE 205).

MAKES 2½ dozen sandwich cookies

SPECIAL EQUIPMENT: 2-inch round scalloped-edge cookie cutter; 12- or 14-inch pastry bag with a ½-inch plain round tip

COOKIES

½ cup (2½ ounces) hazelnuts

½ cup (3½ ounces) granulated sugar

1½ cups (6¾ ounces) all-purpose flour

¼ teaspoon kosher or fine-grained sea salt

6 ounces (1½ sticks, 12 tablespoons) unsalted butter, chilled

3 ounces gianduia chocolate, finely chopped

1 tablespoon plus 1 teaspoon heavy whipping cream

1 teaspoon pure chocolate extract

GIANDUIA FILLING

10 ounces bittersweet chocolate (66 to 72% cacao content), finely chopped

⅔ cup heavy whipping cream.

¼ cup (2½ ounces) Luscious Hazelnut Paste (page 205)

CENTER a rack in the oven and preheat the oven to 350°F. Place the hazelnuts in a cake or pie pan and toast for 15 minutes. Turn the hazelnuts out of the pan into a kitchen towel. Wrap the towel around the nuts and rub them together to remove most of the skins.

POSITION the oven racks to the upper and lower thirds. Line two baking sheets with parchment paper or nonstick liners.

PULSE together the hazelnuts and sugar in the work bowl of a food processor fitted with the steel blade until the hazelnuts are finely ground, about 2 minutes. Add the flour and salt and pulse briefly to blend. Cut the butter into small pieces and add along with the gianduia chocolate. Pulse until the butter is cut into tiny pieces and the chocolate is finely ground, about 1 minute.

IN a small bowl, combine the cream and chocolate extract. With the food processor running, pour this mixture through the feed tube. Process until the dough wraps itself around the blade, about 30 seconds. Form the dough into a disk, wrap tightly in a double layer of plastic wrap, and chill until firm, about 2 hours.

ON a smooth, flat surface, roll out the cookie dough between sheets of lightly floured waxed or parchment paper to a large rectangle ¼-inch thick. Peel off the top piece of paper, brush off any excess flour, and use a 2-inch round scalloped-edge cutter to cut out the cookies. Gather together the scraps, reroll, and cut out more cookies as needed. Place the cookies on the baking sheets leaving at least 1 inch of space between them.

BAKE the cookies for 6 minutes. Switch the pans and bake another 6 minutes, until the cookies are firm.

keeping

Store the unfilled cookies in an airtight plastic container at room temperature up to 3 days. Store the filled cookies in an airtight plastic container between layers of waxed paper at room temperature up to 2 days.

streamlining

The cookie dough can be stored tightly covered in plastic wrap in the refrigerator up to 4 days. Bring it to room temperature before using. To freeze up to 4 months, place the wrapped dough in a freezer bag and seal tightly. Use a large piece of masking tape and an indelible marker to label and date the contents. Thaw overnight in the refrigerator and bring to room temperature before using.

The ganache filling can be made up to 4 days in advance and kept in a tightly sealed container in the refrigerator. To freeze up to 3 months, place the container in a plastic freezer bag. Use a large piece of masking tape and an indelible marker to label and date the contents. If frozen, thaw overnight in the refrigerator and bring to room temperature before using.

making a change

Replace the gianduia chocolate with bittersweet chocolate (66 to 72% cacao content).

REMOVE the baking sheets from the oven and transfer them to racks to cool completely.

FOR THE FILLING, place the bittersweet chocolate in a large heat-safe bowl. In a small saucepan, heat the cream until it begins to bubble around the edges. Pour the cream over the chocolate and let stand for 30 seconds. Stir together with a heat-safe silicone spatula until smooth. Add the hazelnut paste and blend together thoroughly. Cover the bowl tightly with plastic wrap and chill until thick but not firm, about 15 minutes.

FIT a 12- or 14-inch pastry bag with a ½-inch plain round tip and fill the bag partway with the filling. Pipe about a tablespoon of filling on the flat side of half of the cookies, then top the filling with the remaining cookies, pressing them together to spread the filling to the outer edges. Or use a small offset metal spatula to spread the filling on the flat side of half of the cookies.

milk chocolate–almond sandwich cookies

TWO ALMOND AND DARK MILK CHOCOLATE COOKIES ENCLOSE A CREAMY DARK MILK CHOCOLATE GANACHE FILLING TO MAKE THESE SANDWICH COOKIES. THE COOKIES ARE MADE WITH FINELY GROUND ALMONDS, ALSO CALLED ALMOND MEAL, WHICH CAN BE FOUND IN MANY NATURAL FOOD STORES IN BULK BINS OR PREMEASURED BAGS. BUT IT'S EASY ENOUGH TO MAKE YOUR OWN FINELY GROUND ALMONDS BY PULSING SLICED ALMONDS WITH A TABLESPOON OF SUGAR IN THE WORK BOWL OF A FOOD PROCESSOR. FOR THIS RECIPE GRIND 1¼ CUPS (3¾ OUNCES) SLICED ALMONDS TO EQUAL 1 CUP GROUND ALMONDS.

MAKES 2 dozen sandwich cookies

SPECIAL EQUIPMENT: 2-inch round scalloped-edge cookie cutter

COOKIES

4 ounces (8 tablespoons, 1 stick) unsalted butter, softened

½ cup (3½ ounces) granulated sugar, divided

2 large egg yolks, at room temperature

1 teaspoon pure chocolate extract

1 cup (3½ ounces) finely ground almonds, blanched or unblanched

4 ounces dark milk chocolate (38 to 42% cacao content), finely chopped

1⅔ cups (7½ ounces) all-purpose flour

¾ teaspoon ground cinnamon

¼ teaspoon kosher or fine-grained sea salt

DARK MILK CHOCOLATE FILLING

8 ounces dark milk chocolate (38 to 42% cacao content), finely chopped

½ cup heavy whipping cream.

BEAT the butter in the bowl of an electric stand mixer using the flat beater attachment or in a large mixing bowl using a handheld mixer until fluffy, about 2 minutes. Add ¼ cup of the sugar and cream together until thoroughly blended.

WHISK the egg yolks and chocolate extract together in a small bowl. Add this mixture to the butter mixture, blending thoroughly.

IN the work bowl of a food processor fitted with the steel blade pulse together the remaining ¼ cup sugar, the ground almonds, and dark milk chocolate until the chocolate is finely ground, about 1 minute. Add this mixture to the butter mixture, blending completely.

OVER a bowl, sift together the flour and cinnamon. Add the salt and toss to blend. Add this mixture to the butter mixture in 3 stages, blending thoroughly. Form the dough into a disk, wrap it tightly in plastic wrap, and chill until firm enough to roll out, about 2 hours.

POSITION the oven racks in the upper and lower thirds and preheat the oven to 375°F. Line two baking sheets with parchment paper or nonstick liners.

ON a smooth, flat surface roll out the pastry dough between sheets of lightly floured waxed or parchment paper to a large rectangle ¼ inch thick. Peel off the top piece of paper, brush off any excess flour, and use a 2-inch round scalloped-edge cutter to cut out the cookies. Gather together the scraps, reroll, and cut out more cookies as needed. Place the cookies on the baking sheets, leaving at least 1 inch of space between them.

BAKE the cookies for 5 minutes. Switch the baking pans and bake another 5 to 7 minutes, until the cookies are firm. Remove the baking sheets from the oven and transfer them to racks to cool completely.

FOR THE FILLING, place the milk chocolate in a large heat-safe bowl. In a small saucepan, heat the cream until it begins to bubble around the edges. Pour the cream over the chocolate and let stand for 30 seconds. Stir together with a heat-safe silicone spatula until smooth. Cover the bowl tightly with plastic wrap and chill until thick but not firm, 45 minutes to 1 hour.

USE a small offset metal spatula to spread about 1 tablespoon of filling on the flat side of half of the cookies, then top the filling with the remaining cookies, pressing them together to spread the filling to the outer edges. Serve the cookies at room temperature.

keeping

Store the unfilled cookies in an airtight plastic container between layers of waxed paper at room temperature up to 3 days. Store the filled cookies in an airtight plastic container between layers of waxed paper at room temperature up to 2 days.

streamlining

The cookie dough can be stored tightly covered in plastic wrap in the refrigerator up to 4 days. Bring it to room temperature before using. To freeze up to 4 months, place the wrapped dough in a freezer bag and seal tightly. Use a large piece of masking tape and an indelible marker to label and date the contents. Thaw overnight in the refrigerator and bring to room temperature before using.

The ganache filling can be made up to 4 days in advance and kept in a tightly sealed container in the refrigerator. To freeze up to 3 months, place the container in a plastic freezer bag. Use a large piece of masking tape and an indelible marker to label and date the contents. If frozen, thaw overnight in the refrigerator and bring to room temperature before using.

triple chocolate—walnut biscotti

THESE ARE FULL OF CHOCOLATE FLAVOR FROM THE COMBINATION OF DUTCH-PROCESSED COCOA POWDER, BITTERSWEET CHOCOLATE, AND CACAO NIBS. THESE KEEP VERY WELL AND TRAVEL WELL, MAKING THEM PERFECT FOR A PICNIC OR A HOSTESS GIFT. IF YOU WANT TO BE VERY INDULGENT, DIP THEM HALFWAY INTO MELTED BITTERSWEET CHOCOLATE.

MAKES 3½ dozen cookies

1½ cups (6¾ ounces) all-purpose flour

½ cup (1¾ ounces) unsweetened Dutch-processed cocoa powder

2 teaspoons baking soda

Pinch of kosher or fine-grained sea salt

½ cup (3½ ounces) granulated sugar

⅓ cup (2¼ ounces) firmly packed light brown sugar

3 large eggs, at room temperature

1 teaspoon pure vanilla extract

1 teaspoon pure chocolate extract

3 ounces bittersweet (66 to 72% cacao content), cut into small chunks

½ cup (2¼ ounces) lightly toasted walnuts, finely chopped (see page 10)

½ cup (2 ounces) cacao nibs

POSITION the oven racks in the upper and lower thirds and preheat the oven to 350°F. Line two baking sheets with parchment paper or nonstick liners.

INTO the bowl of an electric stand mixer or a large mixing bowl, sift together the flour, cocoa powder, and baking soda. Add the salt, granulated sugar, and brown sugar. Use the flat beater attachment or a handheld mixer to stir together briefly.

USING a fork, lightly whisk the eggs with the vanilla and chocolate extracts in a small bowl or liquid measuring cup. Add this mixture to the flour mixture, mixing on low speed until thoroughly combined. Stop occasionally and scrape down the sides and bottom of the bowl with a rubber spatula. Add the chocolate chunks, walnuts, and cacao nibs and stir to blend thoroughly.

DIVIDE the dough into four equal pieces. Dust your hands with flour to keep the dough from sticking and shape each piece into a log about 6 inches long, 2 inches wide, and ¾ inch high. Place two logs on each baking sheet, leaving at least 4 inches between them. Bake for 10 minutes, then switch the baking sheets and bake another 10 minutes, until set.

REMOVE the baking sheets from the oven and rest on cooling racks for 15 minutes. Do not turn off the oven.

CAREFULLY peel the parchment paper from the back of the logs. Place the logs on a cutting board. Using a serrated knife, cut the logs on the diagonal into ½-inch-thick slices. Place the slices back onto the baking sheet on their sides, so the wide part of each faces up. Bake the biscotti for 8 minutes, switch the baking sheets, and bake until firm, 6 to 8 minutes. Transfer the baking pans to racks to cool. Serve the biscotti at room temperature.

Store the biscotti in an airtight plastic container between sheets of waxed paper at room temperature up to 2 weeks.

The biscotti dough can be shaped into the logs and stored tightly covered in plastic wrap in the refrigerator up to 4 days. Bring it to room temperature before using. To freeze up to 4 months, place the wrapped dough in a freezer bag and seal tightly. Use a large piece of masking tape and an indelible marker to label and date the contents. Thaw overnight in the refrigerator and bring to room temperature before using.

making a change
adding style

Replace the walnuts with almonds, pecans, or coarsely chopped toasted, skinned hazelnuts.

Dip one flat end of each biscotti in melted bittersweet chocolate (see page 9). Place the biscotti on a baking sheet and chill for 15 minutes to set the chocolate.

milk chocolate chunk–pecan biscotti

THIS VARIATION OF CLASSIC BISCOTTI BRINGS TOGETHER DARK MILK CHOCOLATE AND PECANS, WHICH ARE THE PERFECT MARRIAGE. THEY ARE CRISP AND CRUNCHY, IDEAL FOR DUNKING INTO A GLASS OF MILK OR A CUP OF HOT CHOCOLATE (PAGES 198, AND 200). LIKE ALL BISCOTTI, THESE KEEP VERY WELL IN A TIGHTLY SEALED CONTAINER UP TO 2 WEEKS.

MAKES *about 4 dozen cookies*

2 cups (8½ ounces) all-purpose flour

¾ cup (5½ ounces) granulated sugar

⅓ cup (2¼ ounces) firmly packed light brown sugar

2 teaspoons baking powder

¼ teaspoon kosher or fine-grained sea salt

2 large eggs, at room temperature

1 teaspoon pure vanilla extract

4 ounces (8 tablespoons, 1 stick) unsalted butter, melted

1 cup (3¾ ounces) lightly toasted pecans, coarsely chopped (see page 10)

6 ounces dark milk chocolate (38 to 42% cacao content), cut into small chunks

POSITION the oven racks in the upper and lower thirds and preheat the oven to 350°F. Line two baking sheets with parchment paper or nonstick liners.

IN the bowl of an electric stand mixer using the flat beater attachment or in a large mixing bowl using a handheld mixer, combine the flour, granulated sugar, brown sugar, baking powder, and salt and stir together briefly.

USING a fork, lightly whisk the eggs with the vanilla extract in a small bowl or liquid measuring cup. Add this mixture and the melted butter to the flour mixture, mixing on low speed until thoroughly combined. Stop occasionally and scrape down the sides and bottom of the bowl with a rubber spatula. Add the pecans and dark milk chocolate and stir to blend thoroughly.

DIVIDE the dough into four equal pieces. Dust your hands with flour to keep the dough from sticking and shape each piece into a log about 6 inches long, 2 inches wide, and ¾ inch high. Place two logs on each baking sheet, leaving at least 4 inches between them. Bake for 13 minutes, then switch the baking sheets and bake another 12 minutes, until set.

REMOVE the baking sheets from the oven and rest on cooling racks for 15 minutes. Do not turn off the oven.

CAREFULLY peel the parchment paper from the back of the logs. Place the logs on a cutting board. Using a serrated knife, cut the logs on the diagonal into ¾-inch-thick slices. Place the slices back onto the baking sheet on their sides, so the wide part of each faces up. Bake the biscotti for 8 minutes, switch the baking sheets, and bake until firm, 6 to 8 minutes.

TRANSFER the baking pans to racks to cool. Serve the biscotti at room temperature.

keeping

Store the biscotti in an airtight plastic container between sheets of waxed paper at room temperature up to 2 weeks.

The biscotti dough can be shaped into the logs and stored tightly covered in plastic wrap in the refrigerator up to 4 days. Bring it to room temperature before using. To freeze up to 4 months, place the wrapped dough in a freezer bag and seal tightly. Use a large piece of masking tape and an indelible marker to label and date the contents. Thaw overnight in the refrigerator and bring to room temperature before using.

making a change

Replace the pecans with almonds, walnuts, or coarsely chopped toasted hazelnuts.

bittersweet chocolate-coconut-almond biscotti

THE COMBINATION OF BITTERSWEET CHOCOLATE CHUNKS, CACAO NIBS, SWEETENED SHREDDED COCONUT, AND SLICED ALMONDS GIVES THESE BISCOTTI A VERY CRUNCHY TEXTURE AS WELL AS A SLIGHTLY TROPICAL FLAVOR. BISCOTTI ARE ALWAYS GOOD FOR DIPPING, ESPECIALLY INTO HOT FUDGE SAUCE (PAGE 202).

MAKES *about 2 dozen cookies*

2 cups (8½ ounces) all-purpose flour

1 cup (2 ounces) sweetened shredded coconut

1 cup (3 ounces) sliced almonds, blanched or unblanched

⅔ cup (4 ounces) granulated sugar

4 ounces bittersweet chocolate (66 to 72% cacao content), cut into small chunks

½ cup (2 ounces) cacao nibs

2 teaspoons baking powder

¼ teaspoon kosher or fine-grained sea salt

2 large eggs, at room temperature

1 teaspoon pure vanilla extract

4 ounces (8 tablespoons, 1 stick) unsalted butter, melted

CENTER a rack in the oven and preheat the oven to 350°F. Line a baking sheet with parchment paper or a nonstick liner.

IN the bowl of an electric stand mixer using the flat beater attachment or in a large mixing bowl using a handheld mixer, combine the flour, coconut, sliced almonds, sugar, bittersweet chocolate, cacao nibs, baking powder, and salt and stir together briefly.

USING a fork, lightly whisk the eggs with the vanilla extract in a small bowl or liquid measuring cup. Add this mixture and the melted butter to the flour mixture, mixing on low speed until thoroughly combined. Stop occasionally and scrape down the sides and bottom of the bowl with a rubber spatula.

DIVIDE the dough into three equal pieces. Dust your hands with flour to keep the dough from sticking and shape each piece into a log about 8 inches long, 2 inches wide, and ¾ inch high. Place the logs on the baking sheet, leaving at least 2 inches between them. Bake the biscotti for 25 to 28 minutes, until the loaves are light golden and set.

REMOVE the baking sheet from the oven and rest it on a cooling rack for 15 minutes.

CAREFULLY peel the parchment paper from the back of the logs. Place the logs on a cutting board. Using a serrated knife, cut the logs on the diagonal into ½-inch-thick slices. Place the slices back on the baking sheet on their sides, so the wide part of each faces up. Bake the biscotti for 15 to 18 minutes, until firm.

TRANSFER the baking pan to a rack to cool. Serve the biscotti at room temperature.

keeping Store the biscotti in an airtight plastic container between sheets of waxed paper at room temperature up to 2 weeks.

The biscotti dough can be shaped into the logs and stored tightly covered in plastic wrap in the refrigerator up to 4 days. Bring it to room temperature before using. To freeze up to 4 months, place the wrapped dough in a freezer bag and seal tightly. Use a large piece of masking tape and an indelible marker to label and date the contents. Thaw overnight in the refrigerator and bring to room temperature before using.

adding style Dip one flat end of each biscotti in melted bittersweet chocolate (see page 9). Place the biscotti on a baking sheet and chill for 15 minutes to set the chocolate. Or dip one long end of each biscotti diagonally into melted bittersweet chocolate and proceed as above.

white chocolate shortbread coins

PURE WHITE CHOCOLATE SHORTBREAD IS FORMED INTO LOGS, CHILLED, THEN SLICED AND BAKED. ONCE COOLED, THE COOKIES ARE DIPPED HALFWAY IN MELTED WHITE CHOCOLATE, GIVING THEM AN EXTRA ACCENT AND DECORATION. INSTEAD OF DIPPING THE SHORTBREAD COINS, YOU CAN LEAVE THEM PLAIN AND USE THEM TO MAKE SANDWICH COOKIES WITH A FILLING OF WHITE OR BITTERSWEET CHOCOLATE GANACHE (PAGES 104 AND 93) ICE CREAM, OR RASPBERRY PRESERVES.

MAKES *about 3½ dozen cookies*

COOKIES

5 ounces white chocolate (31 to 35% cacao content), broken into small pieces

1½ cups (6¾ ounces) all-purpose flour

¼ teaspoon kosher or fine-grained sea salt

5 ounces (10 tablespoons, 1¼ sticks) unsalted butter, softened

¼ cup firmly packed (1½ ounces) light brown sugar

¼ cup (1½ ounces) superfine sugar

GARNISH

3 ounces white chocolate (31 to 35% cacao content), finely chopped

PULSE the white chocolate, flour, and salt in the work bowl of a food processor fitted with the steel blade until the white chocolate is very finely ground, about 2 minutes.

BEAT the butter in the bowl of an electric stand mixer using the flat beater attachment or in a large mixing bowl using a handheld mixer on medium speed until fluffy, about 2 minutes.

ADD the brown sugar and superfine sugar and beat together. Stop occasionally and scrape down the sides and bottom of the bowl with a rubber spatula.

WITH the mixer speed on low, add the flour mixture to the butter mixture in 3 stages, mixing completely after each addition. Stop and scrape down the sides and bottom of the bowl with a rubber spatula.

PLACE two large sheets of waxed paper on a flat surface, divide the dough in half evenly, and place each half onto a sheet of the waxed paper. Use the waxed paper to shape and roll the dough into cylinders about 13 inches long and 1 inch in diameter. Wrap the cylinders tightly with the waxed paper, then wrap each in plastic wrap. Chill in the freezer for 45 minutes or in the refrigerator for at least 4 hours, until firm enough to slice.

POSITION the oven racks in the upper and lower thirds and preheat the oven to 300°F. Line two baking sheets with parchment paper or nonstick liners.

PLACE a dough cylinder on a cutting board. Use a sharp knife to cut each cylinder into ½-inch-thick slices. Cut straight down and rotate the cylinder a quarter-turn after every six slices so it will keep its round shape. If the dough becomes soft while working with it, rewrap it, chill for another 10 to 15 minutes, then continue slicing.

PLACE the slices on the baking sheets, leaving at least 1 inch of space between them. Bake for 10 minutes. Switch the pans and bake another 10 to 12 minutes, until set and lightly colored.

REMOVE the baking sheets from the oven and cool the cookies on the baking sheets on racks.

FOR THE GARNISH, melt the white chocolate in a microwave-safe bowl on low power in 30-second bursts, stirring with a heat-safe silicone spatula after each burst. Line a baking sheet with parchment or waxed paper. Dip a shortbread coin halfway into the melted white chocolate. Lift the shortbread out of the chocolate and let any excess drip off. Place the shortbread flat on the baking sheet. Continue with the remaining coins. To set the chocolate, place the baking sheet in the refrigerator for 15 minutes.

keeping

Store the shortbread in an airtight plastic container between layers of waxed paper at room temperature up to a week. To freeze up to 3 months, wrap the container in several layers of plastic wrap and aluminum foil. Use a large piece of masking tape and an indelible marker to label and date the contents. If frozen, thaw overnight in the refrigerator and bring to room temperature before serving.

streamlining

The dough cylinders can be made and kept in the refrigerator up to 3 days before baking. They can also be kept in the freezer up to 3 months. To refrigerate, wrap the cylinders tightly in several layers of plastic wrap. To freeze, wrap the same way and place each cylinder in a plastic freezer bag. You can take them directly from the freezer and slice for baking, or thaw the cylinders overnight in the refrigerator.

making a change

Add ½ cup (2¼ ounces) finely chopped pecans or walnuts to the dough before shaping into cylinders.

adding style

Make sandwich cookies using ice cream, White Chocolate Ganache (page 104), Bittersweet Chocolate Ganache (page 93), White Chocolate–Passion Fruit Frosting (page 33), or raspberry or apricot preserves.

cocoa—almond wafers

COCOA POWDER AND SLICED ALMONDS ARE USED TO MAKE THESE UNUSUAL WAFERS THAT ARE SIMILAR TO BISCOTTI BECAUSE THEY ARE BAKED TWICE. FIRST THEY ARE BAKED IN A LOAF PAN; AFTER THE LOAF IS COOLED IT IS SLICED VERY THIN AND THE SLICES ARE DRIED IN THE OVEN, MAKING THEM VERY CRISP. THE WAFERS ARE A WONDERFUL ACCOMPANIMENT TO ICE CREAM. I ALSO LIKE TO SPREAD THEM WITH A THIN LAYER OF BITTERSWEET CHOCOLATE GANACHE (PAGE 93) OR RASPBERRY PRESERVES.

MAKES about 2½ dozen wafers

SPECIAL EQUIPMENT: 9 x 5 x 3-inch loaf pan

1 tablespoon unsalted butter, softened

6 large egg whites, at room temperature

¼ teaspoon cream of tartar

1 cup (6½ ounces) superfine sugar

1⅓ cups (6 ounces) all-purpose flour

⅓ cup (1¼ ounces) unsweetened cocoa powder (natural or Dutch-processed)

1 cup (3 ounces) sliced almonds, blanched or unblanched

CENTER a rack in the oven and preheat the oven to 300°F. Line the loaf pan with aluminum foil, letting it hang about 2 inches over the sides. Use a paper towel or your fingers to coat the inside of the foil with the softened butter.

WHIP the egg whites and cream of tartar together in the grease-free bowl of an electric stand mixer using the wire whip attachment or in a large grease-free mixing bowl using a handheld mixer until frothy. Gradually sprinkle on the superfine sugar and continue to whip the egg whites until they hold glossy and firm but not stiff peaks.

OVER a separate bowl, sift together the flour and cocoa powder and fold into the egg whites in 4 stages. The mixture will be very thick. Fold in the sliced almonds.

TRANSFER the mixture to the prepared loaf pan, using a rubber spatula to spread it out evenly. Bake the loaf for 45 to 50 minutes, until a cake tester or toothpick inserted in the center comes out clean.

REMOVE the pan from the oven and cool completely on a rack. Position the oven racks in the upper and lower thirds and lower the oven temperature to 275°F. Line two baking sheets with parchment paper or nonstick liners.

LIFT the cooled loaf from the pan by holding the edges of the foil. Carefully peel the foil from the loaf. Place the loaf on a cutting board. Using a serrated knife, cut the loaf into ¼-inch-thick slices. Place the slices flat on the baking sheets. Bake the wafers for 15 to 20 minutes. Turn the wafers over and bake another 15 to 20 minutes, until firm.

TRANSFER the baking sheets to racks to cool. The wafers will become crisp as they cool. Serve them at room temperature.

keeping

Store the wafers in an airtight plastic container at room temperature up to 2 weeks.

streamlining

The loaf can be baked a day before slicing and drying in the oven. After it is completely cooled, cover it tightly with aluminum foil and hold at room temperature.

adding style

Spread one side of each wafer with Bittersweet Chocolate Ganache (page 104) or with raspberry preserves.

white chocolate-vanilla madeleines

WHITE CHOCOLATE AND VANILLA BEAN PASTE COMBINE SUPERBLY IN THESE CLASSIC FRENCH SHELL-SHAPED COOKIES. THEY ARE MOIST AND FLAVORFUL, PERFECT WITH A CUP OF TEA OR WHITE HOT CHOCOLATE (PAGE 200). MADELEINES CAN BE MADE INTO SANDWICH COOKIES WITH A VARIETY OF FILLINGS, SUCH AS WHITE CHOCOLATE GANACHE (PAGE 104) OR RASPBERRY OR APRICOT PRESERVES.

MAKES 2 dozen cookies

SPECIAL EQUIPMENT: two 12-cavity (3 inches long) madeleine pans

1 tablespoon unsalted butter, melted and slightly cooled

4 ounces white chocolate (31 to 35% cacao content), finely chopped, divided

3 ounces (6 tablespoons, ¾ stick) unsalted butter, cut into small pieces

1 tablespoon pure vanilla bean paste

2 large eggs, at room temperature

⅓ cup (2 ounces) superfine sugar

½ cup (2¼ ounces) all-purpose flour

¼ teaspoon kosher or fine-grained sea salt

POSITION the oven racks in the upper and lower thirds and preheat the oven to 350°F. Use a pastry brush or a paper towel to coat the inside of each cavity of both madeleine pans with the melted butter.

MELT 2 ounces of the white chocolate and the butter together in the top of a double boiler over low heat, stirring often with a rubber spatula to ensure even melting. Or place the chocolate and butter in a microwave-safe bowl and melt on low power in 30-second bursts, stirring after each burst. Remove the top pan of the double boiler, if using, and wipe the bottom and sides very dry. Add the vanilla bean paste and stir until thoroughly blended. Stir the chocolate-butter mixture with a rubber spatula occasionally to prevent a skin from forming on top.

WHIP the eggs in the bowl of an electric stand mixer using the wire whip attachment or in a large mixing bowl using a handheld mixer on medium speed until frothy, about 1 minute. Add the superfine sugar and whip together on medium-high speed until the mixture is very thick and pale yellow and holds a slowly dissolving ribbon when the beater is lifted, about 5 minutes.

PULSE the remaining 2 ounces white chocolate, the flour, and salt in the work bowl of a food processor fitted with a steel blade until the chocolate is very finely ground, about 1 minute. With the mixer speed on low, add this flour mixture to the egg mixture in 3 stages, blending well after each addition. Stop and scrape down the sides and bottom of the bowl with the rubber spatula a few times while mixing.

POUR the melted white chocolate mixture into the batter and blend thoroughly. Transfer the batter to a 2-cup liquid measuring cup. Pour the batter slowly into each cavity of the madeleine pans, filling them ¾ full. Place each madeleine pan on a baking sheet.

BAKE the madeleines for 6 minutes. Switch the baking sheets and bake for another 6 to 8 minutes, until the tops of the madeleines spring back lightly when touched.

REMOVE the baking pans from the oven. Holding the madeleine pans upside down over cooling racks, gently shake them to release the cookies. Cool completely on the racks.

SERVE the madeleines at room temperature.

keeping

Store the madeleines in an airtight plastic container between layers of waxed paper at room temperature up to 3 days. To freeze up to 3 months, wrap the container tightly in several layers of plastic wrap and aluminum foil. Use a large piece of masking tape and an indelible marker to label and date the contents. If frozen, thaw overnight in the refrigerator and bring to room temperature before serving.

making a change

Add ½ cup (2¼ ounces) toasted, finely chopped pecans or walnuts to the batter before turning into the pans to bake.

adding style

Make madeleine ganache sandwiches by spreading the flat side of one cookie with White Chocolate Ganache (page 104) and topping it with the flat side of another cookie.

Make madeleine sandwiches by spreading a thin layer of raspberry or apricot preserves on the flat side of one cookie and topping it with the flat side of another cookie.

Drizzle the cooled madeleines with thin lines of melted bittersweet, milk, or white chocolate. Let the chocolate set in the refrigerator for 15 minutes before serving or storing.

Half-dip the madeleines in melted white chocolate (see page 9). Let the chocolate set in the refrigerator for 15 minutes before serving or storing.

white chocolate chunk-toasted pecan cookies

CHUNKS OF WHITE CHOCOLATE AND TOASTED PECANS ADD FLAVOR AND TEXTURE TO THESE CHEWY COOKIES. THESE ARE VERY TEMPTING BECAUSE YOU CAN SEE THE CHUNKS OF WHITE CHOCOLATE AND PECANS.

MAKES *about 4 dozen cookies*

SPECIAL EQUIPMENT: *1¼-inch-diameter ice cream scoop*

¾ cup (3 ounces) coarsely chopped pecans (see page 10)

8 ounces (16 tablespoons, 2 sticks) unsalted butter, softened

1 cup (6 ounces) firmly packed light brown sugar

1 large egg, at room temperature

2 teaspoons pure vanilla extract

2 cups (9 ounces) all-purpose flour

¾ teaspoon baking soda

½ teaspoon baking powder

½ teaspoon kosher or fine-grained sea salt

8 ounces white chocolate (31 to 35% cacao content), cut into small chunks

POSITION the oven racks in the upper and lower thirds and preheat the oven to 350°F. Line three baking sheets with parchment paper or nonstick liners. Place the pecans in a cake or pie pan and toast in the oven for 7 to 8 minutes, until golden. Remove the pan from the oven and cool on a rack.

BEAT the butter in the bowl of an electric stand mixer with the flat beater attachment or in a large mixing bowl using a handheld mixer until fluffy, about 1 minute. Add the brown sugar and beat together until thoroughly blended.

USING a fork, lightly beat the egg and vanilla together in a small bowl or liquid measuring cup. Add to the butter mixture and blend thoroughly. Stop and scrape down the bottom and sides of the bowl with a rubber spatula to ensure even mixing.

OVER a bowl, sift together the flour, baking soda, and baking powder. Add the salt and toss to blend. Add this mixture to the butter mixture in 4 stages, stopping to scrape down the sides and bottom of the bowl with the rubber spatula after each addition.

ADD the white chocolate and toasted pecans and stir to distribute evenly. Use a 1¼-inch-diameter ice cream scoop to scoop out small mounds. Place the mounds on the baking sheets, leaving at least 2 inches of space between them. Chill one sheet of the cookies while baking the other two.

BAKE the cookies for 5 minutes. Switch the pans and bake another 5 to 6 minutes, until the cookies are firm.

REMOVE the baking sheets from the oven and transfer them to racks to cool completely. Serve the cookies at room temperature.

Store the cookies in an airtight plastic container at room temperature up to 4 days. To freeze up to 3 months, wrap the container tightly in several layers of plastic wrap and aluminum foil. Use a large piece of masking tape and an indelible marker to label and date the contents. If frozen, thaw overnight in the refrigerator and bring to room temperature before serving.

streamlining

The cookie dough can be and stored tightly covered in plastic wrap in the refrigerator up to 4 days. Bring it to room temperature before using. To freeze up to 4 months, place the wrapped dough in a freezer bag and seal tightly. Use a large piece of masking tape and an indelible marker to label and date the contents. Thaw overnight in the refrigerator and bring to room temperature before using.

making a change

Replace the pecans with walnuts.

milk chocolate–dulce de leche bars

THESE POTENT BARS HAVE THREE LAYERS: A COCONUT AND BROWN SUGAR CRUST, A DULCE DE LECHE (CARAMEL) FILLING, AND A GLAZE OF DARK MILK CHOCOLATE. YOU CAN CUT THESE INTO SMALLER BITE-SIZE PIECES, IF YOU LIKE.

MAKES 2½ dozen 1 x 2½-inch bars

SPECIAL EQUIPMENT: 9 x 13-inch baking pan

CRUST

4 ounces (8 tablespoons, 1 stick) unsalted butter, cut into small pieces

1 cup (2 ounces) sweetened shredded coconut

1 cup (6 ounces) firmly packed light brown sugar

1 cup (4½ ounces) all-purpose flour

1 teaspoon baking powder

⅛ teaspoon kosher or fine-grained sea salt

DULCE DE LECHE FILLING

One14-ounce can sweetened condensed milk

1 ounce (2 tablespoons, ¼ stick) unsalted butter, softened

1 tablespoon light corn syrup

GLAZE

13 ounces dark milk chocolate (38 to 42% cacao content), finely chopped

CENTER a rack in the oven and preheat the oven to 350°F. Line the inside of a 9 x 13-inch baking pan with parchment paper, pressing it into the pan and letting it hang about 2 inches over the short sides.

FOR THE CRUST, melt the butter in a 1-quart saucepan over low heat. Place the coconut, brown sugar, flour, baking powder, and salt in a 2-quart mixing bowl and toss to blend thoroughly. Pour the melted butter into this mixture and use a rubber spatula to stir until the dry ingredients are moistened. Transfer the mixture to the baking pan and press it in evenly, making sure it reaches into the corners.

BAKE the crust for 15 to 18 minutes, until lightly golden and set. Remove the baking pan from the oven and cool it completely on a rack. Do not turn off the oven.

FOR THE DULCE DE LECHE FILLING, combine the sweetened condensed milk, butter, and corn syrup in a 2-quart heavy-duty saucepan. Stir the mixture constantly over medium heat until it thickens and turns a deep beige, about 5 minutes. Pour the filling over the cooled crust, using an offset metal spatula to spread it evenly. Return the baking pan to the oven and bake for 12 to 14 minutes, until the filling begins to bubble. Remove the baking pan from the oven and transfer it to a rack to cool completely.

FOR THE GLAZE, melt the milk chocolate in the top of a double boiler over warm water, stirring occasionally with a rubber spatula to ensure even melting. Or melt the chocolate in a microwave-safe bowl on low power in 30-second bursts, stirring after each burst. Remove the top pan of the double boiler, if using, and wipe the bottom and sides very dry.

POUR the melted chocolate over the top of the dulce de leche filling and use an offset metal spatula to quickly spread it evenly. Tap the pan gently on the countertop to release any air bubbles in the chocolate. Chill the pan for 10 minutes to begin to set the chocolate, then let it set completely at room temperature.

LIFT the bars from the pan by holding the edges of the parchment paper, then peel the parchment paper away from the bars. Use a chef's knife dipped in hot water and dried to trim off about ¼ inch from all of the edges, making them even and clean. Use a ruler to help measure where to cut. Cut into 1-inch slices across the width of the pan, then cut each slice into 2½-inch bars along the length of the pan, cleaning the knife between each cut.

SERVE the bars at room temperature.

keeping

Store the bars in an airtight plastic container between layers of waxed paper at room temperature up to 3 days.

streamlining

The crust and the filling can be baked the day before adding the dark milk chocolate glaze. Store the pan tightly covered with aluminum foil at room temperature.

CHAPTER SIX

*custards, mousses,
and puddings*

cocoa and bittersweet chocolate pudding

CHOCOLATE PUDDING IS THE COMFORT FOOD WE ALL GREW UP EATING THAT BRINGS BACK FOND MEMORIES. THIS IS AN UPDATE ON THE CLASSIC. IT IS RICH, INTENSELY FLAVORED, CREAMY, AND SMOOTH— JUST PERFECT FOR DESSERT ANY TIME.

MAKES eight ½-cup servings

SPECIAL EQUIPMENT: eight ½-cup bowls, custard cups, or ramekins; 10- or 12-inch pastry bag and large open star tip

PUDDING

5 ounces bittersweet chocolate (70 to 72% cacao content), finely chopped

½ cup (3½ ounces) granulated sugar

¼ cup (¾ ounce) unsweetened cocoa powder (natural or Dutch-processed), sifted

3 tablespoons cornstarch, sifted

⅛ teaspoon kosher or fine-grained sea salt

2 cups milk (whole or 2%), divided

4 large egg yolks, at room temperature

1 cup heavy whipping cream

2 tablespoons unsalted butter, softened

1 teaspoon pure vanilla extract

1 teaspoon pure chocolate extract

GARNISH

¼ cup heavy whipping cream

½ teaspoon pure vanilla extract

1 tablespoon finely shaved bittersweet chocolate (70 to 72% cacao content)

FOR THE PUDDING, melt the bittersweet chocolate in a microwave-safe bowl on low power for 30-second bursts. Stir with a rubber spatula after each burst. Set aside while preparing the rest of the pudding, stirring occasionally to prevent a skin from forming on top.

PLACE the sugar in a large bowl. Into the bowl, sift together the cocoa and corn-starch, then add the salt and toss to blend. Add ½ cup of the milk and whisk until smooth. Lightly whisk the egg yolks in a separate bowl and stir into the mixture.

COMBINE the cream and remaining milk in a large heavy-duty saucepan. Bring to a boil over medium heat. Remove the saucepan from the heat and slowly whisk the sugar mixture into the milk mixture until blended. Place the saucepan back over medium heat and stir the mixture constantly with a heat-safe silicone spatula until thick, about 5 minutes.

STRAIN the mixture into a large heat-safe bowl, add the butter, and whisk until the butter has melted. Add the vanilla and chocolate extracts and the melted chocolate and whisk until smooth.

POUR the pudding into a large liquid measuring cup or use a 2-inch-diameter ice cream scoop to transfer the pudding into bowls. Cover the bowls tightly with plastic wrap and chill about 2 hours.

FOR THE GARNISH, whip the cream until frothy in the bowl of an electric stand mixer using the wire whip attachment or in a mixing bowl using a handheld mixer. Add the vanilla and continue to whip until the cream holds soft peaks. Fit a 10- or 12-inch pastry bag with a large open star tip and fill partway with the whipped cream. Pipe

Store the undecorated pudding tightly covered with plastic wrap in the refrigerator up to 3 days.

making a change

Add 1 teaspoon ground cinnamon to the cocoa mixture.

a star of whipped cream in the center of each cup and sprinkle with shaved chocolate. Or use a spoon to place a large dollop of whipped cream in the center of each pudding and garnish with shaved chocolate.

SERVE the pudding at room temperature.

mighty mocha mousse

IT'S HARD TO BEAT THE FLAVOR COMBINATION OF COFFEE AND BITTERSWEET CHOCOLATE. THIS LIGHT AND CREAMY MOUSSE IS REVVED UP BY USING INSTANT ESPRESSO POWDER AND CHOCOLATE EXTRACT. MOUSSE IS DELICATE AND SHOULD BE PREPARED NO MORE THAN 1 DAY IN ADVANCE OF SERVING.

MAKES ten ½-cup servings

SPECIAL EQUIPMENT: instant-read thermometer; ten ½-cup bowls, custard cups, or ramekins or one 1½-quart bowl

MOUSSE

8 ounces bittersweet chocolate (66 to 72% cacao content), finely chopped

1¾ cups heavy whipping cream, divided

1 tablespoon instant espresso powder

1 teaspoon pure vanilla extract

1 teaspoon pure chocolate extract

3 large egg whites, at room temperature

½ cup (3½ ounces) granulated sugar

GARNISH

¼ cup heavy whipping cream

½ teaspoon pure vanilla extract

1 tablespoon finely shaved bittersweet chocolate, optional

or

Ten small chocolate disks, optional

PLACE the bittersweet chocolate in a 2-quart heat-safe bowl. In a small saucepan, heat ¾ cup of the cream to a boil. Turn off the heat, add the espresso powder, cover, and steep for 10 minutes. Remove the cover and bring the cream to a boil again. Strain the cream through a fine-mesh strainer over the chocolate, let it stand for 30 seconds, then stir together with a heat-safe silicone spatula until all the chocolate is melted and the mixture is smooth. Add the vanilla and chocolate extracts and stir to blend completely.

PLACE the egg whites in the grease-free bowl of an electric stand mixer or a large grease-free mixing bowl and place the bowl over a pan of simmering water. Stirring constantly, heat the egg whites until they register 160°F on an instant-read thermometer. Remove the bowl from the water and wipe the bottom dry. Using the wire whip attachment or a handheld mixer, whip the egg whites until they are frothy. Slowly sprinkle on the sugar and whip the whites until they hold firm but not stiff peaks. Fold the whipped egg whites into the chocolate mixture in 3 stages, blending completely.

WHIP the remaining cup of the cream to soft peaks in the bowl of an electric stand mixer with the wire whip attachment or in a mixing bowl using a handheld mixer. Fold the cream into the chocolate mixture in 3 stages, blending thoroughly. Divide the mousse evenly among ten ½-cup serving bowls or pour it into a 1½-quart bowl. Cover tightly with plastic wrap and chill until set, about 2 hours.

FOR THE GARNISH, whip the cream in an electric mixer with the wire whip attachment or in a bowl using a handheld mixer until frothy. Add the vanilla and continue to whip the cream until it holds soft peaks. Serve each mousse with a dollop of

whipped cream on top. If using the optional shaved chocolate, sprinkle a little over the whipped cream on top of each mousse. If using the optional chocolate disks, center one in the whipped cream on top of each serving.

keeping   Store the mousse tightly covered with plastic wrap in the refrigerator up to 1 day.

bittersweet chocolate-caramel mousse

BITTERSWEET CHOCOLATE AND CREAMY CARAMEL SAUCE COME TOGETHER TO MAKE A MOUSSE WITH A PERFECT BALANCE OF FLAVOR AND TEXTURE. MAKE THIS AT LEAST 2 HOURS BEFORE SERVING SO IT HAS TIME TO SET.

MAKES six ½-cup servings

SPECIAL EQUIPMENT: six ½-cup bowls, custard cups, or ramekins or one 1½-quart bowl; 12-inch pastry bag and large open star tip

4 ounces bittersweet chocolate (66 to 72% cacao content), finely chopped

½ cup (3½ ounces) granulated sugar

½ cup (3 ounces) firmly packed light brown sugar

¼ cup water

2 teaspoons honey

1 teaspoon pure vanilla bean paste

2 cups heavy whipping cream, divided

2 ounces (4 tablespoons, ½ stick) unsalted butter, softened

MELT the bittersweet chocolate in the top of a double boiler over low heat, stirring frequently with a rubber spatula to ensure even melting. Or melt the chocolate in a microwave-safe bowl on low power in 30-second bursts, stirring after each burst. Remove the top pan of the double boiler, if using, and wipe the bottom and sides very dry. Set aside the chocolate, stirring occasionally.

COMBINE the granulated sugar, brown sugar, water, honey, and vanilla paste in a 3-quart heavy-duty saucepan. Cook over high heat until the mixture comes to a boil. Dip a pastry brush in water and run it around the inside of the pan at the point where the mixture meets the sides of the pan to prevent sugar crystallization. Repeat once more. Cook the mixture without stirring until it turns amber, 6 to 8 minutes.

WHILE the sugar is cooking bring ⅔ cup of the cream to a boil over medium heat.

SLOWLY add the hot cream to the caramel mixture, stirring constantly with a long-handled heat-safe silicone spatula. Be careful, because the mixture will bubble and foam. Remove the saucepan from the heat. Stir in the butter until it is completely melted, then stir in the melted chocolate thoroughly. Transfer this mixture to a heat-safe bowl, cover tightly with plastic wrap, place on a cooling rack, and cool to room temperature.

WHIP the remaining 1⅓ cups cream to soft peaks in the bowl of an electric stand mixer with the wire whip attachment or in a mixing bowl using a handheld mixer. Reserve ½ cup of the whipped cream for the garnish. Fold the remaining whipped cream into the chocolate mixture in 3 stages, blending thoroughly.

DIVIDE the mousse evenly among the serving bowls or pour it into a 1½-quart bowl. Cover tightly with plastic wrap and chill until set, about 2 hours.

FOR THE GARNISH, fit a 12-inch pastry bag with a large open star tip and fill with the reserved whipped cream. Pipe a rosette or star of cream on top of each serving of mousse and serve immediately.

keeping

Store the mousse, without the whipped cream garnish, tightly covered with plastic wrap in the refrigerator up to 1 day.

milk chocolate–cinnamon mousse

CINNAMON IS THE PERFECT FOIL FOR THE RICHNESS OF DARK MILK CHOCOLATE IN THIS MOUSSE. THE TEXTURE IS LIGHT AND FLUFFY, LIKE EATING A CHOCOLATE CLOUD.

MAKES 3 cups, six ½-cup servings

SPECIAL EQUIPMENT: instant-read thermometer; six ½-cup bowls, custard cups, or ramekins or one 1½-quart bowl; 10- or 12-inch pastry bag and large open star tip

MOUSSE

5 ounces dark milk chocolate (38 to 42% cacao content), finely chopped

1¼ cups heavy whipping cream, divided

½ teaspoon pure vanilla extract

½ teaspoon pure chocolate extract

1 teaspoon ground cinnamon

2 large egg whites, at room temperature

¼ cup (1½ ounces) superfine sugar

2 teaspoons unsweetened cocoa powder (natural or Dutch-processed)

GARNISH

1 tablespoon finely shaved dark milk chocolate (38 to 42% cacao content)

FOR THE MOUSSE, place the dark milk chocolate in a 2-quart heat-safe bowl. In a small saucepan, heat ¼ cup of the cream to a boil. Pour the hot cream over the chocolate, let it stand for 30 seconds, then stir together with a heat-safe silicone spatula until all the chocolate is melted and the mixture is smooth. Add the vanilla and chocolate extracts and the cinnamon and stir to blend completely.

WHIP ½ cup of the cream to soft peaks in the bowl of an electric stand mixer with the wire whip attachment or in a mixing bowl using a handheld mixer. Fold the cream into the chocolate mixture in 3 stages, blending thoroughly.

PLACE the egg whites in the grease-free bowl of an electric stand mixer or a large grease-free mixing bowl and place the bowl over a pan of simmering water. Stirring constantly, heat the egg whites until they register 160°F on an instant-read thermometer. Remove the bowl from the water and wipe the bottom dry. Using the wire whip attachment or a handheld mixer, whip the egg whites until they are frothy. Slowly sprinkle on the sugar and whip the egg whites until they hold firm but not stiff peaks. Fold the whipped egg whites into the chocolate mixture in 3 stages, blending completely.

SPRINKLE the cocoa powder on the mousse and fold in thoroughly. Divide the mousse evenly among six ½-cup bowls or pour it into a 1-quart bowl. Cover tightly with plastic wrap and chill until set, about 2 hours.

WHIP the remaining ½ cup of cream to soft peaks in the bowl of an electric stand mixer with the wire whip attachment or in a mixing bowl using a handheld mixer. Fit a 10- or 12-inch pastry bag with a large open star tip. Pipe a rosette in the center of each bowl of mousse. Garnish the top of the mousse with finely shaved dark milk chocolate.

keeping Store the mousse, without whipped cream garnish, tightly covered with plastic wrap in the refrigerator up to 1 day.

white chocolate mousse and blueberry sauce parfait

CREAMY, LIGHT, AND AIRY WHITE CHOCOLATE MOUSSE IS COMBINED WITH SCRUMPTIOUS BLUEBERRY SAUCE TO MAKE A STRIKING AND DELECTABLE DESSERT. THE BLUEBERRY SAUCE CAN BE MADE A FEW DAYS IN ADVANCE OF ASSEMBLING THE PARFAIT.

MAKES 4 servings

SPECIAL EQUIPMENT: 4 tall wine glasses (1¼-cup capacity)

WHITE CHOCOLATE MOUSSE

5 ounces white chocolate (31 to 35% cacao content), finely chopped

2 tablespoons water

¾ cup heavy whipping cream

BLUEBERRY SAUCE

1⅓ cup (7 ounces) fresh or fresh-frozen blueberries

⅔ cup (4 ounces) firmly packed light brown sugar

2 tablespoons freshly squeezed lemon juice

½ teaspoon kosher or fine-grained sea salt

1 teaspoon pure vanilla extract

FOR THE MOUSSE, combine the white chocolate and water in the top of a double boiler over low heat and melt together, stirring frequently with a rubber spatula to ensure even melting. Or melt the chocolate and water in a microwave-safe bowl on low power in 30-second bursts, stirring after each burst. Remove the top pan of the double boiler, if using, and wipe the bottom and sides completely dry.

WHIP the cream to soft peaks in the bowl of an electric stand mixer with the wire whip attachment or in a mixing bowl using a handheld mixer. Fold the cream into the white chocolate mixture in 3 stages, blending thoroughly. Cover tightly with plastic wrap and chill until set, about 2 hours.

FOR THE BLUEBERRY SAUCE, combine the blueberries, brown sugar, lemon juice, and salt in a 2-quart saucepan. Bring the mixture to a boil and cook, stirring often, until the berries burst. Continue to stir and cook the mixture until it is reduced by half, about 5 minutes. Remove the saucepan from the heat and stir in the vanilla. Transfer the sauce to a heat-safe bowl, cover tightly with plastic wrap, and chill.

TO ASSEMBLE THE PARFAITS, spoon half of the mousse into 4 tall wine glasses. Spoon half of the blueberry sauce over the mousse. Add the remaining mousse to the glasses and drizzle with the remaining blueberry sauce. Serve the parfaits immediately.

streamlining

Store the mousse tightly covered with plastic wrap in the refrigerator up to 1 day.
Store the blueberry sauce in a tightly covered container in the refrigerator up to 4 days.

making a change

Replace 1 tablespoon of the water with Grand Marnier or another orange liqueur.
To make Blackberry Sauce, replace the blueberries with the same amount of blackberries.

milk chocolate–toasted coconut crème brûlée

THIS CRÈME BRÛLÉE HAS A BOTTOM LAYER OF LIGHTLY TOASTED COCONUT AND A TOPPING OF CRISP, BRITTLE CARAMELIZED SUGAR. IN BETWEEN IS VELVETY-TEXTURED, LUSCIOUSLY FLAVORED CUSTARD. CRÈME BRÛLÉE IS BAKED IN A WATER BATH THAT HELPS TO MAINTAIN ITS CREAMY TEXTURE. IT'S BEST TO CARAMELIZE THE TOPPING RIGHT BEFORE SERVING. AFTER THE TOPPING IS CARAMELIZED IT BECOMES TOO STIFF IF REFRIGERATED AND TOO SOFT IF LEFT AT ROOM TEMPERATURE LONGER THAN AN HOUR.

MAKES *eight ½-cup servings*

SPECIAL EQUIPMENT: *eight ½-cup heat-safe ramekins, custard cups, or bowls; 3-quart baking dish or roasting pan; propane or butane kitchen torch (optional)*

CRÈME BRÛLÉE

½ cup (1 ounce) sweetened shredded coconut

3 cups heavy whipping cream

⅓ cup (2 ounces) superfine sugar

8 ounces dark milk chocolate (38 to 42% cacao content), finely chopped

1 teaspoon pure chocolate extract

6 large egg yolks, at room temperature

⅛ teaspoon kosher or fine-grained sea salt

1 quart boiling water

GARNISH

½ cup (2½ ounces) superfine sugar

CENTER a rack in the oven and preheat the oven to 350°F. Place the coconut in a cake or pie pan and toast for 8 to 12 minutes, stirring every 3 minutes, until lightly golden. Remove the pan from the oven and cool on a rack.

LOWER the oven temperature to 300°F. Place the ramekins in a 3-quart baking dish or roasting pan.

PLACE the cream and sugar in a 2-quart saucepan and bring to a boil over medium heat, stirring occasionally with a heat-safe silicone spatula to blend evenly. Turn off the heat, add the chocolate and let it stand for 1 minute. Stir the mixture together using the heat-safe silicone spatula, a whisk, or immersion blender until very smooth. Add the chocolate extract and blend well.

PLACE the egg yolks and salt in a medium mixing bowl. Whisk or stir together until smooth. Add the chocolate mixture and whisk or stir together until thoroughly combined. Strain the mixture through a fine-mesh strainer into a large liquid measuring cup.

PLACE 1 tablespoon of toasted coconut in the bottom of each ramekin. Pour the custard mixture into the ramekins, dividing it evenly. Carefully pour the boiling water into the baking dish until it reaches halfway up the sides of the ramekins. Tightly cover the pan with aluminum foil. Bake the custards for 1 hour, until a cake tester inserted in the center comes out slightly moist.

REMOVE the baking dish from the oven and remove the aluminum foil. Remove the ramekins from the water bath and place them on a rack to cool completely. Cover each ramekin tightly with plastic wrap. Chill in the refrigerator for at least 2 hours before serving.

FOR THE GARNISH, sprinkle the top of each custard evenly with a teaspoon or two of the superfine sugar. If desired, use a propane kitchen torch to caramelize the top of the custards. Hold the torch a few inches above the custard and move it around the top. The sugar will become bubbly and golden brown. Or place the custards on a baking sheet or roasting pan and place them under the broiler for 2 to 3 minutes. Watch carefully, because the sugar can burn quickly.

SERVE the custard immediately or hold at room temperature up to 1 hour.

 Store the baked custard without the caramelized sugar topping tightly covered with a double layer of plastic wrap in the refrigerator up to 3 days. Caramelize the top of the custard before serving.

white chocolate crème caramel

THIS CLASSIC CRÈME CARAMEL IS DRESSED UP WITH THE SUBTLE YET NOTABLE FLAVOR OF WHITE CHOCOLATE. THE BOTTOM OF THE CUSTARD CUPS ARE LINED WITH CARAMEL THAT RUNS OVER THE TOP AND BECOMES A SAUCE WHEN THE CUSTARDS ARE INVERTED AFTER BAKING. BE PATIENT WHEN INVERTING THESE BECAUSE IT MAY TAKE A FEW SECONDS FOR THE CUSTARD TO DROP ONTO THE PLATE.

MAKES six ½-cup servings

SPECIAL EQUIPMENT: six ½-cup heat-safe custard cups, ramekins, or bowls; 3-quart baking dish or roasting pan

CARAMEL
¾ cup (5 ounces) granulated sugar
⅓ cup water

WHITE CHOCOLATE CUSTARD
1½ cups milk (whole or 2%)
½ cup heavy whipping cream
1 teaspoon pure vanilla bean paste
8 ounces white chocolate (31 to 35% cacao content), finely chopped
3 large eggs, at room temperature
½ cup (3½ ounces) granulated sugar
1 quart boiling water

CENTER a rack in the oven and preheat the oven to 350°F. Place the custard cups in a 3-quart baking dish or roasting pan.

FOR THE CARAMEL, combine the sugar and water in a 1-quart saucepan over medium-high heat. Bring the mixture to a boil and stir to dissolve the sugar. Cook the mixture without stirring until it turns a rich golden brown, about 8 minutes.

DIVIDE the caramel evenly among the custard cups. Tilt and rotate each cup so the caramel completely covers the bottom.

FOR THE CUSTARD, place the milk, cream, and vanilla bean paste in a 2-quart heavy-duty saucepan. Warm the mixture over medium heat to the point when tiny bubbles become visible at the edges. Remove the pan from the heat and stir in the white chocolate until it is completely melted.

PLACE the eggs in the bowl of an electric stand mixer or in a large mixing bowl. Use the wire whip attachment or a handheld mixer to whisk together until they are frothy. With the mixer on medium speed slowly sprinkle on the sugar.

IN a steady stream pour the warm milk mixture into the egg mixture and blend together thoroughly. Strain the custard through a fine-mesh strainer into a large liquid measuring cup and pour it into the cups, dividing it evenly.

PLACE the roasting pan on the oven rack. Carefully pour the boiling water into the pan until it reaches halfway up the sides of the cups. Reduce the oven temperature to 325°F. Cover the roasting pan with aluminum foil. Bake the custard for 35 minutes, remove the foil and bake another 5 to 8 minutes, until the custards wiggle slightly when the side of the pan is touched. Remove the roasting pan from the oven and transfer the cups to a rack to cool.

TO UNMOLD THE CUSTARDS, run a thin-bladed knife around the edges of the cups. Place a serving plate over the top of a cup and invert the custard onto the plate. Repeat with each cup.

SERVE the custards immediately or refrigerate until ready to serve.

keeping

Store the baked custard in the cups, tightly covered with a double layer of plastic wrap in the refrigerator up to 3 days.

adding style

Decorate the top of the custard with rosettes or dollops of whipped cream and scatter shaved white chocolate over the cream.

bittersweet chocolate–hazelnut soufflés with hazelnut whipped cream

THESE SOUFFLÉS ARE MADE WITH A COMBINATION OF UNSWEETENED CHOCOLATE AND BITTERSWEET CHOCOLATE. BECAUSE THE TEXTURE IS SO DENSE, THE SOUFFLÉ FALLS VERY LITTLE AFTER IT IS OUT OF THE OVEN FOR A WHILE. THE ADDITION OF HAZELNUT WHIPPED CREAM ADDS AN EXTRA FLAVOR DIMENSION THAT MAKES THIS DESSERT EXTRAORDINARY. WHEN THE SOUFFLÉ IS SERVED HOT, STRAIGHT FROM THE OVEN, THE WHIPPED CREAM BEGINS TO MELT ON TOP OF IT, CREATING A LUSCIOUS TEXTURE. AS WITH OTHER CHOCOLATE SOUFFLÉS, THESE CAN BE MIXED A DAY IN ADVANCE AND KEPT TIGHTLY COVERED IN THE REFRIGERATOR UNTIL YOU ARE READY TO BAKE AND SERVE THEM.

MAKES *eight ½-cup servings*

SPECIAL EQUIPMENT: *2-inch-diameter ice cream scoop; eight ½-cup heat-safe ramekins or bowls*

HAZELNUT WHIPPED CREAM

1 cup heavy whipping cream

3 tablespoons finely chopped toasted hazelnuts (see page 10)

2 tablespoons superfine sugar

SOUFFLÉS

1 tablespoon unsalted butter, softened

1 tablespoon granulated sugar

6 ounces bittersweet chocolate (66 to 72% cacao content), finely chopped

2 ounces unsweetened chocolate, finely chopped

3 ounces (6 tablespoons, ¾ stick) unsalted butter, cut into small pieces

1½ teaspoons pure vanilla extract

¼ teaspoon kosher or fine-grained sea salt

4 large eggs, separated, at room temperature

3 large egg whites, at room temperature

¼ teaspoon cream of tartar

½ cup (2½ ounces) superfine sugar

1 cup (4 ounces) finely ground toasted hazelnuts (see page 10)

FOR THE HAZELNUT WHIPPED CREAM, place the cream in a 1-quart heavy-duty saucepan and bring to a boil over medium-high heat. Pour the cream into a heat-safe bowl and stir in the hazelnuts. Cover the bowl tightly with plastic wrap and chill overnight.

CENTER a rack in the oven and preheat the oven to 375ºF. Use a paper towel or your fingers to coat the inside of the ramekins with the softened butter. Sprinkle the inside of each with sugar. Tilt the ramekins so the sugar sticks to the butter. Set aside while preparing the soufflé batter.

MELT the bittersweet chocolate, unsweetened chocolate, and butter together in the top of a double boiler over hot water, stirring often with a rubber spatula to ensure even melting. Or place the chocolates and butter in a microwave-safe bowl and melt on low power in 30-second bursts, stirring after each burst. Remove the top pan of the double boiler, if using, and wipe the bottom and sides very dry.

ADD the vanilla and salt to the chocolate mixture and stir until well blended. Let the mixture cool, stirring occasionally with a rubber spatula to prevent a skin from forming on top.

PLACE the 4 egg yolks in a 1-quart mixing bowl and stir briefly to break them up, then pour them into the chocolate mixture and blend together thoroughly.

PLACE all 7 egg whites in the grease-free bowl of an electric stand mixer or in a large grease-free mixing bowl. Using the wire whip attachment or a handheld mixer, whip the egg whites on medium-high speed until they are frothy. Add the cream of tartar and continue to whip. When soft peaks form, gradually sprinkle on the ½ cup superfine sugar and continue to whip until the egg whites hold glossy and firm but not stiff peaks.

FOLD the whipped egg whites into the chocolate mixture in 4 stages, then fold in the hazelnuts. Use a 2-inch-diameter ice cream scoop to divide the mixture evenly among the ramekins.

PLACE the ramekins on a baking sheet and bake for 14 to 16 minutes, until the soufflés are puffed over the top, look set, and the centers wiggle a little. You can also test for doneness with a cake tester inserted into the center of a soufflé. It should come out moist, but not runny.

WHILE the soufflés are baking, strain the hazelnuts out of the whipping cream. In the bowl of an electric stand mixer using the wire whip attachment or in a large mixing bowl using a handheld mixer, whip the cream until frothy. Add the 2 tablespoons superfine sugar and whip until the cream holds soft peaks.

SERVE each soufflé immediately with a scoop of hazelnut whipped cream on top.

streamlining

Prepare the soufflé batter and place it into the ramekins. Tightly cover the ramekins with plastic wrap and refrigerate up to 1 day before baking.

making a change

To make Milk Chocolate–Hazelnut Soufflés, replace the bittersweet chocolate with 12 ounces dark milk chocolate (38 to 42% cacao content) and reduce the sugar to ¼ cup.

milk chocolate–dulce de leche pots de crème

DULCE DE LECHE IS A STAPLE OF LATIN AMERICAN CUISINE. IT IS AN INCREDIBLY DELECTABLE, CREAMY MIXTURE MADE BY COOKING SWEETENED CONDENSED MILK UNTIL IT THICKENS AND CARAMELIZES. THIS RECIPE COMBINES DULCE DE LECHE WITH A DARK MILK CHOCOLATE MIXTURE TO MAKE A SENSUAL POT DE CRÈME. BE SURE TO PREPARE THE POTS DE CRÈME AT LEAST 3 HOURS IN ADVANCE OF SERVING SO THEY HAVE TIME TO COOL AND CHILL.

MAKES eight ½-cup servings

SPECIAL EQUIPMENT: 8-inch square baking pan or pie pan and 3-quart baking pan or roasting pan; eight ½-cup heat-safe custard cups, ramekins, or bowls; 12- or 14-inch pastry bag and large open star tip

DULCE DE LECHE

One 14-ounce can sweetened condensed milk

POTS DE CRÈME

8 ounces dark milk chocolate (38 to 42% cacao content), finely chopped

1½ cups heavy whipping cream

1 teaspoon pure vanilla extract

1 teaspoon pure chocolate extract

6 large egg yolks, at room temperature

2 tablespoons granulated sugar

⅛ teaspoon kosher or fine-grained sea salt

1 quart boiling water

GARNISH

½ cup heavy whipping cream

2 teaspoons confectioners' sugar, sifted

2 tablespoons finely shaved dark milk chocolate (38 to 42% cacao content)

FOR THE DULCE DE LECHE, center a rack in the oven and preheat the oven to 425°F. Place the sweetened condensed milk in an 8-inch square baking pan or a pie pan. Cover the pan tightly with foil and put the pan into a larger baking or roasting pan. Pour hot water halfway up the sides of the smaller baking pan.

BAKE until the mixture is thick and caramel brown, 1 hour and 15 minutes to 1½ hours. Maintain the level of water in the larger pan by adding more hot water if necessary as the mixture bakes.

REMOVE the baking pan from the water bath, uncover the pan, and place it on a rack to cool completely. Cover the mixture tightly with plastic wrap and chill in the refrigerator. Bring to room temperature before mixing with the pot de crème custard.

FOR THE POTS DE CRÈME, lower the oven temperature to 325°F. Place the custard cups in a 3-quart baking dish or roasting pan.

PLACE the chopped chocolate in a large heat-safe bowl. Place the cream in a saucepan and bring to a boil over medium heat. Pour the cream over the chocolate and let it stand for 1 minute. Stir the mixture together using a heat-safe silicone spatula, whisk, or immersion blender until very smooth. Add the vanilla and chocolate extracts and blend well.

WHISK together the egg yolks, granulated sugar, and salt in a medium mixing bowl until smooth and the sugar is dissolved, about 1 minute. Add the chocolate mixture and whisk or stir together until thoroughly combined. Strain the mixture through a fine-mesh strainer into a large bowl, then stir in ½ cup of the dulce de leche until the mixture is smooth and thoroughly blended.

POUR this mixture into the custard cups, dividing it evenly. Carefully pour boiling water into the baking dish until it reaches halfway up the sides of the cups or bowls. Tightly cover the pan with aluminum foil. Bake the custards for 25 to 30 minutes, until they look set on the edges but jiggle slightly in the center.

REMOVE the baking dish from the oven and remove the aluminum foil. Remove the cups from the water bath and place them on a rack to cool completely. Cover the cups tightly with plastic wrap. Chill in the refrigerator for at least 2 hours before serving, which helps them to set.

FOR THE GARNISH, whip the cream in the chilled bowl of an electric stand mixer or a medium mixing bowl, using the wire whip attachment or a handheld mixer, until it is frothy. Add the confectioners' sugar and continue to whip the cream on medium speed until it holds firm peaks.

FIT a 12- or 14-inch pastry bag with a large open star tip and fill partway with the whipped cream. Hold the pastry bag straight up and down about 1 inch above the top of the custard, and pipe a star or rosette in the center. Scatter shaved dark milk chocolate on the top of the custards. Serve the custards chilled.

keeping

streamlining

Store the baked pots de crème in the cups tightly covered with a double layer of plastic wrap in the refrigerator up to 3 days.

The dulce de leche can be made up to 4 days in advance and kept in a tightly covered container in the refrigerator. To freeze up to 4 months, wrap the container tightly in several layers of plastic wrap and aluminum foil. Use a large piece of masking tape and an indelible marker to label and date the contents. If frozen, thaw overnight in the refrigerator and bring to room temperature before using.

truffles and candies

bittersweet chocolate-marzipan truffles

MAKING THESE TRUFFLES COULDN'T BE ANY EASIER. MARZIPAN MIXED WITH MELTED BITTERSWEET CHOCOLATE MAKES UP THE CENTERS. ONCE THIS MIXTURE IS ROLLED INTO BALLS, THE TRUFFLES ARE DIPPED IN BITTERSWEET CHOCOLATE AND ROLLED IN FINELY CHOPPED TOASTED ALMONDS. ROLLS OF MARZIPAN ARE AVAILABLE IN THE BAKING SECTION OF GROCERY STORES.

MAKES 1½ dozen truffles

SPECIAL EQUIPMENT: truffle dipper or plastic fork; 18 fluted paper candy cups

¾ cup (2½ ounces) sliced almonds, blanched or unbalanced

8 ounces bittersweet chocolate (66 to 72% cacao content), finely chopped, divided

One 7-ounce roll marzipan

CENTER a rack in the oven and preheat the oven to 350°F. Place the sliced almonds in a cake or pie pan. Toast them in the oven for 8 minutes, stirring every 2 minutes, until they are lightly golden. Remove the pan from the oven and cool on a rack. Use a large chef's knife to chop the almonds fine. Place them in a 1-quart bowl.

MELT 2 ounces of the bittersweet chocolate in a microwave-safe bowl on low power for 30 second bursts, stirring with a heat-safe silicone spatula after each burst.

BREAK the roll of marzipan into several small pieces and place in the bowl of an electric stand mixer or a large mixing bowl. Use the flat beater attachment or a handheld mixer on medium speed to completely smooth out the marzipan. Add the melted chocolate and mix together until completely blended, about 1 minute.

LINE two baking sheets with waxed or parchment paper. Pinch off walnut-size pieces of the marzipan mixture and roll into balls. Place the truffles on one of the baking sheets.

MELT 5 ounces of the remaining bittersweet chocolate in a microwave-safe bowl on low power for 30 second bursts, stirring with a heat-safe silicone spatula after each burst. Add the remaining ounce of finely chopped chocolate to the melted chocolate in 2 stages, stirring until the first addition is completely melted before adding the next.

PLACE a truffle in the melted chocolate and swirl it around to coat completely. Use a truffle dipper or plastic fork with the middle tines broken out to remove the truffle from the chocolate. Holding the truffle over the bowl, let the excess chocolate drip off, then place the truffle in the bowl of chopped almonds. Shake the bowl to cover the truffle completely with almonds. Lift out the truffle with another truffle dipper or fork and place it on the other baking sheet. Repeat with the remaining truffles.

LET the truffles set up at room temperature or refrigerate them for 15 minutes.

PLACE each truffle in a fluted paper candy cup and serve at room temperature.

keeping

Store the truffles in an airtight plastic container between layers of waxed paper in the refrigerator, away from strongly flavored foods, up to 2 weeks. To freeze up to 3 months, wrap the container tightly in several layers of plastic wrap and aluminum foil. Use a large piece of masking tape and an indelible marker to label and date the contents. If frozen, thaw overnight in the refrigerator and bring to room temperature before serving.

making a change

Replace the bittersweet chocolate with dark milk chocolate (38 to 42% cacao content).

bittersweet chocolate–salted caramel truffles

THESE TRUFFLES ARE MADE FROM THE SAME RECIPE THAT IS USED FOR SALTED CARAMEL–BITTERSWEET CHOCOLATE SAUCE. THE COMBINATION OF THE FLAVORS OF SALTED CARAMEL AND BITTERSWEET CHOCOLATE IS ONE OF MY FAVORITES. THE SALT BRINGS OUT THE BEST IN BOTH THE CARAMEL AND THE CHOCOLATE. THESE HAVE A VELVETY TEXTURE AND WILL MELT IN YOUR MOUTH.

MAKES *about 3 dozen truffles*

SPECIAL EQUIPMENT: *1-inch-diameter round ice cream scoop; about 3 dozen fluted paper candy cups*

1 recipe (2 cups) Salted Caramel–Bittersweet Chocolate Sauce (page 203)

3 tablespoons unsweetened cocoa powder (natural or Dutch-processed)

MAKE the sauce and allow it to cool, then chill in the refrigerator at least 1 hour.

LINE a baking sheet with waxed or parchment paper. Place the cocoa powder in a small bowl.

USE a 1-inch-diameter ice cream scoop to scoop out the truffles and place them onto the lined baking sheet. Roll the truffles into balls between your palms, then roll each ball in cocoa powder, coating them completely. Replace the truffles on the baking sheet.

SERVE them at room temperature in fluted paper candy cups.

keeping

Store the truffles in an airtight plastic container between layers of waxed paper in the refrigerator, away from strongly flavored foods, up to 2 weeks. To freeze up to 3 months, wrap the container tightly in several layers of plastic wrap and aluminum foil. Use a large piece of masking tape and an indelible marker to label and date the contents. If frozen, thaw overnight in the refrigerator and bring to room temperature before serving.

bittersweet chocolate-guava truffles

IF YOU LIKE GUAVA, THESE TRUFFLES
ARE FOR YOU. GUAVA PUREE IS
BLENDED WITH BITTERSWEET
CHOCOLATE TO CREATE THE
DELECTABLE CENTERS THAT ARE
DIPPED IN BITTERSWEET CHOCOLATE.

MAKES *about 3 dozen truffles*

SPECIAL EQUIPMENT: *1-inch-diameter round ice cream scoop; truffle dipper or plastic fork; about 3 dozen fluted paper candy cups*

20 ounces bittersweet chocolate (66 to 72% cacao content), finely chopped, divided

½ cup heavy whipping cream

⅔ cup guava puree (see Sources, page 209)

2 tablespoons unsweetened cocoa powder, natural or Dutch-processed, sifted

PLACE 8 ounces of the bittersweet chocolate in a 2-quart heat-safe bowl. Warm the cream in a small saucepan over medium-high heat until bubbles form around the edges. Immediately pour the hot cream over the chopped chocolate and let stand for 30 seconds. Stir together with a heat-safe silicone spatula until completely smooth and all the chocolate is melted. Stir in the guava puree and blend thoroughly. Cover the bowl tightly with plastic wrap, cool to room temperature, then chill in the refrigerator until thick but not stiff, about 1 hour.

LINE a baking sheet with waxed or parchment paper. Use a 1-inch-diameter ice cream scoop to scoop out the truffles and place them onto the lined baking sheet. If the truffles are soft at this point, chill them in the refrigerator for 15 to 30 minutes.

DUST your hands with cocoa powder and roll the truffles into balls between your palms. Replace the truffles on the baking sheet and chill briefly.

PLACE 9 ounces of the bittersweet chocolate in the top of a double boiler over hot water. Stir often with a rubber spatula to ensure even melting. Or melt the chocolate in a microwave-safe bowl on low power in 30-second bursts, stirring after each burst. Remove the top pan of the double boiler, if using, and wipe the bottom and sides very dry.

STIR in the remaining chocolate in 3 stages, making sure each batch is melted before adding the next.

LINE another baking sheet with parchment or waxed paper. Use a truffle dipper or a plastic fork with the two middle tines broken out to dip each truffle into the chocolate. Holding the truffle over the bowl, let the excess chocolate drip off. Place the truffle on the second baking sheet. Repeat with the remaining truffles.

LET the chocolate set at room temperature or in the refrigerator for 15 minutes.

PLACE the truffles in fluted paper candy cups and serve at room temperature.

keeping Store the truffles in an airtight plastic container between layers of waxed paper in the refrigerator, away from strongly flavored food, up to 2 weeks. To freeze up to 3 months, wrap the container tightly in several layers of plastic wrap and aluminum foil. Use a large piece of masking tape and an indelible marker to label and date the contents. If frozen, thaw overnight in the refrigerator and bring to room temperature before serving.

luscious gianduia squares

A BLEND OF BITTERSWEET CHOCOLATE, DARK MILK CHOCOLATE, HAZELNUT PASTE, AND CHOPPED TOASTED HAZELNUTS CREATES A CANDY THAT FILLS THE MOUTH WITH INTENSE FLAVOR. THESE GO VERY WELL WITH COFFEE OR TEA AFTER DINNER.

MAKES sixty-four 1-inch squares

SPECIAL EQUIPMENT: 8-inch square baking pan

1 cup (5 ounces) hazelnuts

6 ounces bittersweet chocolate (66 to 72% cacao content), finely chopped

3 ounces dark milk chocolate (38 to 42% cacao content), finely chopped

1½ cups (12 ounces) Luscious Hazelnut Paste (page 205), at room temperature

CENTER a rack in the oven and preheat the oven to 350°F. Place the hazelnuts on a jelly-roll pan and toast in the oven for 15 to 18 minutes, until the skins split and the nuts are light golden brown. Remove the pan from the oven and immediately pour the hazelnuts into a towel. Wrap the towel around the hazelnuts and rub them together to remove most of the skins. Place the hazelnuts in the work bowl of a food processor fitted with the steel blade and chop them very coarsely.

LINE an 8-inch square baking pan with waxed paper, letting it hang about 2 inches over the sides.

MELT 5 ounces of the bittersweet chocolate and the dark milk chocolate in the top of a double boiler over hot water, stirring often with a rubber spatula to ensure even melting. Or melt the chocolates in a microwave-safe bowl on low power in 30-second bursts, stirring after each burst. Remove the top pan of the double boiler, if using, and wipe the bottom and sides of the pan dry. Stir in the remaining chocolate in 3 stages, making sure each batch is melted before adding the next.

WHEN the chocolate is completely blended, add the hazelnut paste and chopped hazelnuts and stir to blend together thoroughly. Transfer the mixture to the lined pan, spreading it evenly into the corners with an offset metal spatula. Lightly tap the pan on the countertop to eliminate any air bubbles. Cover the pan tightly with plastic wrap and chill until firm, about 1 hour.

LIFT the candy from the pan by holding the waxed paper, then peel the waxed paper off the candy. Place the gianduia on a cutting board and use a large chef's knife, dipped in hot water and dried, to cut it into 8 rows in each direction, forming squares.

SERVE the squares at room temperature.

keeping

Store the squares between layers of waxed paper in an airtight plastic container in the refrigerator, away from strongly flavored food, up to 2 weeks. To freeze up to 3 months, wrap the container in several layers of plastic wrap and aluminum foil. Use a large piece of masking tape and an indelible marker to label and date the contents. If frozen, thaw overnight in the refrigerator and bring to room temperature before serving.

making a change

Replace the bittersweet chocolate and dark milk chocolate with an equal amount of gianduia chocolate.

streamlining   The gianduia mixture can be kept in the baking pan tightly covered with plastic wrap in the refrigerator, away from strongly flavored food, up to 2 weeks. Cut the candy into squares before serving.

The toasted hazelnuts and the hazelnut paste can be made in advance and kept in tightly covered containers in the refrigerator up to 1 month. Bring them to room temperature before using.

white chocolate–lime truffles

THESE VELVETY SMOOTH TRUFFLES BRING TOGETHER TWO FLAVORS THAT ARE A PERFECT MATCH, BUT ARE RARELY USED TOGETHER: WHITE CHOCOLATE AND LIME. WHEN BITING INTO ONE OF THESE, YOU WILL EXPERIENCE THE PLEASURE OF THE SUBTLE TANGY FLAVOR.

MAKES 3½ dozen truffles

SPECIAL EQUIPMENT: 1-inch-diameter round ice cream scoop; 3½ dozen fluted paper candy cups

12 ounces white chocolate (31 to 35% cacao content), very finely chopped

½ cup heavy whipping cream

Finely grated zest of 4 large limes

½ cup (1½ ounces) confectioners' sugar, sifted

PLACE the finely chopped white chocolate in a 2-quart heat-safe bowl.

IN a ½-quart saucepan bring the cream to a boil over medium heat. Add the lime zest, cover the pan, turn off the heat, and steep for 15 minutes. Uncover the pan and bring the cream back to a boil over medium heat. Strain the cream through a fine-mesh strainer over the chocolate. Stir together with a heat-safe silicone spatula until the chocolate is melted and the mixture is smooth. Cover the bowl tightly with plastic wrap and chill in the refrigerator until thick but not stiff, about 40 minutes.

LINE a baking sheet with waxed or parchment paper and place the confectioners' sugar in a small bowl. Use a 1-inch-diameter ice cream scoop to scoop out the truffles and place them onto the lined baking sheet. Roll the truffles into balls between your palms, then roll each ball in confectioners' sugar, coating them completely. Replace the truffles on the baking sheet.

SERVE the truffles at room temperature in fluted paper candy cups.

keeping Store the truffles in an airtight plastic container between layers of waxed paper in the refrigerator, away from strongly flavored food, up to 2 weeks. To freeze up to 3 months, wrap the container tightly in several layers of plastic wrap and aluminum foil. Use a large piece of masking tape and an indelible marker to label and date the contents. If frozen, thaw overnight in the refrigerator and bring to room temperature before serving.

bittersweet chocolate-lemon ganache squares

MY GOOD FRIEND AND COLLEAGUE KITTY MORSE GROWS FLAVORFUL MEYER LEMONS AND OFTEN BRINGS ME A BAGFUL WHEN SHE COMES TO VISIT. I USED THE FRESHLY GRATED ZEST OF THOSE LEMONS TO ADD LIVELY FLAVOR TO BITTERSWEET CHOCOLATE GANACHE FOR THESE CANDIES. THE SQUARES CAN BE FINISHED BY ROLLING THEM IN COCOA POWDER OR DIPPING IN CHOCOLATE.

MAKES sixty-four 1-inch squares

SPECIAL EQUIPMENT: 8-inch square baking pan; truffle dipping fork or plastic fork; 64 fluted paper candy cups (optional)

LEMON GANACHE SQUARES

10 ounces bittersweet chocolate (70 to 72% cacao content), finely chopped

2 ounces unsweetened chocolate, finely chopped

1¼ cups heavy whipping cream

Finely minced or grated zest of 4 Meyer lemons

GARNISH

¼ cup unsweetened cocoa powder (natural or Dutch-processed)

or

12 ounces bittersweet chocolate (70 to 72% cacao content), finely chopped

Finely grated zest of 1 Meyer lemon

LINE an 8-inch square baking pan with waxed paper, letting it hang about 2 inches over the sides.

FOR THE GANACHE, place the bittersweet chocolate and unsweetened chocolate in a large heat-safe bowl. Warm the cream in a small saucepan over medium heat until it bubbles around the edges. Immediately pour the cream over the chocolate. Let it stand 30 seconds, then stir together with a heat-safe silicone spatula until very smooth and the chocolate is completely melted. Stir in the lemon zest and blend thoroughly.

TRANSFER the mixture to the lined pan, spreading it evenly into the corners with an offset metal spatula. Lightly tap the pan on the countertop to eliminate any air bubbles. Cover the pan tightly with plastic wrap and chill until firm, about 1 hour.

LIFT the candy from the pan by holding the waxed paper, then peel the waxed paper off the candy. Place the candy on a cutting board and use a large chef's knife, dipped in hot water and dried, to cut the ganache into 8 rows in each direction, forming squares.

LINE a baking sheet with waxed or parchment paper. For the garnish, sift the cocoa powder into a small bowl. Separate the squares and roll each in the cocoa powder, coating completely. Place the rolled squares on the baking sheet.

TO GARNISH the squares with chocolate instead of cocoa powder, melt 9 ounces of the bittersweet chocolate in the top of a double boiler over hot water, stirring frequently with a rubber spatula to ensure even melting. Or melt the chocolate in a microwave-safe bowl on low power in 30-second bursts, stirring after each burst. Remove the top pan of the double boiler, if using, and wipe the bottom and sides very dry. Stir the remaining bittersweet chocolate into the melted chocolate in 3 batches, making sure each batch is completely melted before adding the next.

USE a truffle dipper or a plastic fork with the two middle tines broken out to dip each square into the chocolate. Holding the square over the bowl, let the excess chocolate drip off. Slide the square onto the baking sheet. After dipping 4 or 5 squares, sprinkle a bit of the lemon zest in the center of each before the chocolate sets up. Repeat with all the squares, then chill them briefly to set the chocolate.

PLACE each square in a fluted paper candy cup and serve them at room temperature.

keeping

Store the squares between layers of waxed paper in an airtight plastic container in the refrigerator, away from strongly flavored food, up to 2 weeks. To freeze up to 3 months, wrap the container in several layers of plastic wrap and aluminum foil. Use a large piece of masking tape and an indelible marker to label and date the contents. If frozen, thaw overnight in the refrigerator and bring to room temperature before serving.

making a change

Replace the lemon zest with orange zest.

cacao nib brittle

THIS UNUSUAL BRITTLE IS MADE USING CACAO NIBS INSTEAD OF NUTS. THE SWEETNESS OF THE SUGAR SYRUP TAKES THE BITTER EDGE OFF THE NIBS AND MAKES THIS A YUMMY CANDY. TRY IT BROKEN INTO TINY PIECES OR FINELY GROUND, SPRINKLED OVER ICE CREAM.

MAKES *about 30 pieces (11½ ounces)*

1 tablespoon canola or safflower oil
1 cup (6½ ounces) granulated sugar
¼ cup water
¼ teaspoon cream of tartar
1¼ cups (5 ounces) cacao nibs

USE a paper towel to coat the back of a baking sheet with the oil.

PLACE the sugar, water, and cream of tartar in a 2-quart heavy-duty saucepan. Over high heat, bring the mixture to a boil. Run a damp pastry brush around the inside edges of the pan where the mixture meets the sides, to prevent crystallization. Do this twice. Cook the mixture until it turns a deep amber color, about 8 minutes.

IMMEDIATELY stir in the cacao nibs using a heat-safe silicone spatula, coating the nibs completely with the caramel. Work quickly and turn the mixture out onto the oiled baking sheet. Use the spatula to spread the mixture to a thickness of about ¼ inch. Let the brittle set for 30 minutes.

GENTLY lift the brittle from the back of the pan and break in into pieces. Serve at room temperature.

keeping

Store the brittle between layers of waxed paper in an airtight plastic container at room temperature up to 2 weeks.

bittersweet chocolate clusters with almonds and dried cherries

THE TANGINESS OF THE DRIED
CHERRIES MAKES THESE CLUSTERS
STAND OUT, WITH THE TOASTED
ALMONDS ADDING A GOOD BALANCE
OF FLAVOR AND TEXTURE. IF YOU
WANT TO GET THE MOST OUT OF
THESE CANDIES, I SUGGEST USING
THE HIGHEST CACAO CONTENT
BITTERSWEET CHOCOLATE YOU CAN
FIND.

MAKES 2½ dozen clusters

SPECIAL EQUIPMENT: 2½ dozen
fluted paper candy cups

1 cup (5 ounces) dried tart cherries

1 cup (5 ounces) whole unblanched
almonds, toasted (see page 10)

7 ounces bittersweet chocolate (66 to
85% cacao content), finely chopped

LINE a baking sheet with waxed paper. Combine the cherries and almonds in a bowl
and stir together.

PLACE 5 ounces of the chocolate in the top of a double boiler over hot water. Stir
often with a rubber spatula to ensure even melting. Or melt the chocolate in a microwave-safe bowl on low power in 30-second bursts, stirring after each burst. Remove
the top pan of the double boiler, if using, and wipe the bottom and sides very dry.
Stir in the remaining chocolate in 3 stages, making sure each batch is melted before
adding the next.

WHEN the chocolate is completely blended, add the cherry-almond mixture and
stir to coat them completely. Use a spoon to drop 1-inch clusters onto the lined
baking sheet. Let the clusters set up at room temperature or chill them briefly in the
refrigerator for 10 to 15 minutes.

GENTLY peel the clusters off the waxed paper. Serve at room temperature in fluted
paper candy cups.

keeping

Store the clusters between layers of waxed paper in an airtight plastic container in the
refrigerator, away from strongly flavored food, up to 2 weeks. To freeze up to 3 months, wrap
the container in several layers of plastic wrap and aluminum foil. Use a large piece of masking
tape and an indelible marker to label and date the contents. If frozen, thaw overnight in the
refrigerator and bring to room temperature before serving.

making a change

Replace the bittersweet chocolate with dark milk chocolate or white chocolate.
    Replace half of the almonds with cacao nibs.

assorted bittersweet chocolate coins

THESE CHOCOLATE COINS ARE BASED ON CLASSIC FRENCH *MENDIANTS*. THEY ARE A MINIMALIST CANDY THAT IS EASY TO MAKE AND ALLOWS YOUR CREATIVITY TO SHINE. WHEN ASSEMBLING THE COINS, USE ANY COMBINATION OF THE INGREDIENTS YOU LIKE.

MAKES 3½ dozen 1-inch coins

6 ounces bittersweet chocolate (66 to 72% cacao content), finely chopped

½ ounce each of 3 or more of the following:

   toasted pistachios, walnuts, or peanuts, coarsely chopped

dried tart cherries, candied orange peel, or crystallized ginger, coarsely chopped

sea salt flakes

freshly ground nutmeg

freshly ground black pepper

LINE a baking sheet with waxed paper. Place 5 ounces of the chocolate in the top of a double boiler over hot water. Stir often with a rubber spatula to ensure even melting. Or melt the chocolate in a microwave-safe bowl on low power in 30-second bursts, stirring after each burst. Remove the top pan of the double boiler, if using, and wipe the bottom and sides very dry.

STIR in the remaining chocolate in 3 stages, making sure each batch is melted before adding the next.

WHEN the chocolate is completely blended, drop 1-teaspoon-size coins onto the lined baking sheet. Make 3 or 4 coins at a time. Top each coin with a few pieces of nuts, dried fruit, and/or spices, as you choose.

LET the coins set up at room temperature or chill them briefly in the refrigerator for 10 to 15 minutes.

GENTLY peel the coins off the waxed paper. Serve at room temperature.

keeping

Store the coins between layers of waxed paper in an airtight plastic container in the refrigerator, away from strongly flavored food, up to 2 weeks. To freeze up to 3 months, wrap the container in several layers of plastic wrap and aluminum foil. Use a large piece of masking tape and an indelible marker to label and date the contents. If frozen, thaw overnight in the refrigerator and bring to room temperature before serving.

making a change

Replace the bittersweet chocolate with dark milk chocolate or white chocolate.

bittersweet chocolate bark with ginger and apricots

THE COMBINATION OF CHOPPED CRYSTALLIZED GINGER AND CHOPPED DRIED APRICOTS GIVES THIS BARK A LIVELY FLAVOR. THE TEXTURE IS FURTHER ENHANCED BY THE ADDITION OF CACAO NIBS. CRYSTALLIZED GINGER IS AVAILABLE IN MANY HEALTH FOOD STORES, SPECIALTY FOOD SHOPS, AND THROUGH ONLINE SOURCES (SEE PAGE 209).

MAKES *about 4 dozen pieces (1¾ pounds)*

1 cup (5¼ ounces) finely chopped crystallized ginger

1 cup (5½ ounces) finely chopped dried apricots

½ cup (2 ounces) cacao nibs

1 pound bittersweet chocolate (66 to 72% cacao content), finely chopped

LINE a baking sheet with waxed paper or a nonstick liner. Combine the crystallized ginger, apricots, and cacao nibs in a bowl and stir to combine evenly.

PLACE 12 ounces of the chocolate in the top of a double boiler over hot water. Stir often with a rubber spatula to ensure even melting. Or melt the chocolate in a microwave-safe bowl on low power in 30-second bursts, stirring after each burst. Remove the top pan of the double boiler, if using, and wipe the bottom and sides very dry.

STIR in the remaining chocolate in 3 stages, making sure each batch is melted before adding the next.

WHEN the chocolate is completely blended, quickly stir in the ginger, apricots, and cacao nibs with a rubber spatula, coating them completely. Pour the mixture onto the baking sheet and spread it evenly with the spatula to cover most of the sheet. Chill the bark in the refrigerator for 30 minutes to 1 hour, until firm enough to break.

GENTLY peel the waxed paper off the back of the bark and break the bark into pieces by hand. Serve the bark at room temperature.

keeping

Store the bark between layers of waxed paper in an airtight plastic container in the refrigerator, away from strongly flavored food, up to 2 weeks. To freeze up to 3 months, wrap the container in several layers of plastic wrap and aluminum foil. Use a large piece of masking tape and an indelible marker to label and date the contents. If frozen, thaw overnight in the refrigerator and bring to room temperature before serving.

making a change

Replace the crystallized ginger with 1 cup chopped toasted walnuts, pecans, or hazelnuts.
Replace the bittersweet chocolate with milk chocolate or white chocolate.

white chocolate–peppermint bark

STRIPED ROUND PEPPERMINT CANDIES
ARE CRUSHED AND ADDED TO
WHITE CHOCOLATE TO CREATE THIS
REFRESHING CANDY. WITH ONLY TWO
INGREDIENTS, THIS IS VERY EASY TO
MAKE. I LIKE TO SERVE THIS CANDY
AFTER A MEAL WITH TEA OR COFFEE.

MAKES *about 4 dozen pieces*
(1 *pound* 14 *ounces*)

2 cups (14 ounces) round peppermint
candies

1 pound white chocolate (31 to 35% cacao
content), finely chopped

LINE a baking sheet with waxed paper or a nonstick liner.

PULSE the candies in the work bowl of a food processor fitted with a steel blade until they are broken into small pieces. Or place the candies in a plastic freezer bag, seal it, and crush them with a rolling pin.

PLACE 12 ounces of the white chocolate in the top of a double boiler over hot water. Stir often with a rubber spatula to ensure even melting. Or melt the chocolate in a microwave-safe bowl on low power in 30-second bursts, stirring after each burst. Remove the top pan of the double boiler, if using, and wipe the bottom and sides very dry.

STIR in the remaining white chocolate in 3 stages, making sure each batch is melted before adding the next.

WHEN the chocolate is completely blended, quickly stir in the crushed peppermint with a rubber spatula, coating the pieces completely. Pour the mixture out onto the baking sheet and spread it evenly with the spatula to cover most of the sheet. Chill the bark in the refrigerator for 30 minutes to 1 hour, until firm enough to break.

GENTLY peel the waxed paper off the back of the bark and break the bark into pieces by hand. Serve the bark at room temperature.

keeping

Store the bark between layers of waxed paper in an airtight plastic container in the refrigerator, away from strongly flavored food, up to 2 weeks. To freeze up to 3 months, wrap the container in several layers of plastic wrap and aluminum foil. Use a large piece of masking tape and an indelible marker to label and date the contents. If frozen, thaw overnight in the refrigerator and bring to room temperature before serving.

making a change

Replace the peppermint candies with chopped toasted pecans, walnuts, hazelnuts, whole unblanched almonds, toasted, or 2 cups chopped dried fruit.
    Replace the white chocolate with milk chocolate or bittersweet chocolate.

ice creams, sorbets, and frozen desserts

bittersweet chocolate ice cream

THIS IS THE MOST INTENSELY
CHOCOLATE ICE CREAM I'VE
EVER EATEN. BITTERSWEET AND
UNSWEETENED CHOCOLATES GIVE IT
DEEP, FULL FLAVOR. IT IS FABULOUS
ON ITS OWN AND IS SPECTACULAR
WHEN SERVED WITH HOT FUDGE
SAUCE (PAGE 202). IT ALSO MAKES A
GREAT ACCOMPANIMENT FOR CAKES,
CUPCAKES, AND COOKIES.

MAKES 1 quart

SPECIAL EQUIPMENT: ice cream maker;
candy, sugar, or instant-read thermometer

2 cups milk (whole or 2%)

2 cups heavy whipping cream

1 vanilla bean

8 large egg yolks, at room temperature

¾ cup (5 ounces) granulated sugar

8 ounces bittersweet chocolate (70 to
72% cocoa content), finely chopped

2 ounces unsweetened chocolate, finely
chopped

COMBINE the milk and cream in a 3-quart heavy-duty saucepan. Use a small sharp knife to split the vanilla bean lengthwise. Scrape out the seeds and add them and the vanilla bean to the mixture. Warm the mixture over medium heat until small bubbles form around the edges.

IN the bowl of an electric stand mixer using the wire whip attachment or in a large bowl using a handheld mixer, whip the egg yolks and sugar together until the mixture is very thick and pale yellow and holds a slowly dissolving ribbon when the beater is lifted, about 5 minutes.

REHEAT the milk mixture to just below the boiling point. Ladle half of the hot milk mixture into a liquid measuring cup and pour slowly into the egg yolk mixture. whisking constantly, to temper the yolks. Pour this mixture back into the saucepan.

STIR the mixture constantly until it is thick enough to coat the spoon or registers 185°F on a candy, sugar, or instant-read thermometer. Immediately remove the thermometer and strain the custard through a fine-mesh strainer into a heat-safe bowl, then discard the vanilla bean pod.

ADD the bittersweet and unsweetened chocolates to the custard and stir together until completely melted and smooth. Cover the bowl tightly with plastic wrap, place on a cooling rack, and cool to room temperature.

CHILL in the refrigerator for several hours.

PROCESS the mixture in an ice cream maker following the manufacturer's instructions. If the ice cream is soft, chill it in the freezer in a tightly covered container until it is fairly firm before serving.

keeping

Store the ice cream in a tightly covered container in the freezer up to 2 weeks. If it is too firm, soften in the refrigerator for 45 minutes to 1 hour before serving.

streamlining

The ice cream mixture can be made up to 3 days in advance and kept tightly covered in a bowl in the refrigerator before freezing in the ice cream maker.

making a change

Add 4 ounces bittersweet chocolate, chopped into small chunks, halfway through processing in the ice cream maker, when the mixture starts to thicken.

bittersweet chocolate-salted caramel ice cream

THIS RECIPE BRINGS TOGETHER A
PERFECT BALANCE OF BITTERSWEET
CHOCOLATE AND SALTED CARAMEL.
IF YOU HAVEN'T TRIED THIS FLAVOR
COMBINATION, NOW IS YOUR CHANCE
TO EXPERIENCE SOMETHING SPECIAL
THAT I KNOW YOU WILL ENJOY. GREAT
ON ITS OWN, THIS IS ALSO A SUPERB
ACCOMPANIMENT TO MANY CAKES,
BROWNIES, AND COOKIES.

MAKES 1 quart

SPECIAL EQUIPMENT: ice cream maker;
candy, sugar, or instant-read thermometer

1 cup (6½ ounces) granulated sugar

3 tablespoons water

1 cup heavy whipping cream

2 cups milk (whole or 2%)

½ teaspoon pure vanilla extract

½ teaspoon pure chocolate extract

½ teaspoon kosher or fine-grained sea
salt

4 large egg yolks, at room temperature

6 ounces bittersweet chocolate (66 to
72% cacao content), very finely chopped

IN a 3-quart heavy-duty saucepan, combine the sugar and water and bring to a boil
over medium-high heat. Dip a pastry brush in water and run it around the rim of the
pan where the line of the sugar meets the side of the pan, to prevent crystallization.
Do this two times. Continue to cook the sugar without stirring until it turns a deep
amber, about 8 minutes.

AT the same time, heat the cream to a boil in a small saucepan. Slowly pour the cream
into the caramel, stirring with a long-handled heat-safe silicone spatula. Be careful,
because the mixture will bubble and foam. Add the milk and cook the mixture until it
is warm, about 3 minutes. Stir in the vanilla and chocolate extracts and the salt.

PLACE the egg yolks in a 2-quart heat-safe mixing bowl and slowly stir in half of
the milk mixture, whisking constantly. Pour this mixture back into the saucepan and
stir until the mixture thickens and reaches 185°F on a candy, sugar, or instant-read
thermometer.

REMOVE the pan from the heat and stir in the chocolate until it is thoroughly melted
and smooth. Strain the mixture through a fine-mesh strainer into a medium heat-
safe bowl. Cover the bowl tightly with plastic wrap, place on a cooling rack, and cool
to room temperature.

CHILL for several hours or overnight.

PROCESS the mixture in an ice cream maker according to the manufacturer's directions. If the ice cream is soft, chill it in the freezer in a tightly covered container until
it is fairly firm before serving.

keeping

Store the ice cream in a tightly covered container in the freezer up to 2 weeks. If it is too firm,
soften in the refrigerator for 45 minutes to 1 hour before serving.

streamlining

The ice cream mixture can be made up to 3 days in advance and kept tightly covered in a bowl
in the refrigerator before freezing in the ice cream maker.

mocha-chocolate chunk ice cream

BITTERSWEET CHOCOLATE, UNSWEETENED CHOCOLATE, AND INSTANT ESPRESSO POWDER MAKE A DEEPLY FLAVORED ICE CREAM. THE ADDITION OF BITTERSWEET CHOCOLATE CHUNKS ADDS CRUNCHY TEXTURE. I LIKE TO SERVE SCOOPS OF THIS WITH WHITE CHOCOLATE SHORTBREAD COINS (PAGE 139).

MAKES 1 quart

SPECIAL EQUIPMENT: ice cream maker; candy, sugar, or instant-read thermometer

1 cup milk (whole or 2%)

1 cup heavy whipping cream

2 teaspoons pure vanilla bean paste

2 tablespoons instant espresso powder

4 large egg yolks, at room temperature

⅓ cup (2¼ ounces) granulated sugar

3 ounces unsweetened chocolate, finely chopped

4 ounces bittersweet chocolate (70 to 72% cocoa content), finely chopped

4 ounces bittersweet chocolate (70 to 72% cocoa content), cut into small chunks

COMBINE the milk, cream, and vanilla bean paste in a 3-quart heavy-duty saucepan. Warm the mixture over medium heat until small bubbles form around the edges. Add the espresso powder, turn off the heat, cover the pan, and let the mixture steep for 20 minutes.

IN the bowl of an electric stand mixer using the wire whip attachment or in a large bowl using a handheld mixer, whip the egg yolks and sugar together until the mixture is very thick and pale yellow and holds a slowly dissolving ribbon when the beater is lifted, about 5 minutes.

REHEAT the milk mixture to just below the boiling point. Ladle half of the hot milk mixture into a liquid measuring cup and pour slowly into the egg yolk mixture, whisking constantly, to temper the yolks. Pour this mixture back into the saucepan. Stir the mixture constantly until it is thick enough to coat the spoon or registers 185°F on a candy, sugar, or instant-read thermometer. Immediately remove the thermometer and strain the custard through a fine-mesh sieve into a heat-safe bowl.

ADD the finely chopped unsweetened and bittersweet chocolates to the mixture and stir together until completely melted and smooth. Cover the bowl tightly with plastic wrap, place on a cooling rack, and cool to room temperature.

CHILL in the refrigerator for several hours.

PROCESS the mixture in an ice cream maker following the manufacturer's instructions. Halfway through processing, when the mixture begins to thicken, add the chocolate chunks and continue to process the ice cream until it's ready. If the ice cream is soft, chill it in the freezer in a tightly covered container until it is fairly firm before serving.

keeping Store the ice cream in a tightly covered container in the freezer up to 2 weeks. If it is too firm, soften in the refrigerator for 45 minutes to 1 hour before serving.

streamlining The ice cream mixture can be made up to 3 days in advance and kept tightly covered in a bowl in the refrigerator before freezing in the ice cream maker.

gianduia ice cream

THIS ICE CREAM REMINDS ME OF MY TRAVELS TO ITALY WHERE MY FIRST CHOICE FOR GELATO WAS ALWAYS GIANDUIA. BITTERSWEET CHOCOLATE, DARK MILK CHOCOLATE, AND HAZELNUT PASTE COMBINE TO MAKE THIS SCRUMPTIOUS ICE CREAM. THE ULTIMATE TASTE EXPERIENCE IS TO SERVE SCOOPS OF THIS WITH DOUBLE GIANDUIA SANDWICH COOKIES (PAGE 129).

MAKES 1½ quarts

SPECIAL EQUIPMENT: ice cream maker; candy, sugar, or instant-read thermometer

ICE CREAM

5 ounces bittersweet chocolate (66 to 72% cacao content), finely chopped

3 ounces dark milk chocolate (38 to 42% cacao content), finely chopped

⅔ cup Luscious Hazelnut Paste (page 205), at room temperature

2 cups milk (whole or 2%)

2 cups heavy whipping cream

1 vanilla bean

8 large egg yolks, at room temperature

¾ cup (5 ounces) granulated sugar

GARNISH

¼ cup (1¼ ounces) chopped toasted, skinned hazelnuts (see page 10)

MELT the bittersweet chocolate, dark milk chocolate, and hazelnut paste together in the top of a double boiler over hot water, stirring occasionally with a rubber spatula to ensure even melting. Or place the chocolates in a microwave-safe bowl and melt on low power in 30-second bursts, stirring after each burst. When all the chocolate is melted, add the hazelnut paste and stir together until thoroughly blended. Remove the top pan of the double boiler, if using, and wipe the bottom and sides very dry.

COMBINE the milk and cream in a 3-quart heavy-duty saucepan. Split the vanilla bean lengthwise, scrape out the seeds, and add both the seeds and the bean to the milk mixture. Bring the mixture to a simmer over medium heat.

IN the bowl of an electric stand mixer using the wire whip attachment or in a large bowl using a handheld mixer, whip the egg yolks and sugar together until the mixture is very thick and pale yellow and holds a slowly dissolving ribbon when the beater is lifted, about 5 minutes.

LADLE half of the hot milk mixture into a liquid measuring cup and pour slowly into the egg yolk mixture, whisking constantly, to temper the yolks. Pour this mixture back into the saucepan. Stir the mixture constantly until it is thick enough to coat the spoon or registers 185°F on a candy, sugar, or instant-read thermometer. Immediately remove the thermometer and strain the custard through a fine-mesh sieve into a heat-safe bowl, then discard the vanilla bean pod.

ADD the melted chocolate mixture to the custard and stir together until completely blended. Cover the bowl tightly with plastic wrap, place on a cooling rack, and cool to room temperature.

SPRINKLE the top of each serving with some of the chopped hazelnut.

CHILL in the refrigerator for several hours.

PROCESS the mixture in an ice cream maker following the manufacturer's instructions. If the ice cream is soft, chill it in the freezer in a tightly covered container until it is fairly firm before serving.

keeping

Store the ice cream in a tightly covered container in the freezer up to 2 weeks. If it is too firm, soften in the refrigerator for 45 minutes to 1 hour before serving.

streamlining

The ice cream base can be made up to 3 days in advance and kept tightly covered in a bowl in the refrigerator before freezing in the ice cream maker.

making a change

Replace the bittersweet chocolate and dark milk chocolate with 8 ounces of gianduia chocolate (see page 4).

milk chocolate ice cream

MILK CHOCOLATE LOVERS WILL REJOICE WITH THIS RICH AND CREAMY ICE CREAM. THE USE OF DARK MILK CHOCOLATE GIVES IT FULL-BODIED FLAVOR. IT GOES VERY WELL WITH OTHER ICE CREAMS AND WITH ANY CHOCOLATE SAUCE.

MAKES 1½ quarts

SPECIAL EQUIPMENT: *ice cream maker; candy, sugar, or instant-read thermometer*

10 ounces dark milk chocolate (38 to 42% cacao content), finely chopped

2 cups milk (whole or 2%)

2 cups heavy whipping cream

1 teaspoon pure vanilla bean paste

8 large egg yolks, at room temperature

¾ cup (5 ounces) granulated sugar

PLACE the milk chocolate in a large heat-safe bowl.

COMBINE the milk and cream in a 3-quart heavy-duty saucepan. Add the vanilla bean paste and stir to blend. Bring the mixture to a simmer over medium heat.

IN the bowl of an electric stand mixer using the wire whip attachment or in a large bowl using a handheld mixer, whip the egg yolks and sugar together until the mixture is very thick and pale yellow and holds a slowly dissolving ribbon when the beater is lifted, about 5 minutes.

LADLE half of the hot milk mixture into a liquid measuring cup and pour slowly into the egg yolk mixture, whisking constantly, to temper the yolks. Pour this mixture back into the saucepan. Stir the mixture constantly until it is thick enough to coat the spoon or registers 185°F on a candy, sugar, or instant-read thermometer. Immediately remove the thermometer and strain the custard through a fine-mesh strainer into the bowl of chocolate.

STIR with a heat-safe silicone spatula to melt the chocolate until thoroughly blended. Cover the bowl tightly with plastic wrap, place on a cooling rack, and cool to room temperature.

CHILL in the refrigerator for several hours.

PROCESS the mixture in an ice cream maker following the manufacturer's instructions. If the ice cream is soft, chill it in the freezer in a tightly covered container until it is fairly firm before serving.

keeping

Store the ice cream in a tightly covered container in the freezer up to 2 weeks. If it is too firm, soften in the refrigerator for 45 minutes to 1 hour before serving.

streamlining

The ice cream mixture can be made up to 3 days in advance and kept tightly covered in a bowl in the refrigerator before freezing in the ice cream maker.

adding style

Serve a scoop of this ice cream with a scoop of White Chocolate Ice Cream (page 190).
Serve with Hot Fudge Sauce (page 202) or Warm Bittersweet Chocolate Sauce (page 201).

white chocolate ice cream

ALTHOUGH THE IVORY COLOR OF THIS ICE CREAM MAKES IT LOOK LIKE VANILLA, IT'S A DELICIOUS SURPRISE WHEN YOU BITE INTO IT AND EXPERIENCE THE INCOMPARABLE FLAVOR OF PURE WHITE CHOCOLATE. TRY SERVING A SCOOP OF THIS WITH OTHER ICE CREAMS AND HOT FUDGE SAUCE (PAGE 202) OR SALTED CARAMEL–BITTERSWEET CHOCOLATE SAUCE (PAGE 203).

MAKES 1½ quarts

SPECIAL EQUIPMENT: ice cream maker; candy, sugar, or instant-read thermometer

12 ounces white chocolate (31 to 35% cacao content), finely chopped

1 cup milk (whole or 2%)

2 cups heavy whipping cream

1 teaspoon pure vanilla bean paste

6 large egg yolks, at room temperature

⅔ cup (4 ounces) superfine sugar

PLACE the white chocolate in a large heat-safe bowl.

COMBINE the milk and cream in a 3-quart heavy-duty saucepan. Add the vanilla bean paste and stir to blend. Bring the mixture to a simmer over medium heat.

IN the bowl of an electric stand mixer using the wire whip attachment or in a large bowl using a handheld mixer, whip the egg yolks and sugar together until the mixture is very thick and pale yellow and holds a slowly dissolving ribbon when the beater is lifted, about 5 minutes.

LADLE half of the hot milk mixture into a liquid measuring cup and pour slowly into the egg yolk mixture, whisking constantly, to temper the yolks. Pour this mixture back into the saucepan. Stir the mixture constantly until it is thick enough to coat the spoon or registers 185°F on a candy, sugar, or instant-read thermometer. Immediately remove the thermometer and strain the custard through a fine-mesh strainer into the bowl of chocolate.

STIR to melt the chocolate until thoroughly blended. Cover the bowl tightly with plastic wrap, place on a cooling rack, and cool to room temperature.

CHILL in the refrigerator for several hours.

PROCESS the mixture in an ice cream maker following the manufacturer's instructions. If the ice cream is soft, chill it in the freezer in a tightly covered container until it is fairly firm before serving.

keeping

Store the ice cream in a tightly covered container in the freezer up to 2 weeks. If it is too firm, soften in the refrigerator for 45 minutes to 1 hour before serving.

streamlining

The ice cream mixture can be made up to 3 days in advance and kept tightly covered in a bowl in the refrigerator before freezing in the ice cream maker.

adding style

Serve scoops of the ice cream with fresh raspberries or blueberries.

bittersweet chocolate ice cream sandwiches

WHAT'S BETTER THAN ICE CREAM AND COOKIES? THESE NONTRADITIONAL ICE CREAM SANDWICHES ENCLOSE BITTER-SWEET CHOCOLATE ICE CREAM BETWEEN TWO POWER-PACKED CHOCOLATE WA-FERS. IF YOU WANT TO GO OVER THE TOP, ROLL THE EDGES OF THE SANDWICHES IN FINELY CHOPPED TOASTED NUTS BEFORE PLACING THEM IN THE FREEZER.

MAKES 21 to 30 sandwiches

SPECIAL EQUIPMENT: 1½-inch-diameter ice cream scoop

1 recipe (about 60) Chunky Bittersweet Chocolate Wafers (page 122)

1 recipe (1 quart) Bittersweet Chocolate Ice Cream (page 184)

LINE a baking sheet with waxed paper. If the ice cream is very firm, soften it slightly in the refrigerator.

PLACE a scoop of ice cream on the flat side of one cookie and cover the scoop with the flat side of another cookie. Press the cookies together lightly to spread the ice cream to the edges. Use a small flat metal spatula to smooth the ice cream around the sides. Place the ice cream sandwich on the baking sheet. Continue with the remaining cookies and ice cream.

COVER the pan with plastic wrap and chill the ice cream sandwiches in the freezer. Serve cold.

keeping

Store the ice cream sandwiches tightly covered individually in an airtight plastic container in the freezer up to 2 weeks.

making a change

Replace the Chunky Bittersweet Chocolate Wafers with Cacao Nib and Cocoa Shortbread (page 114).

Replace the Bittersweet Chocolate Ice Cream with Bittersweet Chocolate–Salted Caramel Ice Cream (page 185) or Mocha–Chocolate Chunk Ice Cream (page 186).

adding style

Roll the edges of the ice cream sandwiches in finely chopped toasted walnuts before freezing.

cocoa and bittersweet chocolate sorbet

THE BLEND OF COCOA POWDER AND BITTERSWEET CHOCOLATE GIVES THIS SORBET A PROFOUND CHOCOLATE FLAVOR WITH A SILKY SMOOTH TEXTURE. IT IS AN EXCELLENT PARTNER FOR MANY OTHER CHOCOLATE DESSERTS, SUCH AS MILK CHOCOLATE CHUNK–PECAN BISCOTTI (PAGE 134).

MAKES 1 pint

SPECIAL EQUIPMENT: ice cream maker

¼ cup water

¾ cup (5 ounces) superfine sugar

¼ cup (¾ ounce) unsweetened cocoa powder (natural or Dutch-processed), sifted

4 ounces bittersweet chocolate (70 to 72% cacao content), very finely chopped

IN a 2-quart heavy-duty saucepan, combine the water and sugar and bring to a boil over medium heat. Add the cocoa powder and stir with a heat-safe silicone spatula until it is dissolved and the mixture is smooth.

REMOVE the pan from the heat and stir in the bittersweet chocolate until it is thoroughly melted and smooth. Strain the mixture through a fine-mesh strainer into a medium heat-safe bowl. Cover the bowl tightly with plastic wrap, place on a cooling rack, and cool to room temperature.

CHILL for several hours or overnight.

PROCESS the mixture in an ice cream maker according to the manufacturer's directions. If the sorbet is soft, chill it in the freezer in a tightly covered container until it is fairly firm before serving.

keeping

Store the sorbet in a tightly covered container in the freezer up to 2 weeks. If it is too firm, soften in the refrigerator 45 minutes to 1 hour before serving.

streamlining

The sorbet mixture can be made up to 3 days in advance and kept tightly covered in a bowl in the refrigerator before freezing in the ice cream maker.

triple chocolate ice cream sundaes

THIS RECIPE USES WHITE CHOCOLATE ICE CREAM, MILK CHOCOLATE ICE CREAM, AND WARM BITTERSWEET CHOCOLATE SAUCE TO MAKE A SUNDAE THAT IS FAR BEYOND ORDINARY. I LIKE TO SERVE THESE IN TALL STEMMED GLASSES.

MAKES 6 to 8 ice cream sundaes

SPECIAL EQUIPMENT: 1½-inch-diameter ice cream scoop; 6 to 8 tall stemmed glasses or dessert bowls

SUNDAE

1 recipe (1½ quarts) White Chocolate Ice Cream (page 190)

1 recipe (1½ quarts) Milk Chocolate Ice Cream (page 189)

1 recipe (2 cups) Warm Bittersweet Chocolate Sauce (page 201)

GARNISH

2 tablespoons shaved bittersweet chocolate (66 to 72% cacao content)

or

2 tablespoons cacao nibs

or

2 tablespoons finely chopped toasted peanuts or almonds (see page 10)

IF the ice creams are very firm, soften them slightly in the refrigerator.

PLACE 2 tablespoons of chocolate sauce in the bottom of a tall stemmed glass or a bowl. Place 2 scoops of White Chocolate Ice Cream on top of the sauce. Drizzle another tablespoon of the sauce on top of the ice cream and top this with 2 scoops of Milk Chocolate Ice Cream. Drizzle another tablespoon of sauce on top of the ice cream. Garnish with about a teaspoon of shaved bittersweet chocolate, cacao nibs, or nuts. Serve immediately.

making a change

To make Hot Fudge Sundaes, replace the Warm Bittersweet Chocolate Sauce with Hot Fudge Sauce (page 202).

gianduia semifreddo

SEMIFREDDO IS THE ITALIAN WORD FOR HALF-FROZEN. THIS DESSERT IS LIKE A PARTIALLY FROZEN MOUSSE, LIGHT AND DELICATE, BUT FULL OF FLAVOR FROM THE USE OF GIANDUIA CHOCOLATE AND HAZELNUTS. IF YOU CAN'T FIND GIANDUIA CHOCOLATE IT CAN EASILY BE REPLACED WITH A BLEND OF BITTERSWEET AND DARK MILK CHOCOLATES. BE SURE TO MAKE THIS AT LEAST ONE DAY BEFORE SERVING SO IT HAS TIME TO FREEZE.

MAKES one 9 x 5 x 3-inch loaf, 12 to 16 servings

SPECIAL EQUIPMENT: 9 x 5 x 3-inch loaf pan; instant-read thermometer

SEMIFREDDO

5 large eggs, separated, at room temperature

½ cup (3½ ounces) superfine sugar

1 pound gianduia chocolate, melted (see page 9)

1½ cups (7½ ounces) hazelnuts, toasted and skinned (see page 10)

1 tablespoon Frangelico or other hazelnut liqueur

2 cups heavy whipping cream

GARNISH

1 tablespoon unsweetened cocoa powder (natural or Dutch-processed), sifted

---

LINE a 9 x 5 x 3-inch loaf pan with plastic, letting it hang about 2 inches over the sides. Separate the eggs.

IN the bowl of an electric stand mixer using the wire whip attachment or in a large bowl using a handheld mixer, whip the egg yolks and ¼ cup of the sugar together until the mixture is very thick and pale yellow and holds a slowly dissolving ribbon when the beater is lifted, about 5 minutes.

IN the work bowl of a food processor fitted with the steel blade, pulse the hazelnuts to chop them coarsely.

FOLD the melted gianduia chocolate, chopped hazelnuts, and Frangelico into the egg yolk mixture, blending thoroughly.

WHIP the cream in the bowl of an electric stand mixer using the wire whip attachment or in a large mixing bowl using a handheld mixer until it holds soft peaks. Fold the whipped cream into the chocolate mixture in 4 stages.

PLACE the egg whites in a grease-free, heat-safe mixing bowl and place the bowl over a pan of simmering water. Stir the egg whites constantly until they reach 160°F on an instant-read thermometer. Remove the bowl from the pan and wipe it dry. Transfer it to an electric stand mixer or a large mixing bowl and whip with the wire whip attachment or handheld mixer until they form soft peaks. Gradually sprinkle on the remaining ¼ cup sugar and whip until the mixture holds firm but not stiff peaks. Fold this mixture into the chocolate mixture in 4 stages.

TRANSFER the mixture to the loaf pan. Use a rubber spatula to spread the mixture evenly and to smooth the top. Cover the pan tightly with plastic wrap and freeze for several hours or overnight.

TO UNMOLD, remove the plastic wrap from the top of the pan. Turn the pan upside down over a serving plate or cutting board. Let it stand for 2 minutes to begin to soften, then gently lift the pan off. Peel off the remaining plastic wrap. Dust the top of the semifreddo lightly with the cocoa powder. Use a chef's knife, dipped in hot water and dried, to cut ½-inch-thick slices. Place each slice on a serving plate and serve immediately.

keeping

The semifreddo will keep tightly wrapped in the freezer for 2 weeks, either in or out of the loaf pan.

making a change

Replace the gianduia chocolate with 10 ounces bittersweet chocolate (66 to 72% cacao content) and 6 ounces dark milk chocolate (38 to 42% cacao content).

CHAPTER NINE

liquid chocolate

intense hot chocolate

THIS HOT CHOCOLATE IS THICK AND CREAMY. YOU WANT TO SAVOR THIS DELECTABLE BEVERAGE BY SIPPING SLOWLY.

MAKES 4 servings

HOT CHOCOLATE

2 cups whole milk

1 cup heavy whipping cream

¼ cup (¾ ounce) unsweetened cocoa powder (natural or Dutch-processed), sifted

6 ounces bittersweet chocolate (66 to 72% cacao content), very finely chopped

½ teaspoon pure vanilla extract

½ teaspoon pure chocolate extract

GARNISH

¼ cup heavy whipping cream.

2 teaspoons confectioners' sugar, sifted

COMBINE the milk, cream, and cocoa powder in a 2-quart heavy-duty saucepan. Cook over medium heat, stirring with a heat-safe silicone spatula, to dissolve the cocoa powder.

ADD the chocolate and stir until it is thoroughly melted and smooth. Bring the mixture to a simmer, but do not boil. Cook for 5 minutes, stirring often.

REMOVE the saucepan from the heat and stir in the vanilla and chocolate extracts. Continue to stir to cool the mixture slightly, then pour into serving cups.

FOR THE GARNISH, whip the cream in the bowl of an electric stand mixer using the wire whip attachment or in a mixing bowl using a handheld mixer until it is frothy. Sprinkle on the confectioners' sugar and continue to whip until the cream holds soft peaks.

PLACE a large scoop of whipped cream on top of each cup of chocolate and serve immediately.

hot malted milk chocolate

MALTED MILK POWDER COMBINED WITH DARK MILK CHOCOLATE GIVES THIS BEVERAGE A TOASTY UNDERTONE. MALTED MILK POWDER IS AVAILABLE IN MOST GROCERY STORES.

MAKES 4 servings

3 cups heavy whipping cream

½ cup whole milk

1 teaspoon pure vanilla bean paste

½ cup plus 2 tablespoons (2¾ ounces) plain malted milk powder, sifted

4 ounces dark milk chocolate (38 to 42% cacao content), finely chopped

COMBINE the cream and milk in a 2-quart heavy-duty saucepan. Bring to a boil over medium-high heat. Add the vanilla bean paste and stir with a heat-safe whisk or silicone spatula to blend. Reduce the heat to medium and add the malted milk powder and chocolate. Stir until the chocolate is completely melted.

REMOVE the pan from the heat. Pour the hot chocolate into cups or mugs and serve immediately.

adding style Top each serving with a dollop of lightly sweetened whipped cream.

white hot chocolate

THIS ULTRACREAMY, RICH BEVERAGE IS MADE WITH WHITE CHOCOLATE. IT IS PERFECT ON A COLD, BLUSTERY DAY OR ANYTIME YOU WANT TO TREAT YOURSELF TO A LUSCIOUS DRINK.

MAKES 4 servings

8 ounces white chocolate (31 to 35% cacao content), finely chopped

1 quart heavy whipping cream

½ teaspoon pure vanilla bean paste

COMBINE the white chocolate and cream in a 2-quart heavy-duty saucepan. Cook over low heat, stirring with a heat-safe whisk or silicone spatula, until the chocolate is completely melted. Raise the heat to medium and stir until the mixture is completely blended and hot.

REMOVE the pan from the heat and stir in the vanilla bean paste. Pour the hot chocolate into cups or mugs and serve immediately.

adding style Top each serving with a dollop of lightly sweetened whipped cream.

creamy hot mocha

A PERFECT BLEND OF BITTERSWEET CHOCOLATE, HEAVY WHIPPING CREAM, AND ESPRESSO GIVES THIS BEVERAGE EXTREME DEPTH OF FLAVOR. THE TEXTURE IS THICK—ALMOST LIKE A MOUSSE—SO IT'S BEST TO SERVE IT WITH SPOONS.

MAKES 4 servings

8 ounces bittersweet chocolate (70 to 72% cacao content) finely chopped

3 cups heavy whipping cream

1 tablespoon plus 1 teaspoon instant espresso powder

COMBINE the bittersweet chocolate and cream in a 2-quart heavy-duty saucepan. Cook over low heat, stirring with a heat-safe whisk or silicone spatula until the chocolate is completely melted. Raise the heat to medium and stir until the mixture is completely blended and hot.

REMOVE the pan from the heat and stir in the instant espresso powder until completely dissolved. Pour the hot mocha into cups or mugs and serve immediately.

adding style

Top each serving with a dollop of lightly sweetened whipped cream.

warm bittersweet chocolate sauce

THIS IS THE QUINTESSENTIAL CHOCOLATE SAUCE. IT IS DEEPLY FLAVORED WITH BITTERSWEET CHOCOLATE, CREAM, AND LIGHT BROWN SUGAR. IT IS SUPERB WITH ANY CAKE OR ICE CREAM.

MAKES 2 cups

½ cup (3 ounces) firmly packed light brown sugar

¾ cup heavy whipping cream

1 teaspoon pure vanilla extract

Pinch of kosher or fine-grained sea salt

6 ounces bittersweet chocolate (66 to 72% cacao content), finely chopped

1½ ounces (3 tablespoons) unsalted butter, softened

COMBINE the brown sugar, cream, vanilla, and salt in a 2-quart heavy-duty saucepan. Stir to dissolve the sugar, then bring to a simmer over medium heat.

REMOVE the pan from the heat and stir in the chocolate and butter with a heat-safe whisk or silicone spatula until completely melted and smooth.

USE the sauce immediately. Or transfer to a bowl, cover with plastic wrap, and cool on a rack to room temperature. Warm the sauce in the top of a double boiler or in a microwave oven on low power before using.

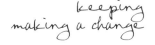

keeping
making a change

Store the sauce in a tightly covered container in the refrigerator up to 1 week.

To make Warm Mocha Sauce, add 1 teaspoon instant espresso powder to the cream mixture.

hot fudge sauce

BRINGING TOGETHER BITTERSWEET
CHOCOLATE AND COCOA POWDER
MAKES THIS SAUCE EXTRAORDINARY.
THIS MOUTHWATERING SAUCE GOES
WELL OVER ICE CREAM, CAKES, AND
BROWNIES.

MAKES 1½ cups

½ cup water

2 ounces (4 tablespoons, ½ stick)
unsalted butter, cut into small pieces and
softened

2 tablespoons unsweetened cocoa
powder (natural or Dutch-processed),
sifted

Pinch of kosher or fine-grained sea salt

4 ounces bittersweet chocolate (66 to
72% cacao content), finely chopped

¼ cup light corn syrup

¼ cup (1½ ounces) granulated sugar

¼ cup (1½ ounces) firmly packed light
brown sugar

1 teaspoon pure chocolate extract

COMBINE the water and butter in a 2-quart heavy-duty saucepan. Bring to a simmer over medium heat.

ADD the cocoa powder and salt and stir with a heat-safe silicone spatula until it is completely blended. Remove the saucepan from the heat and add the bittersweet chocolate. Stir until it is completely melted and the mixture is smooth.

ADD the corn syrup, granulated sugar, and light brown sugar. Return the saucepan to the stovetop and bring to a simmer over medium heat. Cook for 5 minutes, stirring frequently.

REMOVE the saucepan from the heat, add the chocolate extract, and stir to blend thoroughly.

USE the sauce immediately. Or transfer to a bowl, cover with plastic wrap, and cool on a rack to room temperature. Warm the sauce in the top of a double boiler or in a microwave oven on low power before using.

keeping

Store the sauce in a tightly covered container in the refrigerator up to 2 weeks.

salted caramel-bittersweet chocolate sauce

THIS RICH WARM SAUCE COMBINES TWO OF MY FAVORITE FLAVORS, CARAMEL AND BITTERSWEET CHOCOLATE. THE SALT GREATLY ENHANCES BOTH. THIS SAUCE IS AN EXCELLENT ACCOMPANIMENT FOR CAKES, CUPCAKES, AND ICE CREAM. I EVEN USE IT TO MAKE TRUFFLES AFTER IT IS CHILLED (PAGE 170).

MAKES 2 cups

1 cup (6½ ounces) granulated sugar

¼ cup water

1 tablespoon light corn syrup

¾ cup heavy whipping cream

2 ounces (4 tablespoons, ½ stick) unsalted butter, cut into small pieces and softened

½ teaspoon pure vanilla extract

1 teaspoon pure chocolate extract

½ teaspoon fleur de sel or other fine-grained finishing sea salt

3½ ounces bittersweet chocolate (70 to 72% cacao content), finely chopped

COMBINE the sugar, water, and corn syrup in a 2-quart heavy-duty saucepan over high heat. When the mixture begins to bubble around the edges, dip a pastry brush in water and run it around the edges to help prevent crystallization. Continue to cook the mixture, without stirring, until it turns amber, 8 to 10 minutes.

AT the same time, bring the cream to a boil in a small saucepan. Immediately pour the hot cream into the sugar mixture, stirring with a long-handled heat-safe silicone spatula. Be careful, because the mixture may splatter and foam. Add the butter and stir until it is completely melted.

REMOVE the saucepan from the heat and add the vanilla and chocolate extracts, salt, and bittersweet chocolate. Stir until the chocolate is thoroughly melted.

USE the sauce immediately. Or transfer to a bowl, cover with plastic wrap, and cool the bowl on a rack to room temperature. Warm the sauce in the top of a double boiler or in a microwave oven on low power before using.

keeping

Store the sauce in a tightly covered container in the refrigerator up to 2 weeks.

bittersweet chocolate–orange fondue

BITTERSWEET CHOCOLATE IS
ENHANCED BY GRATED ORANGE ZEST
AND GRAND MARNIER TO MAKE
AN UNFORGETTABLE DESSERT. TO
MAINTAIN THE FONDUE'S SILKY
SMOOTHNESS, PREPARE IT JUST
BEFORE SERVING. KEEP IT WARM FOR
DIPPING IN A TRADITIONAL FONDUE
POT OR ON A HOT PLATE. BUT KEEP
THE HEAT LOW SO THE CHOCOLATE
DOESN'T BURN. DEPENDING ON THE
SEASON, YOU CAN VARY THE CHOICES
FOR DIPPING. FONDUE IS A FUN
DESSERT FOR A SMALL GATHERING
BECAUSE GUESTS CAN CHOOSE WHICH
OF THE OFFERED ACCOMPANIMENTS
THEY PREFER TO DIP.

MAKES 1 cup, 3 to 4 servings

SPECIAL EQUIPMENT (OPTIONAL):
fondue pot and forks

making a change

FONDUE

½ cup heavy whipping cream

1½ teaspoons finely grated orange zest

8 ounces bittersweet chocolate (70 to 72% cacao content), finely chopped

Pinch of kosher or fine-grained sea salt

2 tablespoons Grand Marnier or other orange liqueur

ACCOMPANIMENTS FOR DIPPING (CHOOSE A VARIETY)

Eight 1-inch cubes Bittersweet Chocolate Gingerbread (page 28)

Eight 1-inch cubes Cocoa and Cacao Nib Angel Food Cake (page 26)

8 Milk Chocolate Chunk–Pecan Biscotti (page 134)

8 fresh strawberries, hulled

24 fresh raspberries

2 kiwifruits, peeled and cut into ½-inch-thick rounds

1 large banana, cut into 8 rounds

1 large apple, such as Granny Smith or Gala, peeled, cored, and cut into ¼-inch slices

8 dried figs, cut in half

8 dried apricot halves

IN A medium heavy-duty saucepan, bring the cream and orange zest to a simmer. Reduce the heat to low. Add the bittersweet chocolate and salt and whisk until the chocolate is completely melted and smooth. Remove the fondue from the heat and stir in the Grand Marnier.

TRANSFER the fondue to a fondue pot, if using, or a pan set over a tea light candle or hot plate to keep it warm. Serve the fondue with the dipping accompaniments.

To make Milk Chocolate–Orange Fondue, replace the bittersweet chocolate with dark milk chocolate (38 to 42% cacao content).

luscious hazelnut paste

THIS MIXTURE IS THE "SECRET" INGRE-
DIENT THAT IS COMBINED WITH CHOC-
OLATE IN SEVERAL RECIPES TO MAKE
GIANDUIA, THE INCOMPARABLE BLEND
OF HAZELNUTS AND CHOCOLATE.

MAKES 2 cups

SPECIAL EQUIPMENT: food processor

3 cups (15 ounces) hazelnuts

⅓ cup canola, safflower, or hazelnut oil

CENTER a rack in the oven and preheat the oven to 350°F. Place the hazelnuts on a baking sheet and toast in the oven for 15 to 18 minutes, until the skins split and the nuts turn light golden brown. Remove the pan from the oven and immediately pour the hazelnuts into a clean kitchen towel. Wrap the towel around the hazelnuts and rub them together to remove most of the skins.

PLACE the hazelnuts in the work bowl of a food processor fitted with the steel blade. Pulse until the nuts are finely chopped. Add the oil and continue to process until the nuts are finely ground and the mixture is the consistency of peanut butter.

keeping

Store the hazelnut paste in a tightly covered container in the refrigerator up to 1 week. To freeze up to 4 months, place the container in a plastic freezer bag. Use a large piece of masking tape and an indelible marker to label and date the contents. If frozen, thaw overnight in the refrigerator and bring to room temperature before using.

making a change

To make Chocolate Hazelnut Paste, add 6 ounces melted bittersweet chocolate (66 to 72% cacao content) to the hazelnut paste and stir to blend thoroughly.

Replace the hazelnuts with almonds, pecans, or cashews. If using these nuts, use canola or safflower oil.

glossary of chocolate terms

AMELONADO A type of forastero cacao, Amelonado is native to the Amazon basin. Amelonado cacao is either delicate and mild flavored or bitter and acidic, depending on the specific region where it is grown.

ARRIBA This variety of forastero cacao is cultivated in Ecuador. It produces a mild-flavored cacao with a distinctive floral fragrance. Arriba is considered to be one of the finest cacaos in the world. Arriba is also called Nacional.

CACAO Cacao is the name given to a tropical evergreen tree that grows in countries within 20 degrees of the Equator. This tree produces pods that contain cacao beans, which are the source of chocolate. Cacao, rather than cocoa, is the correct name of the tree and its product until it is processed into chocolate.

CACAO BEANS These are the seeds of the pods that grow on cacao trees. When the pods are harvested, they are split open to reveal a milky white membrane containing 20 to 40 almond-shaped cacao beans. The beans and the membrane are spread out to ferment and sun-dry before they are shipped to chocolate factories. Depending on the variety and type of beans, the fermenting and drying process can take up to 2 weeks. All varieties of chocolate are made from cacao beans.

CACAO CONTENT This refers to the percentage of the components of the cacao bean that are in chocolate. These components are chocolate liquor, cocoa butter, and cacao solids, which are bits of the cacao bean ground to a powder. Many chocolate bars are labeled with their percentage of cacao content, such as 62%, 66%, or 70%. Cacao content is exactly the same thing as cacao percentage. Cacao content is also sometimes referred to as cocoa content.

After the cacao content, the remaining components of chocolate are sugar, sometimes a bit (1%) of lecithin, milk solids or powder, for milk chocolate, and often vanilla.

CACAO NIBS are the cracked, roasted, and hulled unsweetened center of cacao beans. They are pure unsweetened chocolate before it is pressed into a liquid and further processed.

CHOCOLATE BLOOM This is a condition in which the cocoa butter in chocolate separates itself from the other ingredients, rises to the surface, and crystallizes. It appears as white streaks and dots or as a gray film. Chocolate bloom is an indication that chocolate has been stored too warm, but it does not mean that the chocolate has gone bad. Once the chocolate is melted it can be used with no loss of quality.

CHOCOLATE LIQUOR After cacao beans are roasted and the outer hulls detached, the remaining inner nibs are ground. This produces a thick, dark, nonalcoholic liquid called chocolate liquor, which is the basis of all chocolate. Chocolate liquor is also called cocoa paste and cocoa mass.

CHOCOLATIER A chocolatier is a person who specializes in making chocolate candies. When this is done on a small scale, it is often referred to as artisanal.

CHUAO This area in the northern coastal region of Venezuela grows some of the world's most highly valued cacao.

COCOA BEANS This is another term for cacao beans, from which all varieties of chocolate are made.

COCOA BUTTER This ivory-colored, natural fat in cacao beans is extracted from chocolate liquor during the process of producing chocolate. Cocoa butter is added back into the mixture to make all types of chocolate, giving them smooth texture. It is the basis for *real* white chocolate.

COMPOUND COATING Also called confectionary coating and summer coating, this is a substitute for pure chocolate. It is made with a fat other than cocoa butter and because of this does not need to be tempered. Compound coating is used primarily for dipping and molding. Because the compound coating contains no cocoa butter, it doesn't have the full flavor of chocolate.

CONCH, CONCHING The conch machine and conching, the technique for stirring liquid chocolate during the final stages of the manufacturing process, are used to make chocolate extremely smooth and palatable. Heavy rollers move back and forth continuously through the liquid to break down any particles and thoroughly blend the ingredients. This results in velvety smooth, melt-in-the-mouth chocolate. The longer the conching time, the smoother the chocolate will be. The best quality chocolates are conched for as long as 72 hours.

COUVERTURE Chocolate that contains a high percentage of cocoa butter (a minimum of 32% cocoa butter) is called couverture. It is used by professionals for dipping, coating, and molding, as well as for baking and eating. Most high cacao content chocolates are considered to be couvertures.

CRIOLLO *Criollo*, which means "native" in Spanish, is the name given to the cacao tree when the Spanish conquered the Aztecs in the sixteenth century. The criollo tree was the original cacao tree cultivated by the Mayans. Today, criollo trees are grown primarily in Central and South America where they originated. The criollo tree produces a full-bodied and very flavorful cacao bean. Criollo is one of the three primary varieties of cacao beans used to produce chocolate. It is a delicate tree that is difficult to grow and produces small yields, so its beans are often combined with other types of cacao beans. Pure criollo beans are extremely rare and are highly prized by chocolate manufacturers. Currently, most criollo cacao is a [varietal] hybrid of the original pure beans.

CRU *Cru* is the French word for "growth." It refers to high-quality cacao beans from a specific plantation or region. Some chocolate manufacturers label their chocolate bars as "Grand Cru," meaning the very best.

ENROBE, ENROBER The technique of coating candies and confections with chocolate in a special machine is called enrobing.

An enrober is a machine that coats candies and confections with chocolate as they pass under a shower of liquid chocolate on a conveyor belt. Excess chocolate flows through the mesh of the conveyor belt on which the confections sit so their bottoms don't sit in a pool of chocolate and form a "foot" (a large base on the bottom of enrobed confections caused by chocolate dripping down and settling at the bottom). Enrobers are used for both small- and large-scale production.

FAIR-TRADE CACAO "Fair trade" means that there is a relationship between cacao farmers, who are mostly small-scale family farmers, and consumers, to guarantee that the farmers receive a fair-value price for their harvest instead of having to sell it to the open market for a miniscule amount of money. Receiving this guaranteed price allows the farmers to invest in their crops so they become sustainable and the farmers can concentrate on bringing out the best flavor of the crops. Certification is available for fair-trade cacao, which means that the cacao beans can be traced to their origin and the farmers who grew them. Currently there are eleven recognized countries that produce fair-trade cacao, including Bolivia, the Dominican Republic, Ghana, and Ecuador.

FORASTERO Forastero cacao, one of the three primary types of cacao beans used to make chocolate, originated in the upper Amazon basin. Forastero is a strong plant species that produces high yields and makes up approximately 90 percent of the world's crop. Because the yield is so large, forastero cacao is known as the "bulk bean." Forastero cacao has a strong, sometimes bitter, flavor, and is most often blended with other beans. There are several hybrids and varieties of forastero cacao, named by their specific places of origin. *Forastero* is a Spanish word for "stranger" or "foreigner."

GANACHE A mixture of chocolate and cream with a smooth texture, ganache is made with different proportions of chocolate and cream depending on the final texture desired and the use for which it is intended. Firm ganache is composed of more chocolate than cream, while soft ganache has more cream than chocolate. Ganache is very versatile and is used as the center for truffles, as the filling for cakes and tarts, and as a glaze or sauce.

GIANDUIA A type of chocolate, gianduia is a commercially made blend of chocolate and roasted hazelnuts with a velvety smooth texture. Often roasted almonds are used in place of hazelnuts. Gianduia is most often made with milk chocolate, but it is also available made with dark and white chocolate. Gianduia is used in the same way as chocolate in recipes. Gianduia is also the name of the flavor combination of hazelnuts and chocolate and the name of a group of candies and confections made with the same flavor combination.

LECITHIN Lecithin is an emulsifier occasionally added to chocolate during manufacturing to help give it a smooth consistency. Lecithin stabilizes fat particles, which keeps them from separating and congealing. The lecithin used in chocolate manufacturing comes from soybeans.

MOCHA The flavor combination of coffee and dark chocolate is called mocha.

OCUMARE A hybrid of criollo and trinitario cacao called Ocumare is grown in a valley of the same name on the central coast of Venezuela. The flavor of Ocumare cacao is light, with a slight sharpness. Ocumare cacao is scarce and is occasionally sold as a single-origin cacao.

ORGANIC CHOCOLATE Chocolate made from cacao grown without the use of any chemical pesticides or fertilizers is considered organic. The other ingredients in organic chocolate must also be certified organic, including sugar, milk, and lecithin. The cacao as well as the other ingredients used to make the chocolate cannot be genetically modified. In addition, organic cacao is typically grown in a sustainable manner.

PORCELANA A type of criollo cacao, porcelana is the most highly prized cacao. It is considered to be mildly flavored, yet complex. Porcelana cacao is native to Venezuela where it is grown in small quantities.

SINGLE ORIGIN Sometimes called single source or estate, this refers to chocolate made from cacao beans grown in one region and often from one farm, plantation, or estate, rather than chocolate made with a blend of cacao beans from a variety of regions. Chocolate made from single-origin cacao beans has a very distinctive flavor profile that is influenced by the climate and soil where the cacao was grown. Chocolate made from single-origin cacao is usually labeled as such.

SNAP This term describes a characteristic of well-tempered chocolate. It breaks cleanly and crisply, with a sharp snap and should not be crumbly or soft.

SUGAR BLOOM This is a white coating of sugar crystals that forms when moisture collects on the surface of chocolate. This moisture draws the sugar in the chocolate to the surface, where it dissolves. Sugar bloom is visible as white stripes and spots, and causes a grainy texture in the chocolate. It is caused by storing chocolate in conditions that are too humid or by storing chocolate too loosely wrapped in the refrigerator so it is exposed to too much moisture.

TEMPERING, TEMPERING MACHINE Tempering, a process of heating, cooling, and heating again, sets the cocoa butter in chocolate at its most stable point. Tempered chocolate has a shiny, even-colored appearance and smooth texture. It sets up rapidly, easily releases from molds, and breaks with a clean, sharp snap. When chocolate is melted it loses its temper and needs to be tempered again for dipping and molding. There are several methods for tempering. The quick or "seeding" method used in this book is the easiest.

The tempering machine is designed specifically to heat and temper chocolate. Tempering machines come in different sizes and capacities and there are some specifically for home use. The machine melts the chocolate, tempers it, and holds the chocolate at the correct temperature for dipping and molding truffles and candies.

THEOBROMA CACAO This Latin name was given to cacao by Linnaeus, the Swedish naturalist who codified the plant world in 1753. Theobroma translates as "food of the gods."

TRINITARIO One of the three primary types of cacao, trinitario is a cross between criollo and forastero. It was created on the island of Trinidad in the early eighteenth century and is now grown throughout the Caribbean region. It has some of the flavor characteristics of criollo and much of the heartiness of forastero, and is considered to have a mild and delicate flavor. As with the other primary types of cacao beans, it has many hybrids and varieties, some of which are named by their exact place of origin.

WINNOWING This process of removing the outer husk of cacao beans to free up the inner nibs during the manufacture of chocolate is also known as hulling. Varying sizes of rollers break the cacao beans before they are sent through a winnowing machine, which blows the husks away with a high-speed blast of air.

intensely chocolate chocolates

The following ingredients were used to develop and test the recipes in this book.

CHOCOLATES
Amano Artisan Chocolate Jembrana 70%
Amano Artisan Chocolate Madagascar 70%
Amano Artisan Chocolate Ocumare 70%
E. Guittard "Crème Française" (white chocolate) 31%
E. Guittard "Soleil d'Or" (dark milk chocolate) 38%
E. Guittard Kokoleka Hawaiian (dark milk chocolate) 38%
E. Guittard Kokoleka Hawaiian 55%
E. Guittard "Lever du Soleil" Chocolate 61%
E. Guittard "Coucher du Soleil" Chocolate 72%
Scharffen Berger Semisweet Chocolate 62%
Scharffen Berger Bittersweet Chocolate 70%
Scharffen Berger Unsweetened Chocolate 99%
Valrhona Ivoire (white chocolate) 35%
Valrhona Gianduia 29%
Valrhona le Lait (dark milk chocolate) 39%
Valrhona Guanaja Lactée (dark milk chocolate) 41%
Valrhona Le Noir 61%
Valrhona Manjari 64%

Valrhona Tainori 64%
Valrhona Alpaco 66%
Valrhona Caraïbe 66%
Valrhona Le Noir 68%
Valrhona Guanaja Grué 70%
Valrhona Araguani 72%
Waialua Estate Chocolate 70%

COCOA POWDERS
Pernigotti (Dutch-processed)
Scharffen Berger (natural)
Valrhona (Dutch-processed)

CACAO NIBS
Amano Artisan Chocolate Accra
Amano Artisan Chocolate Barlovento
Amano Artisan Chocolate Jembrana
Amano Artisan Chocolate Madagascar
Amano Artisan Chocolate Ocumare
Scharffen Berger Chocolate Maker

sources for ingredients and equipment

CHOCOSPHERE
www.chocosphere.com
877-992-4626
This Internet-only store in Portland, Oregon carries a huge variety of chocolate from around the world.

DAGOBA
www.dagobachocolate.com
866-972-39-879, 415-401-0080
fax: 405-401-0087
Dagoba specializes in organic, fair-trade, sustainable chocolate.

THE GINGER PEOPLE
www.gingerpeople.com
800-551-4284
fax: 831-582-2495
The Ginger People specialize in Australian-grown ginger products such as crystallized ginger and ginger spread. Their products are available in many stores and online.

GUITTARD CHOCOLATE
www.guittard.com
800-468-2462, 650-697-4427
fax: 650-692-2761
The E. Guittard line specializes in artisanal chocolates, many of which are single origin. Guittard chocolates are available on the Web site and at many shops throughout the United States.

JB PRINCE COMPANY
www.jbprince.com
36 East 31 Street, New York NY 10016
800-473-0577, 212-683-3553
JB Prince carries a vast variety of professional quality equipment and tools.

KING ARTHUR FLOUR
www.kingarthurflour.com
800-827-6836, 802-649-3361
fax: 802-649-3365
The King Arthur online shop carries a large variety of equipment and ingredients.

PASTRY CHEF CENTRAL, INC.
www.pastrychef.com
561-999-9483, 888-750-2433 (order status only)
fax: 561-999-1282
This Internet-only source supplies a wide variety of ingredients, equipment, and tools.

PERFECT PUREE OF NAPA VALLEY
www.perfectpuree.com
866-787-5233, 707-261-5100
fax: 707-261-5111
The source for fruit purees and concentrates. Their products are also available through Amazon.com and at Whole Foods Markets and other retailers in Northern California.

SCHARFFEN BERGER CHOCOLATE MAKER
www.scharffenberger.com
866-972-6879, 415-401-0080
fax: 415-401-0087
Scharffen Berger chocolate, cocoa powder, and cacao nibs are available through their Web site and at many cookware shops and grocery stores throughout the United States.

SUR LA TABLE
www.surlatable.com
800-243-0852, 866-328-5412
fax: 317-858-5521
Sur La Table carries all kinds of equipment and several types of chocolate and cocoa powder. They have many locations throughout the United States, a catalog and a Web site.

SURFAS RESTAURANT SUPPLY AND GOURMET FOOD
www.culinarydistrict.com
877-641-2661, 310-559-4770
Surfas in Culver City, CA carries a large variety of ingredients and equipment. Surfas products are also available on their Web site.

THE COOK'S WAREHOUSE
www.cookswarehouse.com
800-499-0996, 866-890-5962
The Cook's Warehouse carries a wide variety of equipment. They have three locations in the Atlanta area and a Web site.

VALRHONA
www.valrhona.com
Valrhona makes some of the world's finest chocolates. They are available at many retail outlets throughout the United States and online.

WILLIAMS-SONOMA
www.williams-sonoma.com
877-812-6235
Williams-Sonoma carries a wide variety of equipment and some ingredients. They have stores around the United States, a catalog, and a Web site.

measurements

measurement equivalents

U.S. MEASURING SYSTEM	METRIC SYSTEM
CAPACITY	APPROXIMATE CAPACITY
¼ teaspoon	1.25 milliliters
1 teaspoon	5 milliliters
1 tablespoon	15 milliliters
¼ cup	60 milliliters
1 cup (8 fluid ounces)	240 milliliters
2 cups (1 pint; 16 fluid ounces)	470 milliliters
4 cups (1 quart; 32 fluid ounces)	0.95 liter
4 quarts (1 gallon; 64 fluid ounces)	3.8 liters
WEIGHT	APPROXIMATE WEIGHT
1 ounce	30 grams
2 ounces	60 grams
4 ounces (¼ pound)	112 grams
8 ounces (½ pound)	230 grams
16 ounces (1 pound)	454 grams

liquid measurement equivalents

MEASUREMENT	FLUID OUNCES	OUNCES BY WEIGHT	GRAMS
2 tablespoons	1 fluid ounce	½ ounce	14 grams
¼ cup	2 fluid ounces	1¾ ounces	50 grams
⅓ cup	2⅔ fluid ounces	2 ounces	60 grams
½ cup	4 fluid ounces	4 ounces	113 grams
⅔ cup	5⅓ fluid ounces	5 ounces	140 grams
¾ cup	6 fluid ounces	5¼ ounces	147 grams
1 cup	8 fluid ounces	8 ounces	224 grams

cups to tablespoons

MEASUREMENT	EQUIVALENT
¼ cup (2 fluid ounces)	4 tablespoons
⅓ cup (2⅔ fluid ounces)	5 tablespoons + 1 teaspoon
½ cup (4 fluid ounces)	8 tablespoons
⅔ cup (5⅓ fluid ounces)	10 tablespoons + 2 teaspoons
¾ cup (6 fluid ounces)	12 tablespoons
1 cup (8 fluid ounces)	16 tablespoons

teaspoons and tablespoons to cups

MEASUREMENT	EQUIVALENT
3 teaspoons	1 tablespoon
2 tablespoons	⅛ cup
4 tablespoons	¼ cup
5⅓ tablespoons	⅓ cup
8 tablespoons	½ cup
10⅔ tablespoons	⅔ cup
12 tablespoons	¾ cup
16 tablespoons	1 cup

conversions to and from metric measures

WHEN THIS FACTOR IS KNOWN	MULTIPLY BY	TO FIND
Weight		
Ounces	28.35	Grams
Pounds	0.454	Kilograms
Grams	0.035	Ounces
Kilograms	2.2	Pounds
Measurement		
Inches	2.5	Centimeters
Millimeters	0.04	Inches
Centimeters	0.4	Inches
Volume		
Teaspoons	4.93	Milliliters
Tablespoons	14.79	Milliliters
Fluid ounces	29.57	Milliliters
Cups	0.237	Liters
Pints	0.47	Liters
Quarts	0.95	Liters
Gallons	3.785	Liters
Milliliters	0.034	Fluid ounces
Liters	2.1	Pints
Liters	1.06	Quarts
Liters	0.26	Gallons

	DIVIDE BY	
Milliliters	4.93	Teaspoons
Milliliters	14.79	Tablespoons
Milliliters	236.59	Cups
Milliliters	473.18	Pints
Milliliters	946.36	Quarts
Liters	0.236	Cups
Liters	0.473	Pints
Liters	0.946	Quarts
Liters	3.785	Gallons

index

Page numbers in *italics* indicate photographs.

A

All-purpose flour, 5

Almond(s)

bittersweet chocolate clusters with dried cherries and, 177

bittersweet chocolate tart with candied orange peel and, 93–95, *94*

-cocoa wafers, 141

coconut– biscotti, bittersweet chocolate–, 136–137

frangipane tart, cocoa and bittersweet chocolate, *84*, 85–86

grinding, 131

sandwich cookies, –milk chocolate, 131–132

scones, semisweet chocolate, dried cherry and, 64–65, *65*

in double white chocolate –berry tartlets, 104–105, *105*

in truffles, bittersweet chocolate– marzipan, *168*, 169

in white chocolate –mixed berry muffins, 70, *71*

in white chocolate –sour cream -blueberry scones, 60–61, *61*

Angel food cake, cocoa and cacao nib, 26–27, *27*

Angel food cake pan, 6–7

Apple strudel, bittersweet chocolate, pecan and, 91–92

Apricots, bittersweet chocolate bark with ginger and, 180, *181*

B

Baking pans, 6–7

Baking sheets, 6

Banana

caramelized, –bittersweet chocolate tart, 89–90

-cocoa muffins, 68–69

Bark

bittersweet chocolate, with ginger and apricots, 180, *181*

white chocolate–peppermint, 182

Bars. *See also* Brownies

milk chocolate–dulce de leche, *146*, 147–148

Berry(ies). *See also specific berries*

muffins, white chocolate–mixed berry, 70, *71*

Pavlova, cocoa, with cacao nib whipped cream, 96–97

tartlets, double white chocolate–, 104–105, *105*

Biscotti

bittersweet chocolate–coconut–almond, 136–137

milk chocolate chunk–pecan, 134–135

triple chocolate–walnut, 133–134

Biscuits, cocoa shortcakes with semisweet chocolate whipped cream, *72*, 73–74

Bittersweet chocolate

bark with ginger and apricots, 180, *181*

biscotti, coconut–almond, 136–137

biscotti, triple chocolate–walnut, 133–134

bouchons, cocoa and chocolate, *30*, 31–32

brownie(s)

cake, gianduia, 55–56, *57*

–caramel swirl, *52*, 53–54

fudgy pecan, 46–47

–peanut butter, 50–51

wedges, triple chocolate–toasted coconut, 48–49, *49*

Bundt cake, –toasted walnut, 22–23, *23*

characteristics of, *2*, 3

clusters with almonds and dried cherries, 177

coins, assorted, *178*, 179

–crème fraîche filling, 24

in cupcakes, mocha-walnut, with dulce de leche frosting, 37–38, *39*

extra-bittersweet, *2*, 3

fondue, –orange, 204

ganache filling, 81, *82*, 87–88, 95

ganache squares, –lemon, 175–176

in gianduia filling, 129, 130

in gianduia squares, luscious, 172–173, *173*

gingerbread, 28–29

hot chocolate, intense, 198, *199*

hot fudge sauce, 202

hot mocha, creamy, 201

ice cream, 184

caramel, –salted, 185

gianduia, 187–188

mocha–chocolate chunk, 186

sandwiches, 191

meringue layer cake, and cacao nib, 24–25

in mocha-cinnamon rounds, diamond– studded, *126*, 127–128

in molten mocha cakes, individual, 36–37

mousse, –caramel, 154

mousse, mighty mocha, 152–153, *153*

–peanut butter cookies, 120–121, *121*

piping melted chocolate, 56, *57*

pizza, ganache, 87–88, *88*

pound cake, spiced, and cocoa, 12–13

pudding, and cocoa, 150–151, *151*

sauce, warm, 201

sauce, warm, in ice cream sundaes, triple chocolate, 194

shortbread wedges, mocha, 116–117

sorbet, and cocoa, *192*, 193

soufflé cake, –hazelnut, with hazelnut whipped cream, 16–17

soufflés, –hazelnut, with hazelnut whipped cream, 162–163

strudel, apple, pecan and, 91–92

tart(s)

–caramelized banana, 89–90

–caramel-walnut, 81–83, *83*

frangipane, and cocoa, *84*, 85–86

with orange peel, candied, and almonds, 93–95, *94*

tartlets, crème fraîche–, 111–112

tartlets, –hazelnut and cocoa, 109–110

truffles

–caramel, salted, 170

–guava, 171

–marzipan, *168*, 169

whipped cream, chocolate, 14, 15, *15*

Blueberry(ies)

muffins, white chocolate–mixed berry, 70, *71*

sauce and white chocolate mousse parfait, 156, *157*

scones, –white chocolate–sour cream, 60–61, *61*

Bouchons, cocoa and chocolate, *30*, 31–32

Bowls, 8

Brittle, cacao nib, 176

Brownie(s)

bittersweet chocolate–caramel swirl, *52*, 53–54

bittersweet chocolate–peanut butter, 50–51

cake, gianduia, 55–56, *57*

fudgy pecan, 46–47

wedges, triple chocolate–toasted coconut, 48–49, *49*

white chocolate–macadamia nut, 58–59

Brown sugar, 6

Bundt cake(s)

bittersweet chocolate–toasted walnut, 22–23, *23*

individual chocolate, with white chocolate–passion fruit frosting, 33–34, *35*

about the author

CAROLE BLOOM is a European-trained pastry chef and confectioner who has worked in five-star hotels and restaurants in Europe and the United States. She is the award-winning author of nine other cookbooks, including *Bite-Size Desserts*, *The Essential Baker*, and *Truffles, Candies, and Confections*. Her articles and recipes have appeared in *Bon Appétit, Chocolatier, Cooking Light, Cooking Smart, Eating Well, Fine Cooking, Food & Wine, Gourmet*, and online at Epicurious.com and at Culinate.com. Carole has been a national spokesperson for chocolate groups and associations, as well as a celebrity judge and spokesperson for Sam's Club. She has made many television appearances including the *Today* show, *ABC World News This Morning*, and CNN. She is also a frequent featured speaker at international culinary conferences and trade shows. Carole teaches dessert classes at cooking schools throughout the country.

Carole is a Certified Culinary Professional (CCP) by the International Association of Culinary Professionals (IACP) and a professional member of IACP. She is a founding member and a past president of the San Diego chapter of Les Dames d'Escoffier, an international organization of women of achievement in the culinary industry. She is also the cofounder of the San Diego chapter of Baker's Dozen.

Carole holds a Bachelor of Arts degree in Fine Arts from the University of California at Berkeley. She lives in Carlsbad, California with her husband and their two pampered cats. Please visit her Web site, www.carolebloom.com.